The Peopled Wound:

THE WORK OF HAROLD PINTER

Martin Esslin is head of radio drama for the British Broadcasting Corporation and author of *The Theatre of the Absurd*, *Reflections: Essays on Modern Theatre*, and *Brecht: The Man and His Work*.

The Peopled Wound:

THE WORK OF HAROLD PINTER

BY MARTIN ESSLIN

GARDEN CITY, NEW YORK

DOUBLEDAY & COMPANY, INC.

1970

CONTENTS

The fabric never breaks. The wound is open. The wound is contained. The wound is peopled.

HAROLD PINTER,
"A Note on Shakespeare."

—Do you know what these people do? Len said. They climb from word to word, like stepping stones.

He walked about the room, demonstrating.—Like stepping stones. But tell me this. What do they do when they come to a line with no words in it at all? Can you answer that? What do they do when they come to a line with no words in it at all? Can you tell me that?

HAROLD PINTER,
From the novel *The Dwarfs*,
Chapter 15, p. 79, of the typescript.

Nothing is lost if one does not seek to say the unsayable. Instead, that which cannot be spoken is—unspeakably—*contained* in that which is said!

LUDWIG WITTGENSTEIN,
Letter to Paul Engelmann,
9 April 1917.

INTRODUCTION

Is there any justification for a book on an author who, at the time it was being written, had not yet reached the age of forty? That such a study cannot be the last word on a playwright who may not, as yet, have even started on his most important work is only too obvious. On the other hand the fact that four or five books—or at least booklets—entirely devoted to Harold Pinter have already been published shows that there is a demand for information about the man and analysis and exegesis of his work. On reflection this is natural enough in the case of a playwright like Pinter, who, while obviously interesting and attractive to audiences, directors, amateur groups, and university students, also, and equally obviously, presents them with much that is puzzling, obscure, and evokes a desire for elucidation.

Having devoted a chapter in my study of *The Theatre of the Absurd* to Pinter, I was asked to write a short monograph on him for a series of handbooks on "Dramatists of the World Theatre," published in Germany. This book appeared in November 1967. While the volume now presented to an English-speaking readership is based on that short monograph, it is of necessity a different work. Much that had to be made clear to a German-speaking public could be omitted, as were some features due to the pattern on which that particular series was built. On the other hand far greater emphasis could be laid on Pinter's language and its subtleties, more use could be made of quotations from his work to illustrate it in detail.

Moreover I was fortunate to obtain the help of Harold Pinter himself, who allowed me to see—and in some cases

to quote—some of his hitherto unpublished work: his
early novel *The Dwarfs,* a completed but discarded play,
The Hothouse, and a number of shorter prose pieces. For
this assistance, as for his readiness to check the factual
data in the chronology of his career, I am deeply grateful
to Mr. Pinter. I must, however, emphasise that all the
opinions about Pinter's work voiced in this book are entirely my own and expressed without fear or favour.
Pinter very rightly refrains from commenting on the
"meaning" of his work, and I should not be surprised if
he violently disagreed with some of the interpretations
contained in this book.

The time, clearly, is not yet ripe for a biography of
Harold Pinter. Hence this book opens with an outline of
his career, built up from the main dates of decisive events
in his life, illustrated by quotations from his own recollections contained in interviews with him which have occasionally appeared in periodicals, and with quotations
from characteristic reviews of important performances of
his plays. There follows a chapter that briefly sketches
the background from which Pinter's attitude springs and
the basic assumptions—aesthetic and philosophical—upon
which it rests. Then Pinter's œuvre as a writer is exam-
ined work by work, with special emphasis on his plays.
The sections devoted to individual plays are so arranged
that they can be looked up individually for reference
purposes, yet I should like to stress that, read consecu-
tively, they build up into a coherent account of Pinter's
development and the nature of his subject matter; for
the later plays illumine the earlier ones, while an understanding of the later work is impossible without knowledge of its basis in earlier writings. And the re-emergence
of very early themes in later plays is highly characteristic
of Pinter. His very important early novel, *The Dwarfs,*

for example, is dealt with in the context of the play that is based on passages from it; this section thus sheds light both on Pinter's earliest period as a writer—before he became a dramatist—and on his later work, which is still nourished from that source.

Another point that must be stressed and stressed again in this context concerns the use of a psychoanalytical approach in trying to illumine the subject matter of Pinter's plays and the ways in which the main themes unfold from play to play: I must emphasise that this is done, *not* to give a psychoanalysis of Harold Pinter or to probe his subconscious motivations, but merely to explain the *impact* and *effect* on audiences, who obviously respond to the subconscious content of much that would otherwise remain enigmatic and inexplicable. To say that *Hamlet* derives some of its impact from the presence of an Oedipal theme does not amount to a psychoanalysis of Shakespeare, does not even postulate that Shakespeare must have suffered from a mother complex (which would be a valueless discovery; since most normal men go through such a phase in their life, it would only be a statement of the obvious); it merely explains why a play that, on the surface, has many unsatisfactory features of plot and characterisation, has, through the centuries, retained such a deep fascination over audiences.

The chapter that follows the play-by-play analysis of Pinter's work tries to show some of his ways with language and to point to his important contribution to the art of dialogue. The book is rounded off with a brief attempt to place Pinter in his context, and a bibliography.

For information and help received in writing this book I should like to express my thanks to, apart from Harold Pinter himself, Mr. Emmanuel Wax, Mr. Guy Vaesen,

Mr. Alan Clodd, and Mr. Gerd David, and to the Grove Press for permitting me to quote from Pinter's plays.

In the passages quoted from Harold Pinter's plays, three dots (. . .) signify a pause intended by the author, while four or more dots stand for words omitted in the quotation.

London, September 1969.   MARTIN ESSLIN

The Peopled Wound:

THE WORK OF HAROLD PINTER

CHRONOLOGY OF A CAREER

1930   10 October: Harold Pinter born at Hackney, East
London, the son of Hyman (Jack) Pinter, ladies' tailor,
and his wife Frances (née Mann). Pinter believes that
his father's family might have come to England from
Hungary; the name Pinter does occur among Hungarian Jews. But there is also a family tradition that the
name is of Spanish or Portuguese origin—Pinto, da
Pinto, or da Pinta—so that the Pinters were originally
Sephardic Jews. There is no reason why both these the-
ories might not be correct, as Sephardic Jews frequently
settled in Eastern and Central Europe after the expulsion of the Jews from the Iberian peninsula. (Cf. Pete
and Len talking about Mark's flat in *The Dwarfs:* "LEN:
. . . Everything in this house is Portuguese. PETE:
Why's that? LEN: That's where he comes from. PETE:
Does he? LEN: Or at least, his grandmother on his
father's side. That's where the family comes from . . .")
1930–39   Pinter spends his childhood in the East End.
"I lived in a brick house on Thistlewaite Road, near
Clapton Pond, which had a few ducks in it. It was a
working-class area—some big, run-down Victorian
houses, and a soap factory with a terrible smell, and a
lot of railway yards. And shops. It had a lot of shops.
But down the road a bit from the house there was a
river, the Lea River, which is a tributary of the Thames,
and if you go up the river two miles you find yourself
in a marsh. And near a filthy canal as well. There is a
terrible factory of some kind, with an enormous dirty

chimney, that shoves things down to this canal. . . . My mother was a marvellous cook, as she still is. My father worked terribly hard. He worked a twelve-hour day, making clothes in his shop, but eventually he lost the business and went to work for someone else. In the war he was an air-raid warden." (Pinter in an interview in *The New Yorker*, 25 February 1967.)

1939 At the outbreak of war, Pinter is evacuated to the country. "I went to a castle in Cornwall—owned by a Mrs. Williams—with twenty-four other boys. It had marvellous grounds. And it was on the sea. It looked out on the English Channel, and it had kitchen gardens. All that. But it wasn't quite so idyllic as it sounds, because I was quite a morose little boy. My parents came down occasionally from London. It was over four hundred miles there and back, and I don't know how they made it. It was terribly expensive, and they had no money. I came home after a year or so, and then I went away again—this time with my mother—to a place closer to London." (Pinter, interview in *The New Yorker*, 25 February 1967.)

1944 Return to London. "On the day I got back to London, in 1944, I saw the first flying bomb. I was in the street and I saw it come over. . . . There were times when I would open our back door and find our garden in flames. Our house never burned, but we had to evacuate several times. Every time we evacuated, I took my cricket bat with me." (Pinter, interview in *The New Yorker*, 25 February 1967.)

1947 Pinter leaves Hackney Downs Grammar School. "It was a ten-minute walk from my home. All boys— about six hundred of them. It was a good building. It was pretty awful, but it had great character, and some of the masters had, too. Especially my English master,

Joseph Brearley. He's a very brilliant man. He's a great fellow. He's still there. He was obsessed with the theatre. I played Macbeth when I was sixteen, and he directed me, and then he directed me when I played Romeo. I went in for football and cricket at school, and I was always chosen to run. My main ability was sprinting. I set a new school record—a hundred yards in ten point two—but it's been broken since. The only universities I was thinking about were Oxford and Cambridge. But you had to know Latin, and I didn't know Latin . . ." (Pinter, interview in *The New Yorker*, 25 February 1967.)

1948 Pinter applies for a grant to study acting at the Royal Academy of Dramatic Art. On the recommendation of R. D. (Reggie) Smith, the stage and radio producer, who is acting as assessor, he receives a London County Council grant. "He . . . found he hadn't the sophistication to cope with the other students. To escape he faked a nervous breakdown and, unknown to his parents, tramped the streets for months while continuing to draw a grant." (Anon., "Profile: Playwright on his own," *The Observer*, 15 September 1963.) "I went to RADA for about two terms, then I left of my own free will; I didn't care for it very much. I spent the next year roaming about a bit." (Pinter in conversation with the author, 1967.)

1948–49 On reaching the age of eighteen, when he becomes liable for National Service, Pinter declares himself a conscientious objector. "I was aware of the suffering and of the horror of war, and by no means was I going to subscribe to keeping it going. I said no." (Pinter, interview in *The New Yorker*, 25 February 1967.) He has to appear before two conscientious-objector tribunals. "At my second tribunal, I took one of my close friends, Morris Wernick, to speak for me. The others took reverends. But I had no religious beliefs by then. There were a lot of colonels with mustaches at the tribunal. It was very, very stuffy. I took Wernick, and he made an immortal speech on my behalf. He said, 'Now I *am* going into the Army, so I am not a conscientious objector, but I can assure you, that you will never change *him*. It's a waste of time to try to persuade him to change his mind.'" (Pinter, interview in *The New Yorker,* 25 February 1967.) The tribunals refuse Pinter's application, he receives his call-up papers, but persists in his determination not to go into the Army. Twice he has to appear before a magistrate. "I expected to go to prison, but it was very simple. I was still under twenty-one and it was a civil offence, and the magistrate fined me; then I went on another trial and the same magistrate fined me again— ten pounds and then twenty pounds. It need not have been like that at all, if I had had another magistrate." (Pinter, conversation with the author, 1967.)

1950 *Poetry London,* No. 19, August 1950, publishes two poems by Harold Pinter ("New Year in the Midlands" and "Chandeliers and Shadows"). There is a bad printer's error in this publication, with stanzas from the two poems having got interchanged. So *Poetry London,* No. 20, November 1950, reprints "New Year in the Midlands" together with two new poems ("Rural Idyll" and "European Revels"). But the poet's name now appears as "Harold Pinta." This seems *not* to have been a printer's error, as there is evidence that Pinter signed some letters at that time with the "Portuguese" form of his name.

First efforts to obtain work as an actor. R. D. Smith, who had obtained Pinter his RADA grant, gives him small parts in radio features. 19 September: Pinter's first professional engagement as an actor in a B.B.C. Home Service broadcast, "Focus on Football Pools." 31 October: "Focus on Libraries."

1951 14 January: Pinter's first appearance in Shakespeare. Recording of R. D. Smith's production of *Henry VIII* for B.B.C. Third Programme. Pinter plays the part of Abergavenny. The production is first broadcast on 9 February. Pinter resumes his training as an actor at the Central School of Speech and Drama.

September: Starts his first engagement with Anew McMaster's touring company in Ireland. "He advertised in *The Stage* for actors for a Shakespearean tour . . . . I sent him a photograph and went to see him in a flat near Willesden Junction. . . . He offered me six pounds a week, said I could get digs for twenty-five shillings at the most, told me how cheap cigarettes were and that I could play Horatio, Bassanio and Cassio. It was my first job proper on the stage." (Pinter, *Mac*, London, Pendragon Press: 1968, p. 7/8.)

Poetry London, No. 22, Summer 1951, publishes another poem ("One a Story, Two a Death") by "Harold Pinta."

Sept. 1951–Autumn 1952 Touring Ireland with Anew McMaster. The company includes a number of actors who later achieved prominence: Kenneth Haigh, Patrick Magee, Barry Foster. "Mac travelled by car, and sometimes some of us did too. But other times we went on the lorry with the flats and props, and going into Bandon or Cloughjordan would find the town empty, asleep, men sitting upright in dark bars, cowpads, mud, smell of peat, wood, old clothes. We'd find digs; wash basin and jug, tea, black pudding, and off to the hall, set up a stage on trestle tables, a few rostrum [*sic*] a few drapes, costumes out of the hampers, set up shop, and at night play, not always but mostly to a packed house (where had they come from?) . . ." (Pinter, *Mac*, p. 17.) "Ireland wasn't golden always, but it was golden sometimes and in 1950 it was, all in all, a golden age for me and for others." (*Ibid.*, p. 16.)

1953   Pinter appears in Donald Wolfit's classical season at the King's Theatre, Hammersmith; first meeting with the actress Vivien Merchant (Ada Thomson), with whom Pinter appears in small parts in *As You Like It*. Friendship with the actor—and, later, playwright—Alun Owen, another member of the company.

1954   Pinter decides to assume the stage name David Baron.

1954–57   Acting in provincial repertory theatres: Colchester, Bournemouth, Torquay, Worthing, Richmond, etc.

1956   While acting at Bournemouth, Pinter meets Vivien Merchant again; they play leads opposite each other and get married.

1957   Pinter writes his first play, *The Room*. At a party in London he had come across two men in a small room. One of them, a little man with bare feet, was "carrying on a lively and rather literate conversation, and at the table next to him sat an enormous lorry driver. He had his cap on and never spoke a word. And all the while, as he talked, the little man was feeding the big man—cutting his bread, buttering it, and so on. Well, this image would never leave me." (Pinter, quoted in *Time*, 10 November 1961.) "I told a friend, Henry Woolf, who was studying in the Drama Department of Bristol University, that I would write a play about them. I was working in a repertory company in Torquay, Devon, rehearsing one play in the morning

and playing in another one at night. Woolf telephoned
me and said he had to have the play, so I wrote it. It
was *The Room*. It took me four days, working in the
afternoons. Woolf directed it. On a Sunday night, when
I wasn't acting, I went down to see the play. It seemed
to go well. It excited me. . . ." (Pinter, interview in
The New Yorker, 25 February 1967.)

   The Room, in the production by the Drama Department of Bristol University, was so successful that Bristol's other drama school, attached to the Bristol Old
Vic, also mounted a production, with which it partici-
pated in the *Sunday Times* student drama competition,
held that year at Bristol. Harold Hobson, drama critic
of the *Sunday Times,* who acted as one of the judges
of the competition, was so impressed by the play that
he wrote about its performance (held on 30 December
1957); this drew the attention of a young impresario,
Michael Codron, to Pinter. He asked for any other
plays he might have written. Pinter submitted the two
further plays he had written after *The Room: The
Party,* later *The Birthday Party,* and *The Dumb Waiter.*
Codron expressed interest in the former.

1958   29 January: Birth of Pinter's son, Daniel. "Michael
   Codron took an option on *The Birthday Party* and gave
   me £50 just as Daniel was being born. The play was
   going to go on, I think, in April. Vivien was in hospital;
   we actually had nowhere to go when she came out.
   We had been offered a double job at Birmingham, at
   the Alex [Alexandra Theatre] for the season, that
   would have meant £17 a week each, which would
   have been an enormous salary for us. But I said to
   Vivien: 'I really think we should stay in London, because I have the play coming on.' But she could not
   take it as a concrete thing, it was no more than a dream

for her. However, I insisted and we did stay in London . . . We would in fact have done better to have gone to Birmingham, but we didn't and my life just changed." (Pinter in conversation with the author, 1967.)

February: Pinter takes a flat in Chiswick, London.

28 April: First performance of *The Birthday Party*, at the Arts Theatre, Cambridge. (Meg: Beatrix Lehmann; Stanley: Richard Pearson; Goldberg: John Slater. Directed by Peter Wood.)

19 May: First London performance of *The Birthday Party*, at the Lyric Theatre, Hammersmith. The reviewers of the daily papers unanimously reject the play. Milton Shulman in the *Evening Standard*, 20 May: "*Sorry, Mr. Pinter, you're just not funny enough.* Sitting through *The Birthday Party* at the Lyric, Hammersmith, is like trying to solve a crossword puzzle where every vertical clue is designed to put you off the horizontal. It will be best enjoyed by those who believe that obscurity is its own reward. Others may not feel up to the mental effort needed to illuminate the coy corners of this opaque, sometimes macabre comedy. Not nearly as witty as Simpson's *The Resounding Tinkle* nor nearly as chilling as Ionesco's *The Lesson*, its appeal is based upon the same kind of irreverent verbal anarchy. But the fun to be derived out of the futility of language is fast becoming a cliché of its own. And Mr. Pinter just isn't funny enough. . . ." *The Times* (London): "The first act sounds an offbeat note of madness; in the second the note has risen to a sort of delirium; and the third act studiously refrains from the slightest hint of what the other two may have been about." *The Manchester Guardian:* ". . . . What all this means, only Mr. Pinter knows, for

as his characters speak in non-sequiturs, half-gibberish and lunatic ravings, they are unable to explain their actions, thoughts, or feelings. If the author can forget Beckett, Ionesco and Simpson, he may do much better next time. . . ."

21 May: Pinter in a letter to Donald McWhinnie, assistant head of the B.B.C.'s radio drama department, who had shown interest in getting a radio play from him: ". . . . The play has come a cropper, as you know. What else? The clouds. They are varied, very varied. And all sorts of birds. They come and perch on the window-sill, asking for food! It is touching. Thank you for your encouragement. . . ."

24 May: *The Birthday Party* is taken off after only a week's run. Total receipts for the week: £260 11s. 8d.

25 May: In the *Sunday Times* Harold Hobson comes to the defence of *The Birthday Party:* "One of the actors in Harold Pinter's *The Birthday Party* at the Lyric, Hammersmith announces in the programme that he read History at Oxford and took his degree with Fourth Class Honours. Now I am well aware that Mr. Pinter's play received extremely bad notices last Tuesday morning. At the moment I write these lines it is uncertain even whether the play will still be in the bill when they appear, though it is probable it will soon be seen elsewhere. Deliberately, I am willing to risk whatever reputation I have as a judge of plays by saying that *The Birthday Party* is not a Fourth, not even a Second, but a First, and that Mr. Pinter, on the evidence of this work, possesses the most original, disturbing and arresting talent in theatrical London. I am anxious, for the simple reason that the discovery and encouragement of new dramatists of quality is the present most important task of the British theatre, to put this matter

clearly and emphatically. The influence of unfavourable notices on the box office is enormous; but in lasting effect it is nothing. *Look Back in Anger* and the work of Beckett both received poor notices the morning after production. But that has not prevented those very different writers, Mr. Beckett and Mr. Osborne, from being regarded throughout the world as the most important dramatists who now use the English tongue. The early Shaw got bad notices; Ibsen got scandalous notices. Mr. Pinter is not only in good company, he is in the very best company.

"There is only one quality that is essential to a play. It is the quality that can be found both in *Hamlet* and in *Simple Spymen*. A play must entertain; it must hold the attention; it must give pleasure. Unless it does that, it is useless for stage purposes. No amount of intellect, of high moral intent, or of beautiful writing is of the slightest avail if a play is not in itself theatrically interesting. Theatrically speaking *The Birthday Party* is absorbing. It is witty. Its characters . . . are fascinating. The plot, which consists, with all kinds of verbal arabesques and echoing explorations of memory and fancy, of the springing of a trap, is first rate. The whole play has the same atmosphere of delicious, impalpable and hair-raising terror which makes *The Turn of the Screw* one of the best stories in the world.

"Mr. Pinter has got hold of a primary fact of existence. We live on the verge of disaster. One sunny afternoon, whilst Peter May is making a century at Lords against Middlesex, and the shadows are creeping along the grass, and the old men are dozing in the Long Room, a hydrogen bomb may explode. That is one sort of threat. But Mr. Pinter's is of a subtler sort. It breathes in the air. It cannot be seen, but it enters the room every time the door is opened. There is something in your past—it does not matter what—which will catch up with you. Though you go to the uttermost parts of the earth, and hide yourself in the most obscure lodgings in the least popular of towns, one day there is a possibility that two men will appear. They will be looking for you and you cannot get away. And someone will be looking for *them,* too. There is terror everywhere. Meanwhile it is best to make jokes (Mr. Pinter's jokes are very good), and to play blind man's buff, and to bang on a toy drum, anything to forget the slow approach of doom. *The Birthday Party* is a Grand Guignol of the susceptibilities.

"The fact that no one can say precisely what it is about, or give the address from which the intruding Goldberg and McCann come, or say precisely why it is that Stanley is so frightened by them, is, of course, one of its greatest merits. It is exactly in this vagueness that its spine-chilling quality lies. If we knew what Miles had done, *The Turn of the Screw* would fade away. As it is Mr. Pinter has learned the lesson of the Master. Henry James would recognise him as an equal. . . . Mr. Pinter and *The Birthday Party,* despite their experience last week, will be heard of again. Make a note of their names."

18 July: After his first attempt to write a radio play, *Something in Common,* had—for reasons that are no longer ascertainable—failed to lead to a performance, the B.B.C. commissions another sixty-minute radio play from Pinter.

27 October: The B.B.C. acknowledges receipt of that script—A *Slight Ache.*

1959 28 February: World premiere of *The Dumb Waiter*—in German—at Frankfurt am Main.

1 May: *The Birthday Party* performed by the Tavistock Players at the Tower Theatre, Canonbury, Islington. The semi-amateur cast gives a first-rate performance, which rehabilitates the play in the eyes of some critics.

7 July: Pinter submits the synopsis of a new radio play, *A Night Out,* to the B.B.C.

15 July: *One To Another,* A New Lyric Revue, opens at the Lyric, Hammersmith, containing two sketches by Pinter: "Trouble in the Works," "The Black and White."

29 July: *A Slight Ache* broadcast by the B.B.C. Third Programme. (Edward: Maurice Denham; Flora: Vivien Merchant; directed by Donald McWhinnie.)

9 October: *A Night Out* completed.

10 December: *The Birthday Party* performed at the State Theatre, Braunschweig, Germany.

1960   21 January: *The Room* (Rose: Vivien Merchant; Mr. Kidd: Henry Woolf, at whose instigation the play was written for Bristol; directed by Harold Pinter) and *The Dumb Waiter* (directed by James Roose-Evans) performed at the Hampstead Theatre Club. *The Times* (London): "To find another artist with whom Mr. Pinter may fruitfully be compared one must look farther afield than drama, or even literature, to music—to Webern, in fact, with whose compositions Mr. Pinter's plays have much in common. Like Webern he has a taste for short, compressed forms, as in his revue-sketches which are really complete plays five minutes long, and like Webern he inclines to etiolated pointilliste textures, forever trembling on the edge of silence, and to structures elusive, yet so precisely organized that they possess an inner tension nonetheless potent because its sources are not completely understood."

1 March: *A Night Out* broadcast by the B.B.C. Third Programme. (Albert Stokes: Barry Foster; The Girl: Vivien Merchant; Seeley: Harold Pinter; directed by Donald McWhinnie.)

8 March: *The Room* and *The Dumb Waiter* transferred, with some cast changes, to the Royal Court Theatre. (*The Room* is now directed by Anthony Page.)

22 March: *The Birthday Party,* which had been accepted by Peter Willes, head of Drama at Associated Rediffusion TV, early in 1959 after he had seen a revue sketch by Pinter, is televised by ARD; (Meg: Margery Withers, who played the part in the Tavistock Players production; Stanley: Richard Pearson, who played it in the first stage presentation; directed by Joan Kemp-Welch.)

24 April: *A Night Out* televised by A.B.C.-TV. (Albert Stokes: Tom Bell; The Girl: Vivien Merchant; Seeley: Harold Pinter; directed by Philip Saville.)

27 April: *The Caretaker* opens at the Arts Theatre Club, London. (Mick: Alan Bates; Aston: Peter Woodthorpe; Davies: Donald Pleasence; directed by Donald McWhinnie.) *The Times:* "A SLIGHT PLAY THAT PLEASES AND DAZES. . . . . a slight, unrhetorical play with one set and only three characters . . . . the pleasurable confusion in which Mr. Pinter's writing leaves one. The surface of his works is simple and lucid—none of the individual things his characters say is very subtle or obscure. What is obscure however is the connection between any two things a character says (except on a stream-of-consciousness level) and even more the connection between what one character says and what another says afterwards. Even how the characters come to occupy the same room at the same time (together

without togetherness) is as often as not kept from us. What part does the tramp-caretaker play in the lives of his ex-lunatic host and his brother? Why do they act as they do? How do they communicate, or do they communicate at all? We do not know, and strangely enough, while the play is on, it never occurs to us to worry about not knowing." John Rosselli in the *Guardian:* ". . . a fine play, consistently carried through apart from a few puzzling but not important details. . . . A particular virtue is that nowhere does Mr. Pinter treat non-communication as an extraneous, rather banal 'point' to be made (compare Ionesco's *The Chairs*). It is knit with the people and the action. Yet one must still say that this plunging of audiences into the world of the shut-off mind is something that leads away from the mainstream of art—whose main business, surely, is with the adult relationships we painfully try to keep and deepen. It is a fascinating byway and Mr. Pinter's work literally fascinates; but one hopes he will move on." Patrick Gibbs in the *Daily Telegraph:* ". . . had *Waiting for Godot* never been written, this piece would be judged to be masterly. As it is, it appeared to be excessively derivative, almost to the point of parody."

30 May: *The Caretaker* transfers to the West End, Duchess Theatre.

5 June: Kenneth Tynan in the *Observer:* "With *The Caretaker,* which moved last week from the Arts to the Duchess, Harold Pinter has begun to fulfill the promise that I signally failed to see in *The Birthday Party* two years ago. The latter play was a clever fragment grown dropsical with symbolic content. . . . the piece was full of those familiar overtones that seem to be inseparable from much of avant garde drama. In *The Caretaker* symptoms of paranoia are still detectable

. . . . but their intensity is considerably abated; and the symbols have mostly retired to the background. What remains is a play about people. . . ."

21 July: *Night School,* a new television play by Pinter, broadcast by Associated Rediffusion TV. (Walter: Milo O'Shea; Sally: Vivien Merchant; directed by Joan Kemp-Welch.)

27 July: *The Birthday Party* opens at the Actors Workshop, San Francisco, directed by Glynne Wickham. (First professional performance of Pinter in the U.S.A.)

29 October: *Der Hausmeister* (German version of *The Caretaker*) opens at the Düsseldorf Schauspielhaus.

2 December: The radio play *The Dwarfs* broadcast by the B.B.C. Third Programme. (Len: Richard Pasco; Mark: Alec Scott; Pete: Jon Rollason; directed by Barbara Bray.)

1961 15 January: Recognition from one of the chief upholders of tradition in the British theatre. Noël Coward writes in the *Sunday Times:* ". . . . at the moment . . . . there is only one 'New Movement' straight play playing to good business in a London theatre—*The Caretaker* by Harold Pinter. This, to me, is in no way a strange phenomenon. Mr. Pinter is neither pretentious, pseudo-intellectual nor self-consciously propagandist. True, the play has no apparent plot, much of it is repetitious and obscure, and it is certainly placed in the lowest possible social stratum; but it is written with an original and unmistakable sense of theatre and is impeccably acted and directed. Above all, its basic premise is victory rather than defeat. I am surprised that the critics thought so well of it. Doubtless they were misled by the comfortingly familiar squalour of

its locale and the fact that one of the principal characters is a tramp." (Noël Coward's admiration remained undiminished, and had, indeed, grown five
years later: "Pinter is a very curious, strange element.
He uses language marvellously well. He is what I
would call a genuine original. Some of his plays are a
little obscure, a little difficult, but he's a superb craftsman, creating atmosphere with words that sometimes
are violently unexpected." (Interview in the *Sunday
Telegraph*, 22 May 1966.)

18 January: *A Slight Ache* staged as part of a triple
bill, *Three* (together with one-act plays by John Morti-
mer and N. F. Simpson), at the Arts Theatre Club,
London. (Edward: Emlyn Williams; Flora: Allison
Leggatt; Matchseller: Richard Briers; directed by
Donald McWhinnie.)

27 January: *Le Gardien* (French version of *The
Caretaker*) at the Théâtre de Lutèce in Paris, with
Roger Blin as Davies, poorly received by the critics.
Le Figaro: "[The play] raises *misérabilisme* to a dogma,
promotes starvation to the level of heroism, and glori-
fies the sordid and petty in boredom." *France-Soir:* "Either [the play] is an imposture, or the British have gone
mad." *L'Humanité:* ". . . the rear guard of the avant
garde."

21 February: In the London production of *The Caretaker* Pinter takes over the part of Mick from Alan
Bates for four weeks.

11 May: *The Collection* broadcast by Associated Rediffusion TV (Harry: Griffith Jones; James: Anthony
Bate; Stella: Vivien Merchant; Bill: John Ronane; directed by Joan Kemp-Welch.)

27 May: *The Caretaker* closes its run at the Duchess
Theatre after 425 performances.

17 September: *A Night Out* staged by Leila Blake at the Gate Theatre, Dublin.

2 October: *A Night Out* opens at the Comedy Theatre, London, as part of a triple bill, *Counterpoint,* together with plays by David Campton and James Saunders.

4 October: *The Caretaker* opens at the Lyceum Theatre, New York (with the London cast, except that Robert Shaw had taken Peter Woodthorpe's place as Aston). Howard Taubman in the *New York Times:* "Out of a scabrous derelict and two mentally unbalanced brothers Harold Pinter has woven a play of strangely compelling beauty and passion. *The Caretaker,* which opened last night at the Lyceum, proclaims its young English author as one of the important playwrights of our day. . . . A work of rare originality, *The Caretaker* will tease and cling to the mind. No matter what happens in the months to come, it will lend luster to this Broadway season."

1962 February: *The Caretaker* ends its New York run, having achieved much artistic but little commercial success. *The Collection* opens at the Aldwych Theatre, London, in a double bill with Strindberg's *Playing with Fire.* (Harry: Michael Hordern; James: Kenneth Haigh; Stella: Barbara Murray; Bill: John Ronane; directed by Peter Hall and Harold Pinter.)

7 September: Pinter reads his story *The Examination* on the B.B.C. Third Programme.

November: Joseph Losey's film *The Servant,* after the novel by Robin Maugham, screenplay by Harold Pinter, opens in London.

12 December: Work starts on filming *The Caretaker* in a derelict house (31 Downs Road, Hackney) not far from Pinter's childhood home. The production costs of

about £30,000 have been raised by a group of show-business personalities, including Noël Coward, Richard Burton and Elizabeth Taylor, Peter Sellers, Peter Hall, Leslie Caron, etc. The film is directed by Clive Donner. The cast is the same as that of the New York run.

1963   28 March: *The Lover* broadcast by Associated Rediffusion TV (Richard: Alan Badel; Sarah: Vivien Merchant; directed by Joan Kemp-Welch.)

27 June: First screening of the film version of *The Caretaker* at the Berlin Film Festival.

18 September: *The Lover* and *The Dwarfs* open at the Arts Theatre Club, London. (*The Lover* with Scott Forbes as Richard and Vivien Merchant as Sarah, directed by Harold Pinter; *The Dwarfs* with John Hurt as Len, Michael Forrest as Peter, Philip Bond as Mark, directed by Harold Pinter and Guy Vaesen.)

30 September: Joan Kemp-Welch's production of *The Lover* wins the Prix Italia for Television Drama at Naples.

23 November: Harold Pinter, Alan Badel, and Vivien Merchant receive Guild of British Television Producers and Directors awards for the script and leading performances in *The Lover*.

1964   January: The film version of *The Caretaker* starts its run in New York under the title *The Guest*.

February–March: The B.B.C. Third Programme broadcasts nine short sketches by Pinter, some of which had already been staged in revue, while others had remained unperformed: "Last To Go"; "Applicant"; "Request Stop"; "That's Your Trouble"; "That's All"; "Interview"; "Trouble in the Works"; "The Black and White"; "Dialogue for Three." (Director: Michael Bakewell.)

2 March: Pinter wins the British Screenwriters' Guild award for his screenplay of *The Servant*.

2 June: Pinter reads his story "Tea Party" on the B.B.C. Third Programme.

18 June: *The Birthday Party* revived at the Aldwych Theatre, London. (Meg: Doris Hare; Stanley: Bryan Pringle; Goldberg: Brewster Mason; McCann: Patrick Magee; directed by Harold Pinter.)

1965 30 March: Pinter wins the British Film Academy Award for the best screenplay of 1964 for his adaptation of Penelope Mortimer's novel *The Pumpkin Eater*. (Directed by Jack Clayton, with Peter Finch and Anne Bancroft in the leading parts.)

March: *The Homecoming* starts its pre-London tour.

25 March: The television play *Tea Party* broadcast by B.B.C.-1 in the series "The Largest Theatre in the World," organised by the European Broadcasting Union, through which television organisations throughout Europe co-operate in joint commissions from leading authors. (Robert Disson: Leo McKern; Wendy: Vivien Merchant; Diana: Jennifer Wright; Willy: Charles Gray; directed by Charles Jarrott.) Simultaneously, or in the following week, the play was also screened in France, Luxembourg, Belgium, Switzerland, Austria, Spain, Holland, Denmark, Sweden, Norway.

3 June: *The Homecoming* opens at the Aldwych Theatre, London. (Max: Paul Rogers; Lenny: Ian Holm; Teddy: Michael Bryant; Ruth: Vivien Merchant; directed by Peter Hall.) Harold Hobson in the *Sunday Times:* ". . . Harold Pinter's cleverest play. It is so clever, in fact so misleadingly clever, that at a superficial glance it seems to be not clever enough. This is an appearance only, but it is one for which Mr. Pinter will suffer in the estimation of audiences,

who will perceive an aesthetic defect that does not exist, in the place of a moral vacuum that does. . . . I am troubled by the complete absence from the play of any moral comment whatsoever. To make such a comment does not necessitate an author's being conventional or religious; it does necessitate, however, his having made up his mind about life, his having come to some decision. . . . We have no idea what Mr. Pinter thinks of Ruth or Teddy or what value their existence has. They have no relation to life outside themselves. They live; their universe lives: but not the universe."

October: Pinter achieves his first breakthrough in Paris with the production of *The Collection* and *The Lover* as a double bill, directed by Claude Régy and starring Delphine Seyrig.

15 November: Pinter appears in the part of Garcia in Sartre's *No Exit* on B.B.C. Television, under the direction of Philip Saville.

1966   June: Pinter is awarded the C.B.E. (Commander of the Order of the British Empire) in the Birthday Honours List.

11 October: *Le Retour* (*The Homecoming*) opens. at the Théâtre de Paris. (Max: Pierre Brasseur; Lenny: Claude Rothe; Ruth: Emmanuelle Riva; directed by Claude Régy.)

November: World premiere of the film *The Quiller Memorandum*, after the novel by Adam Hall, screenplay by Harold Pinter (with Alec Guinness, George Segal, Max von Sydow; directed by Michael Anderson).

20 December: *The Homecoming* opens in Boston.

1967   3 January: *The Homecoming* opens in New York, at the Music Box. (The London production and cast, except that Michael Bryant's place in the part of Teddy was taken by Michael Craig.) Walter Kerr in the *New York Times,* 6 January 1967: ". . . Mr. Pinter is one of the most naturally gifted dramatists to have come out of England since the war. I think he is making the mistake, just now, of supposing that the elusive kernel of impulse that will do for a forty-minute play will serve just as suspensefully for an all-day outing. *The Homecoming,* to put the matter as simply as possible, needs a second situation: We could easily take an additional act if the author would only scrap the interminable first. The tide must come in at least twice if we are to be fascinated so long by the shoreline." In spite of this cool notice by the leading New York critic, the heated discussion about the play aroused sufficient interest to ensure it a long run.

28 February: *The Basement* (a television play, originally written as a film script under the title *The Compartment* for a projected film—composed of three short subjects to be written by Beckett, Ionesco, and Pinter —to be produced under the auspices of Grove Press, New York; only one of these, Beckett's *Film,* was completed) broadcast on B.B.C.-TV. (Stott: Harold Pinter; Jane: Kika Markham; Law: Derek Godfrey; directed by Charles Jarrott.)

February: First showing of the film *Accident* (from the novel by Nicholas Mosley, screenplay by Harold Pinter, directed by Joseph Losey; with Dirk Bogarde, Vivien Merchant, Stanley Baker, Delphine Seyrig).

28 March: *The Homecoming* wins the Tony award for the best play on Broadway.

May: *The Homecoming* is voted the best play on Broadway by the New York Drama Critics' Circle and receives the Whitbread Anglo-American award for the best British play on Broadway.

27 July: Robert's Shaw's play, *The Man in the Glass Booth*, directed by Pinter, with Donald Pleasence in the lead, opens in London.

1968   21 January: The London press reports that Pinter refuses to make the cuts demanded by the Lord Chamberlain in his new one-act play, *Landscape*, which is to be staged by the Royal Shakespeare Company at the Aldwych Theatre. Eventually Pinter's insistence that the one or two offending four-letter words are essential leads to the abandonment of the plan to stage the play in the current season.

25 April: As radio is not subject to the Lord Chamberlain's censorship, *Landscape* receives its first, unaltered and uncut, performance in the B.B.C.'s Third Programme. In the stereophonic production, Peggy Ashcroft appears as Beth, Eric Porter as Duff, under Guy Vaesen's direction.

Autumn: Completion of the film version of *The Birthday Party* in London. (Stanley: Robert Shaw; Meg: Dandy Nichols; Goldberg: Sidney Tafler; McCann: Patrick Magee; directed by William Friedkin.)

10 October: Stage versions of *Tea Party* and *The Basement* open at the East Side Playhouse, New York.

9 December: The film of *The Birthday Party* opens in New York.

1969   January: *Silence* completed. Screenplay of the adaptation of L. P. Hartley's novel *The Go-Between* completed.

9 April: The sketch *Night* first performed as part of an evening of one-act plays about marriage by various authors, *Mixed Doubles*, at the Comedy Theatre, London. (Man: Nigel Stock; Woman: Vivien Merchant.)

2 July: *Landscape* and *Silence* open at the Aldwych Theatre, London. (In *Landscape*, Beth: Peggy Ashcroft; Duff: David Waller; in *Silence*, Ellen: Frances Cuka; Rumsay: Anthony Bate; Bates: Norman Rodway; both plays directed by Peter Hall.)

17 September: *Le Gardien* (*The Caretaker*, newly adapted by Eric Kahane) opens at the Théâtre Moderne in Paris. B. Porot Delpech writes in *Le Monde:* "The Théâtre Moderne is a thousand times justified in appealing against the bad reception accorded to *The Caretaker* by press and public in 1961 at the Théâtre de Lutèce. Without a doubt the contact with Pinter was premature then and rendered somewhat astringent by the gloomy production Jean Martin had given it. In the meantime our sensibility has grown accustomed to the new Anglo-Saxon theatre. . . . A great play."

II

BACKGROUND AND BASIC PREMISES

Pinter has at times been accused of being totally apolitical. He himself has occasionally seemed to have wanted to create such an impression. When, during the period of the Macmillan government's first negotiations about Britain's entry into the Common Market, *Encounter* asked a variety of public figures to give their views about the problem, Pinter's reply was the shortest of all: "I have no interest in the matter and do not care what happens." Yet, on closer scrutiny, one will find that neither in his attitude as a citizen nor in his work as a playwright is Pinter so utterly devoid of political content or commitment as some of his detractors tend to maintain. "I'm categorically anti the Americans in Vietnam. And I feel strongly in favour of Israel," he said to an interviewer in April 1968 ("In Search of Harold Pinter," by Kathleen Tynan, *Evening Standard*, London, 26 April 1968). And indeed, behind the highly private world of his plays, there also lurk what, after all, are the basic political problems: the use and abuse of power; the fight for living space; cruelty; terror. Only very superficial observers could overlook this social, this political side of the playwright.

Nor, if one looks at Harold Pinter's background, could these basic preoccupations appear as anything but inevitable. The East End of London, where Pinter grew up as a child in the nineteen-thirties, was a political battlefield. A large Jewish population, mainly refugees from the great Russian pogroms of 1905 but swelled by newer arrivals after the First World War and later by the victims of Hitler, was battling for a foothold and a livelihood among Cockneys, Chinese, Negroes, and Irish. It was in the streets of the East End that Mosley's Fascists clashed with left-wing Jewish militants. And after the end of the Second World War these tensions did not die down.

> Every one [says Pinter] encounters violence in some way or other. I did encounter it in quite an extreme form after the war, in the East End, when the Fascists were coming back to life in England. I got into quite a few fights down there. If you looked remotely like a Jew you might be in trouble. Also, I went to a Jewish club, by an old railway arch, and there were quite a lot of people often waiting with broken milk bottles in a particular alley we used to walk through. There were one or two ways of getting out of it—one was a purely physical way, of course, but you couldn't do anything about the milk bottles—we didn't have any milk bottles. The best way was to talk to them, you know, sort of "Are you all right?" "Yes, I'm all right." "Well, that's all right then, isn't it?" And all the time keep walking towards the lights of the main road. . . . We were often taken for Communists. If you went by, or happened to be passing, a Fascist street meeting and looked in any way antagonistic—this was in Ridley Road market, near Dalston Junction—they'd interpret your very being, especially if you had books under your arms, as evidence of your being a Com-

munist. There was a good deal of violence there, in those days.*

There can be little doubt that Pinter's radical pacifism, which led him, at the age of eighteen, to risk a prison sentence rather than do his National Service, was a reaction to this experience of violence in the years of his boyhood and adolescence. To choose the path of the conscientious objector, however, *is* a deeply political act, but a political act of a peculiarly basic nature, involving as it does a refusal even to listen to the arguments for or against a particular war, a particular political situation. To a radical pacifist of this type all particular arguments pale into nothingness compared to the one essential fact that to be taking part in *any* war, in *any* fighting, must involve the taking of human life. A political decision at this deep, fundamental level can easily appear as a rejection of all politics on the more mundane level of daily debate. Pinter's attitude as a playwright is directly analogous to this paradox: determined to tackle his characters at the very root of their existence, he was led·to a seeming neglect of the less essential aspects of their life and personality. When Kenneth Tynan pressed him on this point in a radio interview in 1960, asking him why his characters never seemed interested in sex (that was before *The Lover* and *The Homecoming*), politics, or general ideas, Pinter replied that he was dealing with characters who stood at essential turning points in their lives: "There is no reason to suppose that at one time or another they didn't listen to a political meeting, or they might even have voted . . . I'm dealing with these characters at the extreme edge of their living, where they are

---

* Lawrence M. Bensky, "Harold Pinter," in *Writers at Work: Paris Review* Interviews, Third Series. New York, Viking Press, 1967; London, Secker & Warburg, 1968, p. 363.

living pretty much alone, at their hearth, their home
hearth . . . We all, I think . . . . may have sexual relationships or go to political meetings or discuss ideas, but
when we get back to our rooms and we are faced with
a bed and we are either alone or with someone else,
then . . . I don't think we go on long about ideas or
political allegiances. . . . I mean, there comes a point,
surely, where this living in *the* world must be tied up
with living in *your own* world, where you are—in your
room . . . Before you manage to adjust yourself to living
alone in your room . . . you are not terribly fit and
equipped to go out and fight the battles . . . which are
fought mostly in abstractions in the outside world." (Pinter, interviewed by Kenneth Tynan in the series "People
Today," B.B.C. Home Service, 28 October 1960; pre-
recorded 19 August 1960.)

Existential adjustment, coming to terms with one's own
being, precedes, and necessarily predetermines, one's attitude to society, politics, and general ideas. Like Beckett
and Kafka, Pinter's attitude here is that of an existentialist: the mode of a man's *being* determines his *thinking.*
Hence, to come to grips with the true sources of their
attitudes, the playwright must catch his characters at the
decisive points in their lives, when they are confronted
with the crisis of adjustment to themselves, which precedes their going out into the world to confront society,
its politics, its ideas and issues.

It is unlikely that Pinter could have been influenced
by, or even been aware of, the philosophy of that origi-
nator of modern existentialism, Martin Heidegger, when
he started to write his plays or to formulate his ideas.
It is all the more significant that Pinter, like Heidegger,
takes as his starting point, in man's confrontation with
himself and the nature of his own being, that fundamen-

tal anxiety which is nothing less than a living being's basic awareness of the threat of non-being, of annihilation. Pinter's people are in a room, and they are frightened, scared. What are they scared of? "Obviously, they are scared of what is outside the room. Outside the room is a world bearing down upon them, which is frightening. . . . We are all in this, all in a room, and outside is a world . . . which is most inexplicable and frightening, curious and alarming." (Pinter, interview with Kenneth Tynan, 1960, as above.)

Yet in Pinter's plays this existential fear is never just a philosophical abstraction. It is, ultimately, based on the experience of a Jewish boy in the East End of London, of a Jew in the Europe of Hitler. In talking about his first play, *The Room,* Pinter himself made this point very clearly: "This old woman is living in a room which, she is convinced, is the best in the house, and she refuses to know anything about the basement downstairs. She says it's damp and nasty, and the world outside is cold and icy, and that in her warm and comfortable room her security is complete. But, of course, it isn't; an intruder comes to upset the balance of everything, in other words points to the delusion on which she is basing her life. I think the same thing applies in *The Birthday Party.* Again this man is hidden away in a seaside boarding house . . . then two people arrive out of nowhere, and I don't consider this an unnatural happening. I don't think it is all that surrealistic and curious because surely *this thing, of people arriving at the door, has been happening in Europe in the last twenty years. Not only the last twenty years, the last two to three hundred."* (Pinter, interviewed by John Sherwood, B.B.C. European Service, 3 March 1960. My italics.)

Man's existential fear, not as an abstraction, not as a

surreal phantasmagoria, but as something real, ordinary, and acceptable as an everyday occurrence—here we have the core of Pinter's work as a dramatist. He acknowledges the influence of a number of writers: "I read Hemingway, Dostoevski, Joyce, and Henry Miller at a very early age, and Kafka. I'd read Beckett's novels too, but I'd never heard of Ionesco until I'd written the first few plays." (Interview with Bensky, see above.) Of these he says Kafka and Beckett made the greatest impression on him: "When I read them it rang a bell, that's all, within me. I thought: something is going on here which is going on in me too." (Pinter, interviewed by John Sherwood, see above.) But whereas both Kafka and Beckett are moving in a surreal world of acknowledged fantasy and dream, Pinter, essentially, remains on the firm ground of everyday reality, even though, in some of his earlier plays, symbolic or even supernatural elements are eventually introduced into the action (the symbolic blind Negro in *The Room,* the mysteriously operated food lift in *The Dumb Waiter,* the enigmatic matchseller in *A Slight Ache,* who may well be merely the emanation of the two other characters' fears); but even in these plays the starting point is always a very real situation with most closely observed real, even hypernaturalistic dialogue, so that the fantasy element, when it does make an appearance, is clearly identifiable as the outward projection, the concretisation of these, very real, characters' dreams and anxieties. In the earliest of Pinter's plays, *The Room,* this attempt to introduce a symbol of death and alienation leads to a break in style and detracts, to some extent, from the play's effect. In the later instances these devices proved more effective; nevertheless Pinter gradually abandoned them and prefers now to remain within a firm framework of "real" events.

And yet: Pinter is not a naturalistic dramatist. This is the paradox of his artistic personality. The dialogue and the characters are real, but the over-all effect is one of mystery, of uncertainty, of poetic ambiguity. An understanding of the cause of this strange paradox will go far towards helping us to find the key to Pinter's method and meaning, and the secret of his impact on the stage.

The first deviation from the usual realistically constructed play lies in the element of uncertainty about the motivation of the characters, their background, their very identity. Frequently this has led critics to accuse Pinter of deliberate mystification: is he withholding information from the audience merely to be able to tease them, like a crime writer who deliberately withholds or distorts the clues to the perpetrator of the crime, in order to obtain cheap suspense?

Pinter's own reply to such accusations of bad faith is a categorical "no." When he received a letter which read: "DEAR SIR, I would be obliged if you would kindly explain to me the meaning of your play *The Birthday Party*. These are the points which I do not understand: 1. Who are the two men? 2. Where did Stanley come from? 3. Were they all supposed to be normal? You will appreciate that without the answers to my questions I cannot fully understand your play," Pinter is said to have replied as follows: "DEAR MADAM, I would be obliged if you would kindly explain to me the meaning of your letter. These are the points which I do not understand: 1. Who are you? 2. Where do you come from? 3. Are you supposed to be normal? You will appreciate that without the answers to your questions I cannot fully understand your letter." (*Daily Mail*, London, 28 November 1967.)

These, to Pinter, are genuine problems: the problem of identity, of motivation, of verification. They are also—so

astonishingly is Pinter in tune with the thinking of our
epoch—the basic problems of contemporary philosophy
and literature.

"Sometimes," Pinter confessed to an interviewer (Marshall Pugh, in the *Daily Mail*, London, 7 March 1964), "I
don't know who I'm looking at in the mirror. There's no
explanation for that face." The question: Who am I? is
intimately linked with the question of motivation. Only
if we know exactly *who* a character is, what his antecedents are, his tastes, his speed of reaction, his vocabulary,
his personal values, can we predict with any accuracy
how he will act in the future. . . . "The explicit form
which is so often taken in twentieth-century drama
is . . . . cheating. The playwright assumes that we have
a great deal of information about all his characters, who
explain themselves to the audience. In fact, what they
are doing most of the time is conforming to the author's
own ideology. They don't create themselves as they go
along, they are being fixed on the stage for one purpose,
to speak for the author, who has a point of view to put
over. When the curtain goes up on one of my plays, you
are faced with a situation, a particular situation, two people sitting in a room, which hasn't happened before, and
is just happening at this moment, and we know no more
about them than I know about you, sitting at this table.
The world is full of surprises. A door can open at any
moment and someone will come in. We'd love to know
who it is, we'd love to know exactly what he has on his
mind and why he comes in, but how often do we know
what someone has on his mind or who this somebody is,
and what goes to make him and make him what he is,
and what his relationship is to others?" (Pinter, interview
with John Sherwood, as above.)

Indeed, in the novel the omniscient narrator, the author who knew every motivation of his characters and freely told his readers about it, went out with Henry James. In drama, where the apparent absence of a narrator, the apparent objectivity of the action presented on the stage, has masked the problem, the omniscient author remained the rule even during the period of naturalism, when the theory underlying the practice of playwriting actually called for total objectivity. Even Ibsen and Gerhart Hauptmann felt compelled to motivate their characters totally and to disclose their motivation to the audience.

It is this cocksureness of the playwrights, their claim to be in a position to know all about their characters and what makes them tick, that Pinter, with his radical and uncompromising attitude of total sincerity, not only rejects but regards as a form of intolerable arrogance on the part of the writers concerned. How, in the present state of our knowledge of psychology and the complexity, the hidden layers, of the human mind, can anyone claim to know what motivates himself, let alone another human being? We do not know, with any semblance of certainty, what motivates our own wives, parents, our own children—why then should we be furnished with a complete dossier about the motivations of any character we casually encounter on the stage? Hence Pinter's rejection of the conventional exposition in drama, which, in a few bold and clever strokes, purports to introduce the principal characters to us with a handy do-it-yourself kit to decipher their origin, background, and motivations—all in the first ten to fifteen minutes of the action.

In the programme brochure of the performance of Pinter's *The Room* and *The Dumb Waiter* at the Royal Court Theatre on 8 March 1960—Pinter's second professional ap-

pearance as a dramatist on the London stage—there lay
a single unsigned, printed sheet of paper, clearly Pinter's
own attempt to forewarn the audience:

> Given a man in a room and he will sooner or
> later receive a visitor. A visitor entering the
> room will enter with intent. If two people in-
> habit the room the visitor will not be the same
> man for both. A man in a room who receives a
> visit is likely to be illuminated or horrified by it.
> The visitor himself might as easily be horrified
> or illuminated. The man may leave with the
> visitor or he may leave alone. The visitor may
> leave alone or stay in the room alone when the
> man is gone. Or they may both stay together in
> the room. Whatever the outcome in terms of
> movement, the original condition, in which a
> man sat alone in a room, will have been sub-
> jected to alterations. A man in a room and no
> one entering lives in expectation of a visit. He
> will be illuminated or horrified by the absence
> of a visitor. But however much it is expected,
> the entrance, when it comes, is unexpected and
> almost always unwelcome. (He himself, of
> course, might go out of the door, knock and
> come in and be his own visitor. It has happened
> before.)
>
> We all have our function. The visitor will
> have his. There is no guarantee, however, that
> he will possess a visiting card with detailed in-
> formation as to his last place of residence, last
> job, next job, number of dependents, etc. Nor,
> for the comfort of all, an identity card, nor a
> label on his chest. The desire for verification is

understandable but cannot always be satisfied. There are no hard distinctions between what is real and what is unreal, nor between what is true and what is false. The thing is not necessarily either true or false: it can be both true and false. The assumption that to verify what has happened and what is happening presents few problems I take to be inaccurate. A character on the stage who can present no convincing argument or information as to his past experience, his present behaviour or his aspirations, nor give a comprehensive analysis of his motives is as legitimate and as worthy of attention as one who, alarmingly, can do all these things. The more acute the experience, the less articulate its expression.

This statement, here reproduced in full, contains the germ of quite a number of Pinter's plays beyond the two which it introduced: certainly *The Birthday Party*, *The Caretaker*, and *The Homecoming* are already present in embryo in the permutations of possibilities arising from someone waiting in a room, who may or may not receive a visitor, may or may not stay with him, may or may not leave. One of the earliest texts by Pinter to have been published, "Kullus," a prose poem in dialogue form dated 1949 (when Pinter was barely more than eighteen years old), already contains this very situation:

I let him in by the back door.
There was a brisk moon.
    —Come in.
He stepped inside, slapping his hands, into the room.
    —Go on Kullus. Go to the fire.
He stooped to the grate and stretched his fingers.

—You do not welcome warmth,
said Kullus.
—I?
—There is no meeting. There is separation. . . .

A girl is introduced into the room. Eventually she asks:

—Which is your room?
she said.
—I am no longer in my room. . . .
("Kullus," in Pinter, *Poems.* London,
Enitharmon Press, 1968, pp. 22–24.)

It is the very same situation that, much later, Pinter developed at length in his television play *The Basement,* but that is present in so many of his other plays.

There is thus a remarkable consistency and continuity in Pinter's basic philosophy. The programme statement, here quoted at length, shows the close affinity between Pinter's ideas and those held by the school of the *nouveau roman* in France. Like these writers, Pinter rejects the author's right to creep inside his characters and pretend to know what makes them act, even how they feel. All he can do is render an account, meticulously accurate, of the movement that takes place; give a description of the situation at the beginning, before the intrusion; and note the changes that have taken place at the end.

But if the playwright cannot claim to know what his characters feel, what makes them act as they do; what, then, can he communicate to an audience? He can convey his impression of the structure, the pattern of a situation, the movement of its change as it unfolds, again in a pattern, like the movement of a dance; and, on observing this, the author can also communicate his own sense of mystery, of wonder at this strange world of patterns and structures, of beings that move by mysterious and unpredictable impulses, like fish in a huge aquarium. Is that *enough* for an author, a playwright, to communicate to an audience which has been accustomed to be offered, in the theatre, complete accounts, with built-in motivation and a full explanation of the actions of well-defined characters?

After all, Pinter might argue, we hardly get more than that in real life. We see two people arguing, perhaps starting to fight, in the street. A crowd gathers around them and watches in fascination. It is most unlikely that this crowd could ever get a clear idea about the issues involved in the quarrel, let alone the antecedents and personalities of the two men themselves. And then, after a police car has arrived and taken the two contenders to the police station, the crowd disperses and may never know what the fight was about. And yet that fight had meaning: it communicated something about the stresses, the violence, the heartbreak of life in a big city; and it had something of a poetical validity: as an expression of the mood, the atmosphere of the time, as a metaphor even for all the unhappiness, the tragedy of the human condition. The bystander whose eyes were open, who was sensitive enough to react to the emotional climate of that street incident, *could* gain an insight, quite a deep insight, into life; a greater awareness of its true nature, perhaps, than if all the facts, all the motivations could have been offered him on a plate (which in reality they hardly ever could); for after all, the opaqueness, the impenetrability of other people's lives, their feelings, their true motivations, is, precisely, an essential feature of the true quality of the world and of our own experience of the world.

There is nothing very unusual in these considerations if we apply them, not to drama, but to a kindred form of literature—poetry. What else is a poem than a pattern, a structure of images, loosely connected, of glimpses of nature, movements, gestures, flashes of insight, snatches of conversation, juxtaposed, not to furnish an argument, an explanation, not even a description of the world, but as metaphors for a mood, an intuition of another human being's inner world.

Pinter's first ambition was to write poetry; basically he has remained a lyric poet whose plays are structures of images of the world, very clear and precise and accurate images, which, however, and this is the point, never aspire to be arguments, explanations, or even coherent stories, aiming to satisfy the audience's craving for vicarious experience through involvement in a nicely rounded incident; instead, Pinter's plays present us with a situation, or a pattern of interlocking situations designed to coalesce into a lyrical structure of moods and emotional insights.

This, however, does not mean that there is not a great deal of dramatic incident, suspense, witty characterisation, or pointed dialogue in Pinter's plays. While the overall effect is lyrical, the detail is intensely dramatic. Indeed, the indeterminacy of the characters, the ambiguity of events, heightens the dramatic tension: is the old man in *The Caretaker* really called Davies, or is he called Jenkins? Why is Stanley in *The Birthday Party* being pursued by two sinister figures? Has Stella in *The Collection* been unfaithful to her husband? Why does Ruth in *The Homecoming* accept the offer to become a prostitute so calmly? These questions are not raised by Pinter to be answered; nor are they, as his critics sometimes suggest, raised gratuitously merely to create spurious curiosity and suspense. They are raised as metaphors of the fact that life itself consists of a succession of such questions that cannot, or will not, be capable of an answer.

"My characters," Pinter has said, "tell me so much and no more, with reference to their experience, their aspirations, their motives, their history. Between my lack of biographical data about them and the ambiguity of what they say there lies a territory which is not only worthy of exploration but which it is compulsory to explore. You and I, the characters which grow on a page, most of the time we're inexpressive, giving little away, unreliable, elusive, evasive, obstructive, unwilling. But it's out of these attributes that a language arises. A language . . . . where, under what is said, another thing is being said." (Pinter, speech to the Seventh National Student Drama Festival in Bristol, *Sunday Times*, London, 4 March 1962.)

Basically a lyric poet, Pinter is deeply concerned with words, their sound, their rhythm, their meaning. "I have mixed feelings about words . . . Moving among them, sorting them out, watching them appear on the page, from this I derive a considerable pleasure. But at the same time I have another strong feeling about words which amounts to nothing less than nausea. Such a weight of words confronts us, day in, day out, words spoken . . . . words written by me and others, the bulk of it a stale, dead terminology; ideas endlessly repeated and permutated become platitudinous, trite, meaningless. Given this nausea, it's very easy to be overcome by it and step back into paralysis. I imagine most writers know something of this kind of paralysis. But if it is possible to confront this nausea, to follow it to its hilt and move through it, then it is possible to say that something

has occurred, that something has even been achieved."
(Pinter, speech at Bristol, as above.)

The tension in Pinter between the delight in words,
the love of vivid, vital language on the one hand, and the
nausea caused by the contemplation of the vast mass of
dead, atrophied language which daily confronts us, is
matched by the tension between his characters' inarticu-
lateness, the spontaneity with which they themselves utter their speech, and his own craftsmanship, his determination to *shape* what he writes.

"Given characters," he says, "who possess a momentum
of their own, my job is not to impose on them, not to
subject them to a false articulation, by which I mean
forcing a character to speak where he could not speak,
making him speak in a way he could not speak, making
him speak of what he could never speak. The relationship between author and characters should be a highly re-
spectful one, both ways. And if it's possible to talk of
gaining a kind of freedom from writing, it doesn't come
by leading one's characters into fixed and calculated postures, but by allowing them to carry their own can, by
giving them a legitimate elbow room. This can be extremely painful. It's much easier, much less pain, not to
let them live.

"I'd like to make quite clear at the same time that I
don't regard my own characters as uncontrolled, or an-
archic. They're not. The function of selection and arrangement is mine. I do all the donkey work, in fact, and
I think I can say that I pay a meticulous attention to the
shape of things, from the shape of a sentence to the over-
all structure of the play. This shaping, to put it mildly, is
of the first importance. I'm not in favour of diarrhea on
the stage. But I think a double thing happens. You arrange *and* you listen, following the clues you leave for

yourself, through the characters. And sometimes a balance is found, where image can freely engender image and where at the same time you are able to keep your sights on the place where the characters are silent and in hiding. It is in the silence that they are most evident to me." (Pinter, speech at Bristol, as above.)

Silence thus is, for Pinter, an essential, an integral part, and often the climax, of his use of language. He has been reproached with a mannerism of silence, an excessive use of long pauses. These strictures are true, but again they seem to me to err insofar as they attribute mercenary motives to what is, to this particular playwright, simply part of his creed as a poet and craftsman, a highly personal way of experiencing, and reacting to, the world around him. And indeed, if we try to listen, with an ear unburdened by an age-old tradition of stage dialogue, to the real speech of real people, we shall find that there are more silences, longer pauses than those allowed by stage convention. And also that a great deal of what *is* spoken, in effect, qualifies as little more than silence: "There are two silences. One when no word is spoken. The other when perhaps a torrent of language is employed. This speech is speaking of a language locked beneath it. That is its continual reference. The speech we hear is an indication of that we don't hear. It is a necessary avoidance, a violent, sly, anguished, or mocking smoke-screen which keeps the other in its place. When true silence falls we are still left with echo but are nearer nakedness. One way of looking at speech is to say it is a constant stratagem to cover nakedness." (Pinter, speech at Bristol, as above.)

The discovery that stage dialogue is a stratagem to cover nakedness, that therefore what is said is merely a chain of rocks and small islands supported by a vast

mountain range beneath the sea's surface, this discovery
is not Pinter's but was first made by Chekhov. In the
fourth act of *The Cherry Orchard* Varya and Lopakhin
actually talk about some article of clothing Varya is looking for, but beneath that trivial exchange there runs
Lopakhin's inability to summon up the courage to pro-
pose to her, *her* inability to give the conversation a turn
that might force him into it. Lopakhin asks her, "What
are you looking for?" Varya replies, "I packed the things
myself, yet I can't remember . . . (*A pause.*)" And in
that pause, that hesitation on both sides to speak the first
word, to end the silence, lies the turning point of the
destiny of these characters. The example—and one could
find dozens of others in Chekhov—shows the relation between this kind of "oblique" dialogue and the pause. It
is the pause that shows the audience that the real preoccupation of the characters, the unspoken subtext, is going
on beneath the surface, but that it is unable to come into
the open. Pinter has developed this Chekhovian technique much further than his master. In Chekhov's plays
there is still a very great deal that is explicit in the traditional conception of stage dialogue; Pinter is able to put
far more into the form of "oblique" dialogue, to let far
more of the real emotional tension of a situation shine
through the interstices of monosyllabic utterance.

One of the labels that has bedevilled criticism of Pinter
is that of a theatre of non-communication. Lopakhin's
failure to declare himself, Varya's inability to make him
speak, would clearly also come into this category, so that,
even if the label fitted, the thing itself could by no means
be regarded as a novelty, an invention of the mid-fifties
of this century. But, of course, what is involved is not
a failure, let alone an impossibility of communication,
merely a *difficulty* of explicit communication. "I think,"

Pinter has said, "that we communicate only too well, in our silence, in what is unsaid, and that what takes place is continual evasion, desperate rear-guard attempts to keep ourselves to ourselves. Communication is too alarming. To enter into someone else's life is too frightening. To disclose to others the poverty within us is too fearsome a possibility. I'm not suggesting that no character in a play can ever say what he in fact means. Not at all. I have found that there invariably does come a moment when this happens, where he says something, perhaps, which he has never said before. And where this happens, what he says is irrevocable, and can never be taken back." (Pinter, speech at Bristol, as above.)

A playwright so fascinated by the difficulty, the terror, the pitfalls of communication will inevitably be fascinated by words and their multifarious uses to disclose and to disguise meaning. Pinter's theatre is a theatre of language; it is from the words and their rhythm that the suspense, the dramatic tension, the laughter, and the tragedy spring. Words, in Pinter's plays, become weapons of domination and subservience, silences explode, nuances of vocabulary strip human beings to the skin. Not even his severest critics have ever cast doubt on Pinter's virtuosity in the use of language. His "tape-recorder" ear has often been praised. And rightly: few English playwrights before him have displayed so acute an observation of the mannerisms, repetitions, and nonsensicalities of the vernacular as it is actually spoken. But there is more to Pinter's use of language than merely accurate observation. In fact, what sounds like tape-recorded speech is highly stylised, even artificial. It is his ability to combine the appearance of utter reality with complete control of rhythm and nuance of meaning that is the measure of Pinter's stature as a poet. Pinter's dialogue is as tightly—perhaps more tightly—controlled than verse. Every syllable, every inflection, the succession of long and short sounds, words and sentences, is calculated to a nicety. And precisely the repetitiousness, the discontinuity, the circularity of ordinary vernacular speech are here used as formal elements with which the poet can compose his linguistic ballet. And yet, because the ingredients from which he takes the recurring patterns and artfully broken rhythms *are* fragments of a brilliantly observed, and often hitherto overlooked, reality, he succeeds in creating the illusion of complete naturalness, of naturalism.

An introductory chapter is not the place for a detailed study of Pinter's linguistic techniques. We shall return to the subject after an analysis of Pinter's work, play by play. What must be stressed at this point is the essentially *dramatic* nature of his use of language. Brecht demanded that the language of drama should be *gestural;* i.e., that the syntax and rhythm of each sentence alone should force the actor into making the appropriate gesture and movement. Pinter's use of language eminently fulfills Brecht's requirement. The speech rhythms of the tramp Davies in *The Caretaker* positively cry out for the impotent stabbing movement of his gesture; Aston's casual style of speech in the same play totally implies and dictates the slowness of his movements, his stillness while endlessly trying to fix an electric plug.

Equally dramatic is the way in which Pinter uses language as a vehicle and instrument of dramatic *action.* Words become weapons in the mouths of Pinter's characters. The one who gets hold of the more elaborate or more accurate expression establishes dominance over his partner; the victim of aggression can be swamped by language that comes too thick and fast, or is too nonsensical to be comprehended: this happens, above all, to Stanley in *The Birthday Party,* who is subjected to a process of brainwashing through a torrent of incomprehensible questions and assertions fired at him by the two terrorists.

The precision, economy, and control Pinter exercises over the language of his dialogue firmly links him to the tradition of English high comedy. No wonder that Noël Coward, the leading contemporary representative of that tradition, has saluted Pinter as the one among the "new wave" of British dramatists whose craftsmanship in the use of language he respects and admires. The fact that he can quite legitimately be related to Kafka and Beckett on the one hand, and to Oscar Wilde and Noël Coward on the other, is highly characteristic of Pinter's originality, his ability to work on a multiplicity of different levels. Insofar as his plays are firmly rooted in real speech and real situations he appears naturalistic—and was, in fact, originally lumped together with the social-realist "kitchen sink" school; insofar as he eschews motivation and questions the very nature of reality his plays can be seen as structures of lyrical images of an unverified, unverifiable, and therefore dreamlike world between fantasy and nightmare; insofar as his observation of linguistic quirks is uncannily sharp, his dialogue must be considered as one of the most realistic representations of the genuine vernacular of the mid-twentieth century; but because the real speech of real people is to a large extent composed of solecism and tautology, it can also be likened to nonsense-poetry and the literature of the absurd. From one angle of vision, this world of inhibited, half-conscious, inarticulate people surrounding themselves with irrational anxieties is grotesque and comic;

from another point of view, it will appear pitiable and tragic.

This kind of ambivalence, indeed of multivalence, Pinter might argue, is in itself a realistic trait; for reality itself is equally multivalent. When Leonard Russell, during the run of *The Caretaker* in London, addressed an open letter to Pinter, deploring the gales of laughter about the unhappy plight of the old tramp in the play, Pinter replied: "An element of the absurd is, I think, one of the features of the play, but at the same time I did not intend it to be merely a laughable farce. If there hadn't been other issues at stake the play would not have been written. Audience reaction can't be regulated, and no one would want it to be; nor is it easy to analyse. But where the comic and the tragic (for want of a better word) are closely interwoven, certain members of an audience will always give emphasis to the comic as opposed to the other, for by so doing they rationalise the other out of existence. On most evenings at the Duchess there is a sensible balance of laughter and silence. Where, though, this indiscriminate mirth is found, I feel it represents a cheerful patronage of the characters on the part of the merrymakers, and thus participation is avoided. This laughter is in fact a mode of precaution, a smoke-screen, a refusal to accept what is happening as recognisable (which I think it is) and instead to view the actors (a) as actors always and not as characters, and (b) as chimpanzees. From this kind of uneasy jollification I must, of course, dissociate myself . . . . As far as I'm concerned, *The Caretaker* is funny, up to a point. Beyond that point it ceases to be funny, and it was because of that point that I wrote it." (Pinter, *Sunday Times*, London, 14 August 1960.)

This statement is the definition of Pinter's own, personal brand of tragicomedy: plays that can be very funny up to the point when the absurdity of the characters' predicament becomes frightening, horrifying, pathetic, tragic. "Comedies of menace" they have been called (in a term first used in 1957 by David Campton, in the subtitle of his play *The Lunatic View*, and first applied to Pinter by Irving Wardle in an article which appeared in *Encore* in September 1958). The term, which echoes the sobriquet "comedy of manners," has its justification. For, as Pinter pointed out in his letter to Leonard Russell, much of the laughter that accompanies his plays up to that point where they cease to be funny is already the laughter of precaution against panic, the whistling in the dark of people who are trying to protect themselves against the menace, the horror, which lies at the core of the action they are witnessing. Even when that laughter tends to be patronising, when it displays the audience's delight in their superiority over characters who are struggling to express even the simplest things in intelligible language, even there it is mingled with the uneasy realisation that, basically, even the more articulate among us have the same difficulties with vocabulary, syntax, and the logical arrangement of our thought. But this is only one, and the least frightening, aspect of Pinter's tragicomic vision of the world. The real menace which lies behind the struggles for expression and communication, behind the closed doors which might swing open to reveal a frightening intruder, behind the sinister gunmen and terrorists, behind the violence, the menace behind all these menacing images is the opaqueness, the uncertainty, and precariousness of the human condition itself. How can we know who we are, how can we verify what is real and what is fantasy, how can we know what we are saying, what is being said to us? "I'm speaking," Pinter once said as he began to make a speech, "knowing that there are at least twenty-four possible aspects of any single statement, depending on where you're standing at the time or on what the weather is like." (Pinter, speech at Bristol, as above.) This is a jocular expression of a state of affairs, but it cannot hide the fact that the state of affairs—which is a true one—is disconcerting and a potential source of terror.

A writer who—naïvely—believes that reality is simple and clearly defined, and can be tackled with confidence from a firm viewpoint, can plan and calculate his work with far greater confidence and foresight than a poet of Pinter's cast of mind, who sees the world as mysterious, multifaceted, and unfathomable. Such a poet can merely follow the outlines of his vision; his working method will have to be highly intuitive. "All I know," Pinter has said, "is that blank sheet of paper in front of me, and then, when it's filled, I can't believe it. I don't throw away many sheets of paper that are filled. I do, of course, go over the sheets of paper many times. I regard myself as an old-fashioned writer. I like to create character and follow a situation to its end. I write quite visually—I can say that. I watch the invisible faces quite closely. The characters take on a physical shape. I watch the faces as closely as I can. And the bodies. I can't see a consistency in my work. I have no idea whether the plays have a consistency or have not. Each play is quite a different world. The problem is to create a unique world in each case with a totally different set of characters. With a totally different environment. It's a great joy to do that." (Pinter, interview in *The New Yorker*, 25 February 1967.)

The starting point is sometimes no more than a situation. Two people in a room. A few words. At the time when he had just begun work on what later became the play *Landscape*, Pinter is quoted as having said: "I've started a couple of pages of something quite different. A new form and I'm diving. It's simply, as it stands, about a woman around fifty. That's all I bloody well know. I don't know where she is . . ." (Kathleen Tynan, "In Search of Harold Pinter," *Evening Standard*, London, 26 April 1968.) So intuitive a writer could not possibly have an axe to grind, a philosophy to propagate. "I only formulate conclusions after I've written the plays. I've no idea what I'm obsessed with—just so pleased to see the words on paper . . ." (*Ibid.*)

It is from the conjunction of this type of obsessive vision and an accomplished craftsman's sense of form and style that this kind of work must spring. The method of work also illumines the seeming contradiction between the meticulous outward reality of the characters and their speech, and the dreamlike, nightmarish quality of the plays as a whole. Intuitions of the obsessive intensity that Pinter describes when he talks about his method of work *are* daydreams, almost hallucinations. Their very realism is part of their menace: it is the clarity of outline of the most frightening nightmares. The dreamer of such dreams may not be aware of their inner consistency, yet on closer analysis they will be bound to reveal to the dispassionate observer such a consistency, which is no more and no less than the structure of the dreamer's personality itself. That is why the work of artists of Pinter's stature can also, though not solely or even mainly, be open to a psychoanalytical approach, not to yield any revelations about the author's personality and problems, but to explain the impact of the work on audiences. It is not the private, personal element in such works of art that exercises that appeal, but the element that the author *shares* with the rest of mankind. This is the secret of the impact of *Oedipus* or *Hamlet*. It is the contention of this study that Pinter's work is open to analysis of this kind, precisely because it *has* a similar impact.

In a very early manuscript, which must date back to Pinter's late teens or early twenties, he clearly, brilliantly, in some ways prophetically describes just this quality of a major dramatist. The text is fairly cryptically entitled "A Note on Shakespeare." It starts:

> The mistake they make, most of them, is to attempt to determine and calculate, with the finest instruments, the source of the wound. They seek out the gaps between the apparent and the void that hinges upon it, with all due tautness. They turn to the wound with deference, a lance, and a needle and thread.
>
> At the entrance of the lance, the gap widens. At the use of needle and thread, the wound coagulates and atrophies in their hand.
>
> Shakespeare writes of the open wound, and through him, we know it open and know it closed. We tell when it ceases to beat, and tell it at its highest peak of fever.
>
> In attempting to approach Shakespeare's work in its entirety, you are called upon to grapple with a perspective in which the horizon alternately collapses and re-forms behind you; in which the mind's participation is subject to an intense diversity of atmosphere.

Once the dedication has begun, however, there is no other way but to him.

One discovers a long corridor of postures; fluid and hardened at the quick; gross and god-like; putrescent and copulative; raddled; attentive; crippled and gargantuan; crumbling with the dropsy; heavy with elephantiasis; broody with government; severe; fanatical; paralytic; voluptuous; impassive; musclebound; lissome; virginal; unwashed; bewildered; humpbacked; icy and statuesque. All are contained in the wound which Shakespeare does not attempt to sew up or re-shape, whose pain he does not attempt to eradicate. He amputates, deadens, aggravates at will, within the limits of a particular piece, but he will not pronounce judgement or cure. Such comment as there is, is so variously split up between characters, and so contradictory in itself, that no central point of opinion or inclining can be determined.

He himself is trapped in his own particular order, and is unable to go out at a distance to regulate and forestall abortion or lapses in vraisemblance. He can only rely on a "few well-chosen words" to bring him through any doubtful patch.

He belongs of course, ultimately, to a secret society, a conspiracy, of which there is only one member; himself. . . .

There follows, in this remarkable description of a great playwright's existential situation, a long catalogue of the self-contradictory elements, the multitude of bizarre personalities that that playwright, whom the young author

chooses to call Shakespeare, carried within himself. The
text ends with this summing up:

> The fabric never breaks. The wound is open.
> The wound is contained. The wound is peo-
> pled.

"A Note on Shakespeare" dates back to the time of
Pinter's earliest efforts as a writer. All the more remarkable is its insight into the creative process of the kind of
dramatist into which he, himself, was later destined to
develop. For it is out of the wound of existential anguish
that the playwright's effort springs to come to terms with
the world and its mystery, its suffering, its bewildering
multiplicity. The wound, the playwright's eye, his perception of the world, is open: that is why all the world
enters into it. The wound is the world. And the world is
the wound. And—because the world's suffering and anguish are the anguish and the suffering of other people as
well as of the mind behind the open eye, the open wound
—the wound *is* peopled.

III

ANALYSIS

EARLY POETRY

When he emerged as a dramatist in 1957, Pinter was twenty-seven years old. But he had published poems since before he was twenty. Two poems, "New Year in the Midlands" and "Chandeliers and Shadows," appeared in the August 1950 number of *Poetry London.* Unfortunately the ends of the two poems got confused in the printing. *Poetry London* tried to make amends by publishing "New Year in the Midlands" again in the following number (November 1950), while "Chandeliers and Shadows" had to wait until 1968 to appear in its correct form in the slim volume of *Poems* published by the Enitharmon Press.

"New Year in the Midlands," although couched in a Dylan Thomas-like idiom of concentrated exuberance, already contains Pinter's sharp eye for the dreamlike quality of the world in all its sordid reality:

. . . . and here am I,
Straddled, exile always in one Whitbread Ale town,
Or such.
Where we went to the yellow pub, cramped in an alley
    bin,
A shoot from the market,
And found the thin Luke of a queer, whose pale
Deliberate eyes, raincoat, Victorian,
Sap the answer in the palm. . . .

The thin, pale queer in the raincoat is already a Pinter character in embryo. "Chandeliers and Shadows," on the other hand, with its motto from *The Duchess of Malfi* ("I'le goe hunt the badger by owle-light: 'tis a deed of darknesse")—omitted in the 1968 reprint—contains its intimation of the baroque, fantastic Pinter of plays to come:

. . . Yet I, lunatic from lunatic spheres,
Shall run crazy with lepers,
And bring God down the chimney,
A tardy locust,
To plunder and verminate man's pastures, entirely . . .

("You verminate the sheet of your birth" is one of Goldberg's accusations against Stanley in *The Birthday Party*.) There is much adolescent love of unusual and archaic words in this and other early poems of Pinter's ("floodlit emperies," "palsied stomacher," a "necromantic cauldron of crosses" in this one poem alone), but the imagery is strong and haunting; it betrays the author's grasp of the poetic quality of the *situations* his imagination thrusts upon him. These poems are clearly written in a state of obsession with words, under the spell of an irresistible impulse. Hence some of them are so private in their surrealist automatic writing that they scarcely yield a meaning to the outsider. "One a Story, Two a Death," for example, a longish narrative poem that appeared in the Summer 1951 issue of *Poetry London* and was not reprinted in the collected volume of 1968, starts with the cryptic stanzas:

Brought in a bowl of flaming crocuses
In an ebon mirrorless age,

Let fall to her face
Till her cheeks lit in tongues.

Who would laugh and call Zello,
See how scorched is the boy,
Who would laugh at the arrow
I should plunge in her eye . . .

There is a dead girl in the poem who is visited by the poet, but little more can be discerned in the darkness of its whirling images. Yet here too some of the images of the plays already appear:

The giant negro tones in ether his flute—

foreshadowing the symbolic death figure of the Negro in *The Room.*

Where in his cape walks the negro,
Growing flowers on his groin.

In another poem from *Poetry London* not reprinted in the collected edition, "European Revels," we meet one of the destructive females of the later Pinter as well as violent men, reminiscent of the killers in *The Dumb Waiter,* the terrorists in *The Birthday Party:*

Her men lovers plasterlads, who
Felled rich women in the moon's Zodiac.

There is in these poems, as indeed in the early and hitherto unpublished novel *The Dwarfs* (which will be discussed in connection with the play of the same title), the recurring character of a young man, who, like Len in *The Dwarfs,* like Aston in *The Caretaker,* has a tendency to talk too much and too intensely and fears the moment when society, the outside world, or his own growing up, will put a stop to this stream of exuberant, mad talking:

Only the deaf can hear and the blind understand
The miles I gabble.
Through these my dances of dunce and devil,
It's only the dumb can speak through the rubble.
Time shall drop his spit in my cup,
With this vicious cut he shall close my trap
And gob me up in a drunkard's lap.
All spirits shall haunt me and all devils drink me;
O despite their dark drugs and the digs that they rib me,
I'll tear off my terrible cap.
                    ("I Shall Tear Off My Terrible Cap," 1951)

Note the use of assonant rhymes, alternating between *a* and *u* sounds: gabble/rubble; cup/trap. The parallels, particularly to Aston's situation, seem difficult to overlook. The same is surely true of the short poem "The Anaesthetist's Pin" (1952), which introduces that instrument linked to "the amputator's saw" and ends:

> At that incision sound
> The lout is at the throat
> And the dislocated word
> Becomes articulate.

Which seems to indicate that the operation is—as in the case of Aston in *The Caretaker*—concerned with curing an excess of speech ("the dislocated word"), hence the "amputation" and the "anaesthetist's pin" may well stand for a lobotomy or electric-shock treatment.

The earliest text in the volume of *Poems* is dated 1949, and had remained unpublished until that volume appeared almost twenty years later. This is the dialogue prose poem "Kullus," which has already been discussed

in the previous chapter and contains the *motif* of the
room and the intruder which pervades Pinter's work from
The Room to *The Basement*. Kullus, a character who
clearly played a considerable part in the young writer's
imagination, also makes an appearance in the poem "The
Task" (1954). And again he is linked to the image of the
room:

> The last time Kullus, seen,
> Within a distant call,
> Arrived at the house of bells,
> The leaf obeyed the bud,
> I closed the open night
> And tailormade the room.

The three following stanzas are variations on the key
words—house, night, leaf, bud, open, night, and room:
the house of bells, for example, becomes the house of
night; the leaf, which obeyed the bud, now alarmed the
bud, etc. Thus the poem anticipates the kaleidoscopic
effect of the changes in the furniture and situation in the
room that is the scene of *The Basement*. The character
of Kullus makes a third appearance in the short story
"The Examination," first published in the review *Prospect*
in the summer of 1959. Here the narrator is engaged in
a contest of wills with Kullus, which takes the form of
some sort of examination. As one or the other of the con-
testants attains a position of dominance over the other,
the room in which the contest takes place becomes his
property.

There is nothing surprising in the re-emergence of
early preoccupations and imagery in the mature work of
a writer. Yet the presence of these basic *motifs* helps to
show us some aspects of the genesis of the author's world

and its particular, highly personal atmosphere after "the dislocated word" had "become articulate."

THE ROOM

Pinter's first play shows the emergence of a firm dramatic structure and well-observed characters from the world of lyrical dream images, which pervaded his early poetry, with particular force and clarity.

The basic situation, which was so frequently to recur, is that of a room, a room with a door; and outside the door, a cold, hostile world. The room is warm and light. Outside it is winter, cold and dark. The second basic component of the play is equally characteristic of much of the later Pinter: a couple—the man large, brutal, fifty years old; the woman older than the man, almost sixty, motherly, sentimental. The woman is completely devoted, completely absorbed in looking after the man. The man just sits there, reads his paper, and allows himself to be fed and pampered. He never utters a word. Rose, the woman, seems to be married to the man, Bert Hudd, but that is by no means certain. Already Pinter manages to maintain an aura of ambiguity, uncertainty around his characters. Rose certainly seems very anxious to please Bert, to make herself as useful and agreeable to him as possible. She forces her solicitude upon him. But he shows no reaction whatever.

A warm room surrounded by a cold and hostile world is, in Pinter's case, in itself a very dangerous situation. Somebody will be pushed from the warmth of the room out into the cold. And a couple, man and woman, where the woman so obviously wants to give love and the man so obviously does not accept her gift, must be a dangerous, ominous constellation. The woman is fighting to maintain the relationship. The man remains cold. When will he abandon the woman?

From the very first moments of the play Pinter stresses Rose's fears by her constant insistence on the cosiness and warmth of the room, as against the dampness and obscurity of the basement flat that had at first been offered to them. Again and again she asks herself whether there are any tenants still living in that basement, and congratulates herself on living on the first floor. Bert, who drives a van, still has a delivery to make; he will have to go out into the cold of the winter evening. But even when Mr. Kidd, an elderly man who is hard of hearing and whom Rose treats as the landlord, though he seems to be no more than the caretaker, enters the room, Bert Hudd remains completely silent, so that we ask ourselves whether he will ever speak, whether indeed he can speak at all.

Rose tries to interrogate Mr. Kidd about the tenants down in the basement. But he does not hear her questions—because he is deaf, or perhaps for other, more sinister reasons?—and does not even seem to know how many floors there are in the house: "Well, to tell you the truth, I don't count them now. . . . Oh, I used to count them once. Never got tired of it. I used to keep a tack on everything in this house. . . . That was when my sister was alive. But I lost track a bit, after she died."

There is nothing intrinsically improbable or unreal in an old man who is so dotty that he talks nonsense. And yet, very characteristically already, by an accumulation of such basically realistic detail Pinter succeeds in building up an atmosphere of menace, of Kafkaesque uncertainty. The silent giant van-driver, the anxious woman clinging to the warmth of her room, and the room being

situated in a house of uncertain size, so that it seems
suspended between an unexplored basement and a top
that loses itself in a dim, unending flight of stairs—each
of these details may in itself be explained away; in accumulation they create tension and foreboding.

Mr. Kidd leaves, and so, after a while, does Bert Hudd.
Now Rose is alone. She is about to put the dustbin outside the door. When she opens the door, she is terrified:
there are people standing there, a young man and a girl.
So subtly has Pinter created the atmosphere of menace
that surrounds the room, of the hostility of the cold world
outside it, that the mere presence of people on the land-
ing—an ordinary enough occurrence—strikes not only
Rose but the audience as well with a veritable shock;
with such simple means has a *coup de théâtre* of great
impact been produced.

At first it seems as though all this terror would turn
out to have been a false alarm. The young couple is looking for a room. What could be more normal and reassur-
ing? They were looking for the landlord to ask him
whether there was one available in the house. But Mr.
Kidd, whom Rose regards as the landlord but whose
name is not recognised by the young couple as the one
they have been given as the owner's, has just been saying
that there were no rooms to be let in the house. And
then—to heighten the menace again—Mrs. Sands, the
young woman, tells Rose how in their search for the landlord they had gone down to the basement:

> . . . and we couldn't see where we were go-
> ing, well, it seemed to me it got darker the more
> we went, the further we went in, I thought we
> must have come to the wrong house. So I
> stopped. And Toddy stopped. And then this

voice said, this voice came—it said—well, it gave
me a bit of a fright, I don't know about Tod,
but someone asked if he could do anything for
us. So Tod said we were looking for the landlord
and this man said the landlord would be upstairs. Then Tod asked was there a room vacant.
And this man, this voice really, I think he was
behind the partition, said yes there was a room
vacant. . . .

Even the vagueness and uncertainty with which the
story is told—in Pinter's masterly handling of the vernacular—the very woolliness of the syntax adds to the atmosphere of horror and fear which it must strike in Rose's
mind—and the audience's, now totally identified with her.
When Rose insists that Mr. Kidd told her the house was
full up, Mr. Sands replies:

The man in the basement said there was one.
One room. Number Seven he said.
(*Pause.*)
ROSE: That's this room.

Again, with the simplest of means, a real shock has been
produced. To Rose the very idea that the room which she
regards as hers should be talked about as being to let is
tantamount to a death sentence.

As Rose violently denies that her room is going to become vacant, the visitors leave. Now Mr. Kidd returns,
in a state of considerable excitement. He is so agitated
that he does not even hear Rose's indignant question
how people could get the idea that her room might be
to let. For Mr. Kidd discloses that for days now he has
been plagued by an intruder, who does not give him a
moment's peace, a man who wants to talk to Rose, is con-

stantly asking for her, is lying down there in the basement and refuses to budge. He wants to see Rose as soon
as her husband is out of the room. For two days Mr. Kidd
has been waiting for that moment. That's why he had
come earlier—to see if Bert had not gone yet. Rose refuses to receive the mysterious intruder. She does not
know anyone who might want to talk to her. But when
Mr. Kidd hints that then the stranger might come into
the room when Bert is present, she relents. Let him be
asked to come quickly. Mr. Kidd leaves. Again Rose is
left by herself.

And now again the door has become the focal point
of suspense and tense expectation. When it opens, what
will it disclose?

At last the door does open: a blind Negro enters; Riley
he calls himself. Rose reacts to him with all the symptoms of disgust, fear, even race hatred.

But Riley has a message for Rose. From whom? From
her father: "Your father wants you to come home." And
Riley calls Rose by a different name: "Come home, Sal."
And, indeed, it seems that Riley is not only a messenger
from Rose's—Sal's—father, but that he *is* her father:

> RILEY: I want you to come home.
> ROSE: No.
> RILEY: With me.
> ROSE: I can't.
> RILEY: I waited to see you.
> ROSE: Yes.
> RILEY: Sal.

Now Rose acquiesces in being called Sal, although only
a few moments earlier, she had angrily asked not to be
called by that name. And she even, in what is clearly a
moment of truth, confesses that her life is almost in-

tolerable: "The day is a hump. I never go out." It is a moment of great lyrical intensity, for the phrase is simple but memorable.

At this moment Bert comes back. He has returned from his trip into the night. And—again a shock effect achieved by the simplest of means—for the first time in the play, he speaks. He speaks about having come back safely, although "they got it dark out," although "they got it very icy out." Then, in a speech of some length, he describes how hard he drove his van: "I caned her along. She was good." The erotic overtones of this impassioned outburst about the van, always referred to in the feminine gender, are unmistakable.

> . . . I use my hand. Like that. I get hold of
> her. I go where I go. She took me there. She
> brought me back.

It is only now that Bert becomes aware of the intruder. With a single exclamation: "Lice!" he attacks the Negro, throws him out of his armchair, and kicks his head against the gas stove, until he lies motionless on the floor. Rose clutches her eyes. She has gone blind.

The Room is a remarkable first play. The dialogue is already masterly; each character has his own style of speech and the wittily observed vernacular with its rambling syntax and tautologies is brilliantly modulated into the intensity of the poetic climax between Rose and Riley. The suddenness of the brutal ending, which comes as a complete surprise, also has a tremendous impact.

It is only the use of the perhaps too overtly symbolical and poetic figure of the blind Negro that might be felt as a break in style; for whereas in the rest of the play the dreamlike and poetic quality arises directly from the

realistic detail, here we are confronted with almost a
cliché metaphor, an allegorical figure from a different,
a neo-romantic or Pre-Raphaelite style.

The room, the relationship between the brutal husband
and his sentimental wife, who is tormented by dark fore-
bodings and existential fears, is seen in entirely realistic
and psychologically accurate terms; indeed, the older
couple—Bert and Rose—are subtly contrasted with the
young people, Mr. and Mrs. Sands, who are looking for
a room; their relationship also shows the signs of tension
between a more intelligent woman and a lazy and dull
man who dominates her by sheer brutality. (Mrs. Sands
says she saw a star outside; Mr. Sands has not seen it; he
simply decrees that she did not see a star.) So the young
couple could be Rose and Bert at an earlier stage. The
mystery and dreamlike anxiety that pervade the first
half of the play in fact emerge from the contrasts between the clarity and realism of these well observed features and the layers of darkness that envelop this pool of
light: the night outside, the basement, the large, unexplored house with its uncertain number of floors. This is
a Rembrandtesque technique of chiaroscuro, and most
effective in creating an atmosphere of foreboding and
uncertainty. The blind Negro, on the other hand, who
has been lying in the basement for days and who appears
to bring Rose a message from her past, is all too manifestly a symbol, an allegory. He has been lying down be-
low and had foreknowledge of the future—that Room
No. 7 would soon be vacant. He must therefore be a
being from beyond the confines of this world: a dead
man or a messenger of death, perhaps Rose's own dead
father. His blackness and his blindness reinforce these
allegorical implications. The blindness that strikes Rose

at the end belongs to the same category of symbolism—
it must mean the end of her relationship with Bert, but
probably more than that: her death.

The character of the old caretaker—or landlord?—Mr.
Kidd combines the realistic and the symbolical elements
in a far more successful manner. His inability to recall
the number of floors in the house, for example, certainly
reinforces the eerie, dreamlike atmosphere, yet it also
can be quite realistically explained as the result of his
senility or hardness of hearing. Yet it cannot be just a
physical disability, or even mental deterioration, which
would wholly explain Mr. Kidd's uncertainty about his
own background (about which he has not even been
asked). *"I think my mum was a Jewess. Yes, I wouldn't
be surprised to learn that she was a Jewess."* Not even a
high degree of feeblemindedness would explain this degree of uncertainty, particularly as Mr. Kidd displays no
symptoms of mental incapacity in bringing Rose the message from her visitor, or in persisting in trying to get it
to her. The inference is that Mr. Kidd may simply be an
inveterate liar or mystifier. After all, when he has been
talking a good deal about his sister and has left the room,
Rose's reaction is: "I don't believe he had a sister, ever."
Here Pinter's use of uncertainty about what his characters
say and mean can thus still be seen as somewhat mechanical and arbitrary. He hardly ever makes this kind
of mistake in his later work.

It is very characteristic of Pinter that the element of
race hatred (which, as we know, must have overshad-
owed his childhood in the East End of London) pervades
the play without ever being directly pushed into the
foreground. Mr. Kidd's strange vagueness about his own
origins introduces the subject, which breaks to the sur-

face with brutal clarity when Bert assaults the blind
Negro with the exclamation "Lice!" Here Bert's motivation must be one of racial hatred; after all, he has not
even taken the trouble to find out why the Negro is in
his room. Thus, he must be attacking him merely as an
object of instant racial revulsion. That Rose's father is
sending a Negro to her with his message, or that Rose's
father himself might be that Negro, must surely also be
a fact of considerable significance. The name by which
her father, or his messenger, addresses Rose is Sal—
Sarah?—which might indicate that the woman who now
calls herself Rose—an *English* Rose?—not only lives with
Bert under a false name, but perhaps may also be con-
cealing her true origin and identity; this would give Mr.
Kidd's musings about *his* possible Jewish origin a painful
irony in Rose's eyes. (In Hitler's Germany all Jewish
women were compelled to call themselves Sarah.) And
the knowledge that she is living in Bert's room, in his
household, under false pretences, as an outsider conceal-
ing her hated foreign origin, would also explain Rose's eagerness to please, her fear of the surrounding world, her
terror of discovery and expulsion, the strain under which
she is living, which makes each day a hump to be
climbed. Consciously or subconsciously, as far as the author is concerned, this might be the source of the existential anxiety that pervades the play and so much of Pinter's
other work. Again and again Rose congratulates herself
on living in a warm room rather than downstairs in the
dark and damp basement—in the underworld of the dead,
from which her dead father is calling for her. As a Jew
in the world of Auschwitz she would indeed be a fugitive
from death. Is this the reason why, when she finally shows
her true feelings to the blind Negro, she says, several

times, *"I have been here,"* as though she wanted to say, here, among strangers, in an alien land? The blindness and blackness of the messenger are, in themselves, symbols of death. That he is called Riley might be an additional pointer to his representing Rose's origins among a despised, underprivileged group.

Such speculations should not be taken as more than hints of possible lines of interpretation of just one of the many strands that make up this short but characteristically richly textured play. The poetic quality of such work springs from the very multiplicity of possible approaches, the ambivalence and ambiguity of the images of which it is composed. It must also be stressed that, of course, the audience is neither meant nor required to become consciously aware of all the possible significances of the symbols and images; what comes across is a total impression: the author's anxiety, which he communicates through this texture of images. Another strand, which, however, doubles and reinforces the same existential emotion, could be isolated from the images of Rose's fear that she might lose her man's love, her fear of being abandoned, her feeling of inadequacy. In the final minutes of the play these two strands coalesce: shortly before Bert brutally assaults the racial outcast—and indirectly Rose as a member of his group, whatever it might be—he also unmistakably reveals that she has failed to hold his affection; Bert's account of his trip in his van clearly shows that his sexual energy is no longer focussed on Rose; the van has ousted her from his affections. The journey into the winter night becomes an act of intercourse with its own triumphant orgasm. No wonder Rose is totally annihilated as the play ends.

THE DUMB WAITER

The Dumb Waiter, also in one act, uses the same basic situation as *The Room.* Again we are in a room enclosed by a dark, mysterious world outside. Again the people in the room are watching, in dreadful suspense, a door which is certain to open. Moreover, in this case we are, from quite an early point in the play, made aware of the fact that whoever it will be who enters by the door will have to die. For the two people in the room are professional assassins, Ben and Gus by name, working-class Cockneys. They are working for a mysterious organisation, which sends them from time to time across country on missions of this kind; at first they are told no more than the bare name of the town to which they have to go and the address at which they will have to call; then they just have to stay there and await further instructions. When these arrive they must liquidate their victim. Then they have to get back as quickly as they can; they don't even know who it is that disposes of the bodies, who cleans up the room where the execution has taken place. As soon as they are back at base, they have to stay at home waiting for the next phone call with the next address for the next execution.

This basic situation in *The Dumb Waiter* is a highly contrived one; it is as though it had been worked out *in order* to provide a new and ingenious variation on the room-door-suspense syndrome. On the other hand, hired killers are, after all, a familiar device of the gangster film and the stage thriller; Pinter as a seasoned repertory actor must have regarded it as a pretty commonplace and easily acceptable starting point. In any case, the variation on the opening situation of *The Room* is brilliantly ingenious and intelligent. Rose, in *her* room, looking at *her* door, was clearly a victim-to-be. Ben and Gus are looking at the door waiting for the victim to walk into the trap. This provides a very different element of suspense and a very different focus for the spectator's fears and hopes. Moreover, with the born dramatist's instinct, Pinter has a spectacular surprise up his sleeve. The audience is watching the door, the *only* way into the room. But there *is* another opening, out into the dark, menacing outside world. Neither the people in the room nor the audience have noticed that between the two beds on which the men are lolling, there is a panelled opening. Suddenly that panelling is pulled up and reveals that the basement room must, originally, have been the kitchen of a café or restaurant, for behind it there is a "dumb waiter." We know that the two men are waiting for their victim in a totally uninhabited, derelict house. Who, then, is working the dumb waiter? Moreover, in the tray that comes down, the two killers find chits of paper with orders; at first these are for very ordinary English fare: Soup of the day. Liver and onions. Jam tart. But gradually the orders become more and more outlandish: Macaroni Pastitsio. Ormitha Macarounada. Bamboo Shoots. Water Chestnuts and Chicken. Char Siu and Bean Sprouts. The two killers, who after all are just loyal employees trying to serve their masters and eager to obey orders, make desperate attempts to fill these orders as well as they can. Gus, the more intelligent of the two—and therefore also more tormented by doubt and guilt feelings—ransacks his luggage to find old biscuits, a packet of potato chips, a small bottle of milk, a packet of tea. These efforts reveal to Ben, who clearly is the senior partner, that Gus has been less than candid with him, having concealed the fact that

he had a packet of potato chips so as not to have to
offer him a few. . . .

Gus repeatedly asks how it can happen that demands
for food should come into the kitchen of a derelict building. Again and again the two men try to convince the
supernatural power bombarding them with impossible
demands that they have nothing to send. Finally they
discover that, as is usual in restaurant kitchens, there is
a speaking tube next to the dumb waiter; it even has the
whistle through which one can announce one's desire to
communicate with the other end upstairs. Ben tries to
do so and hears a voice complaining that the Eccles cake
was stale, the chocolate was melted. On top of all this,
the mysterious voice is asking for tea. Now, Ben and Gus
have been trying to make themselves some tea ever since
they arrived; they had discovered that the gas in the flat
was working off a meter, and they did not have a shilling
between them to put in. Gus is indignant about the im-
pertinence of an unseen presence which is asking him to
make tea although it already knows that he has no shilling. Angrily he leaves to drink at least a glass of water
in the kitchen. When he is gone, the speaking tube begins
to whistle. Ben is getting his instructions from above. The
victim, it seems, has arrived. And now the door opens—a
man is pushed in. It is Gus, without his jacket, his holster,
his revolver. So it is Gus who is the victim! The two
partners face each other, staring at each other, as the
curtain falls. Will Ben kill his mate? The question remains
unanswered.

The symbolism, the intervention of supernatural powers, is thus even more obvious in *The Dumb Waiter* than
it is in *The Room*. Nevertheless the play marks a considerable step forward in the development of Pinter's personal style. It is, for instance, far more clear here that

the supernatural forces that come into play are expressions of the subconscious motivations of characters which, in themselves, are drawn with extreme realism. Ben and Gus, the Cockney killers, are sharply observed and most accurately characterised by their use of language.

From the first it is clear that there is a dangerous degree of tension between these two. They don't trust each other. Gus is in the process of developing guilt feelings; his discipline is getting slack. The last victim was a girl and so the job was an unusually messy one:

> What a mess. Honest, I can't remember a mess like that one. They don't seem to hold together like men, women. A looser texture, like. Didn't she spread, eh? She didn't half spread. Kaw!

Thus the dissolution of the partnership is clearly foreshadowed—just like the precariousness of the relationship between Bert and Rose, which finally erupts into symbolic violence in *The Room*—and the violent end becomes the concretisation of this hostility. We are, consequently, in an area of dream imagery. Because the two men are operating in a world whose workings they do not understand (an organisation that functions entirely above their heads), because they carry out instructions that seem without meaning to them, they have become especially irritable; each of them unloads his own insecurity, his guilt feelings, and the boredom that comes from doing incomprehensible things, upon the other.

If we disregard the bizarre detail of the initial assumption behind the occupation Gus and Ben pursue, we can see without any great difficulty what it is that the supernatural trappings of the play describe: no more and no less than the process of alienation to which men are sub-

jected in a highly organised industrial society, which denies to the individual, particularly the individual of low
intelligence and insight in the lower ranks, any real understanding of its working; and the frustration this en-
genders, the violence into which this frustration is bound
to erupt. After all, is an army so different from the organisation that employs Gus and Ben? In an army, too,
men are sent to destinations where they have to await
further orders as to when they are to start to shoot. Nor
does the machinery by which orders pass in an army differ
so very much from the manner in which Gus and Ben
receive their. (Remember, Pinter was a conscientious
objector and is a determined opponent of any organisation that requires its members to use violence.)

These reflections may point towards an interpretation
of *The Dumb Waiter*. But they should not be taken too
far or too literally. It is the essence of dream imagery of
this kind that the concretised metaphors it puts upon
the stage are by their very nature ambiguous, ambivalent,
and significant on a multiplicity of different levels. Ultimately what is being conveyed is a complex existential
situation—through its emotional tone; and in this case it
is the emotional situation of simple people in a social
context that is beyond their powers of comprehension.

The failure—on the part of Gus and Ben—to understand
the workings of their organisation, their frustration and
irritation find their expression in the dialogue, which
bristles with their difficulties of communication. Again
and again they become entangled in linguistic knots
which they are unable to unravel: the famous exchange
about whether one says "I'll light the kettle" or "I'll light
the gas" is just one among many similarly funny and
revealing passages. The battle of wills, the battle between
two different outlooks on life, different temperaments, is

translated into a battle between different views of language.

> BEN: If I say go and light the kettle I mean go and light the kettle.
>
> GUS: How can you light a kettle?
>
> BEN: It's a figure of speech! Light the kettle. It's a figure of speech!
>
> GUS: I've never heard it.
>
> BEN: Light the kettle! It's common usage!
>
> GUS: I think you've got it wrong.
>
> BEN (*menacing*): What do you mean?
>
> GUS: They say put on the kettle.
>
> BEN (*taut*): Who says?
>
> (*They stare at each other, breathing hard.*)
>
> (*Deliberately.*) I've never in all my life heard anyone say put on the kettle.
>
> GUS: I bet my mother used to say it.
>
> BEN: Your mother? When did you last see your mother?
>
> GUS: I don't know, about—
>
> BEN: Well, what are you talking about your mother for?
>
> (*They stare.*)
>
> Gus, I'm not trying to be unreasonable. I'm just trying to point something out to you.
>
> GUS: Yes, but—
>
> BEN: Who's the senior partner here, me or you?
>
> GUS: You.
>
> BEN: I'm only looking after your interests, Gus. You've got to learn, mate.
>
> GUS: Yes, but I've never heard—
>
> BEN (*vehemently*): Nobody says light the gas! What does the gas light?

Gus: What does the gas—?
BEN (*grabbing him with two hands by the throat, at arm's length*): *The kettle, you fool!*

The dispute about language is here quite manifestly a dispute about authority, a fight for dominance. Yet in the very next exchange, Ben is again threatened. Gus has consented to go and make the tea. But he hesitates. He wants to try out the matches (which, mysteriously, have been pushed under the door, when they complained about not having any left—a first intimation that there are mysterious powers about).

Gus: I want to see if they light.
BEN: What?
Gus: The matches.

Ben's "What?" is full of the fear that Gus might be persisting in his error, that he might reply: "If they light *the gas.*" He is relieved at Gus's reply. At first the matches don't light. When they finally are seen to be working, Ben says, "wearily": "Put on the bloody kettle for Christ's sake."

Unconsciously he has surrendered, by using Gus's phrase rather than his own. The stage direction is quite explicit here: "BEN *goes to his bed, but realising what he has said, stops and half turns. They look at each other.*"

This hostile look foreshadows the final confrontation of executioner and victim. *The Dumb Waiter* may thus, ultimately, be about the relationship between a pair of human beings, on the pattern of Beckett's *Nec tecum, nec sine te* in *Waiting for Godot*. There is always a death-wish at the bottom of these insoluble tensions. The supernatural forces driving us to murder our fellow human being are our subconscious desires and fantasies of aggression.

THE BIRTHDAY PARTY

Pinter's first full-length play combines elements from the two one-acters written during the same period of Pinter's career: the room, the safe haven menaced by an intrusion from the cold outside world, is here a seedy boarding house in a seaside resort where Stanley Webber, a not so very young man in his late thirties, has found refuge from the troubles of life. His landlady, Meg, a simple, elderly woman who looks after him with exaggerated solicitude and who obviously regards him as a son—but also as a kind of lover—recalls the character of Rose in *The Room.* And the two emissaries of a mysterious and brutal organisation who arrive to fetch Stanley away from Meg—a Jew, Goldberg, and an Irishman, McCann—have a good deal in common, both in their function and in their manner of operation, with the two hired killers in *The Dumb Waiter.* But these characters have become far more complex in the three-act play. The situation that forms the starting point for the action is also far more realistically treated, at least in its tangible, external detail, and thus acquires considerably greater power as a poetic metaphor.

Meg's husband, Petey, who is almost as silent as Rose's man Bert in *The Room,* but in a kindly, benevolent way, and Lulu, the buxom girl from next door, complete the sextet of characters; they, too, are treated with complete realism. The only area of darkness that remains concerns the reason *why* Stanley is hiding from the world, why Goldberg and McCann have come to spy him out.

Stanley, we learn, had come to the seaside resort in question as the pianist of a concert party who appeared at the pier. He even tells the story of an occasion when, so he claims, he gave a concert on his own in London; in Lower Edmonton, to be exact, which, after all, is anything but a major centre of artistic activity. But now he has been idle for months, hardly goes out of the house (perhaps because he is too lazy to shave and dress, but perhaps because he is afraid of being recognised?), pours contempt upon his landlady, who stifles him with her motherliness, yet seems totally dependent on her—an adult who has regressed to the status of a babe in arms. That Stanley is disappointed in the world which has rejected him becomes clear from his account of a second concert he was supposed to give:

> They carved me up. Carved me up. It was all arranged, it was all worked out. My next concert. Somewhere else it was. In winter. I went down there to play. Then, when I got there, the hall was closed, the place was shuttered up, not even a caretaker. They'd locked it up. . . . A fast one. They pulled a fast one. I'd like to know who was responsible for that. . . . All right, Jack, I can take a tip. They want me to crawl down on my bended knees. Well I can take a tip . . . any day of the week.

We learn this *before* the arrival of the two terrorists; clearly, Stanley *has* offended some powerful force. But who are *they*, who want him to crawl down on his bended knees? And what could he, a harmless pianist, have done to *them?*

On the day on which the action of the play starts— Pinter preserves the unities of time and place and compresses the action into a time-span of about twenty-four hours—Meg, who is always spoiling Stan with her oversolicitous infatuation, wants to surprise him with a gift. To motivate the present, she maintains it is his birthday, although it is almost certainly nothing of the sort, and, indeed, Meg probably does not even know the actual date of his birthday. In the course of the opening scenes of the play Lulu, the girl from next door, arrives with a big parcel containing Stanley's present. She is a girl of vulgar vitality and tries to arouse Stanley's interest, to get him to go out with her. But Stanley will not allow himself to be seduced.

When Goldberg and McCann, who obviously have been looking for Stanley all over the town, arrive, Meg blurts out the fact that it is Stanley's birthday. And Goldberg, who likes playing the part of a highly sociable fellow, suggests they should give him a party, to which Lulu is also to be invited. Stanley, who beat a hasty retreat when the two intruders appeared on the scene, returns after they have gone upstairs; and Meg unveils her present: he is, after all, a musician, and as he has no piano in the house, she is giving him another musical instrument: a drum. A boy's drum. At first Stanley is stupefied. But then he puts the drum round his neck and begins to beat it, in a normal rhythm at first, then more and more wildly. Meg has succeeded in making him regress to the status of a little boy, a child. Thus the savagery of his reaction signifies the depth of his despair; for Stanley seems to understand the meaning of his acceptance of the little boy's drum only too well. His "savage and possessed" drumming concludes the first act.

The second act is devoted to the "birthday party" itself, the ritual of Stanley's destruction by his two pursuers. At first, before the party has started, Stanley still tries to escape. But McCann, the brutal Irish terrorist, blocks his efforts to get out with increasingly open threats of violence. Petey, Meg's quiet husband, a deck-chair attendant on the promenade, will not be present at the party. He has to go to his chess club. But Lulu comes and immediately succumbs to Goldberg's routine seducer's tricks. Stanley, who has been subjected to a weird surrealist cross-examination by his tormentors before the party got under way, follows the proceedings from a corner of the room, where he sits silent and apathetic while the alcohol begins to flow and Goldberg indulges in sentimental recollections of his past family life. (The episodes he recounts are, however, strangely contradictory, even his own first name varies between Nat and Simey.) A game of blindman's buff forms the climax of the party. Stanley has his eyes bandaged, and McCann breaks Stanley's glasses in the process. Blinded, Stanley steps into his newly acquired drum (thus destroying the last vestige of his status as an artist? or putting an end to his being Meg's little boy?). Then, at last, he catches Meg: "His hands move towards her and they reach her throat. He begins to strangle her."

At this point the lights go out. Lulu is heard screaming. When McCann finds a torch, we see Lulu lying spread-eagled on the table and Stanley bending over her. As Goldberg and McCann move towards him, menacingly, he begins to giggle.

> The torch draws closer. His giggle rises and grows as he flattens himself against the wall. Their [i.e. Goldberg's and McCann's] figures converge upon him. CURTAIN.

Thus Stanley, having tried to strangle Meg and to rape Lulu, seems to have gone out of his mind as the avenging representatives of the organisation finally lay hands on him.

Act III: The next morning. Meg, who remained unaware throughout the "party" of what was going on, is
asking Petey whether Stanley is feeling better. Petey,
who witnessed something of the tortures to which Stanley was being subjected upstairs in his room during the
night, tries to keep her in the dark about the true state
of her beloved lodger. Outside the door there stands a
large black car which, as we later learn, belongs to Goldberg. The two intruders appear, and from their conversation we gather that the things that were done to Stanley in the night were pretty horrible and disgusting. Even
McCann refuses to go upstairs and enter Stanley's room.
And Goldberg, who seemed most vigorous the night before, now looks aged, deprived of his vitality. He is on
the point of collapse, McCann has to blow into his mouth
to revive him with a kind of "kiss of life." Lulu comes and
accuses Goldberg of having seduced and exploited her.
Petey feebly tries to protect Stanley from being taken
away by his tormentors. Without any success. Goldberg
says he knows a doctor who can look after Stanley. They
will take him there. And so Stanley is brought downstairs.
He is in a state of catatonic trance, unable to speak,
without any human reaction, but dressed most respectably in "a dark well-cut suit and white collar. He holds
his broken glasses in his hand. He is clean-shaven." Goldberg and McCann subject him to another flood of ver-
biage, reminiscent of the previous brainwashing scene,
but this time composed of clichés about recovery, treatment, recuperation, and success in the conventional
world:

> GOLDBERG: We'll make a man of you.
> McCANN: And a woman.
> GOLDBERG: You'll be re-orientated.

McCANN: You'll be rich.

GOLDBERG: You'll be adjusted.

McCANN: You'll be our pride and joy.

GOLDBERG: You'll be a mensch.

McCANN: You'll be a success.

GOLDBERG: You'll be integrated.

McCANN: You'll give orders.

GOLDBERG: You'll make decisions.

McCANN: You'll be a magnate.

GOLDBERG: A statesman.

McCANN: You'll own yachts.

GOLDBERG: Animals.

But Stanley can only reply with inarticulate gurgles. Then they take him away—to Monty, where he'll get "treatment."

Meg, still unaware of what has happened, returns from her shopping. She asks whether Stanley has come down yet. Petey hasn't the heart to tell her the truth. And Meg muses over the wonderful party they have had: "I was the belle of the ball. . . . Oh yes. They all said I was. Oh, it's true. I was. . . . I know I was."

A play like *The Birthday Party* can be understood only as a complex poetic image. Such an image exists, simultaneously, on a multitude of levels. A complex pattern of association and allusion is assembled to express a complex emotional state; what the poet tries to communicate by such an image is, ultimately, the totality of his own existential anxiety.

It is clear that the chief agent of this anxiety is Goldberg, the dominant partner in the team of terrorists. In his poem "A View of the Party" (dated 1958, the year of the first performance of the play) Pinter himself puts Goldberg into the centre:

> The thought that Goldberg was
> A man she might have known
> Never crossed Meg's words
> That morning in the room.
>
> The thought that Goldberg was
> A man another knew
> Never crossed her eyes
> When, glad, she welcomed him.
>
> The thought that Goldberg was
> A man to dread and know
> Jarred Stanley in the blood
> When, still, he heard his name.

Goldberg thus might be more than merely the *agent* of the evil power pursuing Stanley; he might be that power itself. At the same time, in the second part of the poem, it is suggested that Goldberg and McCann might, essentially, be forces in the mind—*thoughts:*

> The thought that Goldberg was
> Sat in the centre of the room,
> A man of weight and time,
> To supervise the game.
>
> The thought that was McCann
> Walked in upon this feast,
> A man of skin and bone,
> With a green stain on his chest.

So Goldberg and McCann are concrete men of weight and time, skin and bone, and yet they are also essentially thoughts. This ambivalence between the concrete reality of his characters and their simultaneous force as dream images, symbols, thoughts, is of the essence of Pinter's poetic personality; and it is here stated as clearly as he could ever be expected to define it.

Another point made very clear in this remarkable poem, "A View of the Party," is the theme of the room, the home from which Stanley is expelled. Pinter describes the party itself, and then continues:

> And Stanley sat—alone,
> A man he might have known,
> Triumphant on his hearth,
> Which never was his own.
>
> For Stanley had no home.
> Only where Goldberg was,
> And his bloodhound McCann,
> Did Stanley remember his name.

Finally, the image of blindness falling, which we already know from *The Room* and which recurs in a number of Pinter's other plays, is clearly present in *The Birthday Party*. For the poem closes with the lines:

> A man they never knew
> In the centre of the room,
> And Stanley's final eyes
> Broken by McCann.

The breaking of the glasses by McCann thus corresponds to the blinding of Rose in *The Room*.

Pinter's poem is entitled "A View of the Party." Just *a* view, one among many possible ones. What, then, could Goldberg and his organisation represent?

On one level it is fairly clear—particularly from the final image of Stanley in the uniform of respectable, bourgeois gentility—that Stanley is the *artist* whom society claims back from a comfortable, bohemian, "opt-out" existence. This, it seems, is possible because he is an artist who has doubts about his creative ability; he has not worked for a long time; he has come down from a piano to a little boy's drum; and even that he breaks in his clumsiness in the game of blindman's buff.

On another level *The Birthday Party* might be seen as an image of man's fear of being driven out from his warm place of refuge on earth. The play would then, like Beckett's *Endgame,* emerge as a morality about the process of death itself, a kind of modern *Everyman.* In the first act Stanley teases Meg with a threat which seems to be a long-standing one between them:

> STANLEY (*advancing*): They are coming today.
> MEG: Who?
> STANLEY: They are coming in a van.
> MEG: Who?
> STANLEY: And do you know what they've got in that van?
> MEG: What?
> STANLEY: They've got a wheelbarrow in that van.
> MEG (*breathlessly*): They haven't.
> STANLEY: Oh yes, they have.
> MEG: You're a liar.
> STANLEY (*advancing upon her*): A big wheelbarrow. And when the van stops they wheel it out, and they wheel it up the garden path, and then they knock at the front door.
> MEG: They don't.
> STANLEY: They're looking for someone.
> MEG: They're not.

STANLEY: They're looking for someone. A certain person.

MEG (*hoarsely*): No, they're not!

STANLEY: Shall I tell you who they're looking for?

MEG: No!

STANLEY: You don't want me to tell you?

MEG: You're a liar!

At this moment there *is* a knock at the front door. Meg goes out and one hears a voice saying: "Hullo Mrs. Boles. It's come." (A very typically Pinteresque shock effect, after the long build-up about the van and the wheelbarrow!) It turns out that the visitor is Lulu, and what has come is the parcel with Stanley's present. Yet there can be little doubt that the van with the wheelbarrow in it, with which Stanley frightens Meg, is a hearse with a coffin. Stanley does not specify *who* it is that will be taken away in the wheelbarrow. It might be Meg, and Meg's reaction might therefore be her fear of her own death; but Stanley might also be frightening her with the prospect of *his* disappearance. In the light of the later events in the play, it becomes clear that, above all, Stanley's game to frighten Meg is merely a projection of his fear that someone will come to take *him* away. Goldberg's black car at the end would then also represent a hearse, while Stanley's correct dress, his speechlessness, and his blindness would be an image of him laid out and lying in state as a corpse.

In *The Room* Rose's fear of losing her home is clearly the fear of death; the coming of the Negro who calls her home is, therefore, in my view, a signal of her impending death. Goldberg and McCann could also be seen as such messengers, sent out to transport a human being into the nether world: Goldberg with his pronounced Jewish family feelings and his sentimentality could then be seen as a grotesque caricature of Jehovah, the Lord over life and death, while the brutal torturer McCann could represent a projection of Stanley's fears of the physical suffering in the hour of extinction.

On another plane again, that of psychological archetypes, *The Birthday Party* might also be seen as an image, a metaphor for the process of growing up, of expulsion from the warm, cosy world of childhood. That Meg, with her crushing combination of motherliness and senile eroticism, is a mother image seen from the viewpoint of an Oedipus complex needs no particular stress. Stanley is reluctant to leave the warm, though seedy, nest which Meg has built for him. He is afraid, not only of the outside world, but also of sexuality outside the cosy mother-son relationship. That is why he refuses to "go out" with Lulu (in both senses of the phrase: having a girl friend, and going out into the world). And that is why, at the climax of his mental crisis, his "birthday party," he first attacks Meg, the mother figure, perhaps for not *resisting* the destruction of their relationship, not being aware of the meaning of the presence of Goldberg and McCann; why we later find him trying to rape Lulu. He *has* been driven away from infantile sexuality, is being pushed into an adult relationship (hence also Goldberg's provocative love play with Lulu in Stanley's presence). It is because the individual's feelings in this crisis are ambivalent that Stanley's actions are ambivalent and charged with aggression against both the mother figure (whom he despises for the very dependence in which he lives and yet cannot reject because he is too lazy, too weak to brave the world on his own) and the girl, whose attraction frightens him and therefore evokes feelings of hatred and aggression. Moreover, if Meg is a mother figure with overtones of subconscious incestuous yearnings, then Goldberg with his exaggerated Jewish family feelings is a father figure par excellence. In that case Stanley's fear of the avenging angels sent by "the organisation" would be an expression of his guilt feelings for his incestuous impulses, his dread of punishment by the father figure. It is noteworthy that Petey in many ways resembles Bert in *The Room*: he also hardly talks, lets himself be pampered by his wife, goes out of the house for long periods; but while Bert is savage and brutal, Petey is mild. Bert's brutality reappears in that of Goldberg and McCann. In other words, one figure has been split into three components.

Seen from this angle, Stanley's removal in the garb of the respectable, hard-working suburban breadwinner would be an image of the adult's nostalgic leave-taking from the cosy, comfortable, warm, cared-for world of his childhood, his view of the adult world as one of Adam driven out from Paradise to earn his daily bread in the sweat of his brow.

These are just three possible levels of interpretation of a play like *The Birthday Party*. There may be many others. What must be stressed, however, is that there is *no contradiction* between these different aspects. As in all poetic imagery there is a deep and organic connection between the multiple planes on which the layers of ambiguity of the imagery operate. For example, the process of growing up is in itself an image, and a metaphor of dying: one incarnation of the self dies, to make room for another which is being born to take its place. Rites of initiation are also very often closely related to funeral rites. Equally, society driving an artist towards respectable work closely corresponds to the transition from childhood to the workaday world of the adult. All children can be seen as living for play and self-expression, and in that sense all children are artists. The process of growing up is one of losing the emotional range, the irresponsibility and freedom of the artist.

Thus on closer examination the different levels of approach will be seen merely as different aspects of the same immensely complex, immensely relevant, and immensely *true* poetic metaphor for a basic human situation, an existential archetype. And it is precisely the realism, the reality of the concrete situation portrayed, that gives the poetic image its solidity and power. Each of the characters is endowed with his own linguistic personality: the slowness and softness of Meg, Goldberg's mental agility, McCann's brutality—they are all firmly delineated by the way they speak. But here again the language also provides a poetic texture of images that parallel and reinforce the metaphorical aspect of the action. The seemingly nonsensical brainwashing sessions in which Stanley is drowned in a welter of quick-fire questions and statements by the two terrorists contain innumerable references to the main metaphors of the play. ("What would your old mum say, Webber?" "Why did you kill your wife?" "Why did you never get married?" "You contaminate womankind." "You verminate the sheet of your birth"—just to pick a few from a long list of projections of Stanley's guilt feelings, culminating in: "What makes you think you exist? You're dead. You're dead. You can't live, you can't think, you can't love. You're dead. You're a plague gone bad. There's no juice in you. You're nothing but an odour!" These are the *thoughts*, Stanley's thoughts, externalised by the characters of Goldberg and McCann.)

Both in treatment and subject matter *The Birthday Party* shows affinities with another masterpiece that is also a metaphor of an existential crisis of a similar nature: Kafka's *The Trial,* where the hero also suffers from un- accountable guilt feelings and is also, at the end, taken away to his execution by two angels of death in the guise of respectable-looking gentlemen. But Pinter's play, his first mature contribution to dramatic literature, is a wholly individual, wholly original creation.

A SLIGHT ACHE

Originally conceived as a radio play, *A Slight Ache* has also been performed on the stage. But in its radio form the play is bound to be more effective, because then it can remain open whether the central character, the matchseller, who never speaks, actually exists or is no more than a projection of the two other characters' fears.

A Slight Ache is the first of Pinter's plays based on a middle-class idiom: Edward and Flora are an affluent middle-class couple; they live in a large country house surrounded by gardens. Edward used to be in business, but now he regards himself as something of an intellec- tual. He mentions that he is engaged in writing a book on space and time; on another occasion he refers to his plans for a work on the Belgian Congo.

The play starts with Edward and Flora at breakfast; their dialogue about trivial matters shows—just like the opening dialogue between Ben and Gus at the beginning of *The Dumb Waiter*—that there is considerable tension between them. Do wasps "bite" or "sting"? The question leads to a bitter altercation. And the wasp that has strayed onto the breakfast table is trapped in a marmalade jar by Edward and, after prolonged torture, killed by having boiling tea water poured over it. Edward, who has complained about a slight ache in his eyes, rejoices in the thought that the hot water will *blind* the wasp: ". . . Tilt the pot. Tilt. Aah . . . down here . . . right down . . . blinding him . . . that's . . . it."

Again we find the image of blindness—as in *The Room* and *The Birthday Party*—which seems to be equated with sexual inadequacy and death. Also the episode around the wasp shows the depth of bitterness, hatred, and cruelty that lurks behind the polite voices and formal manners in this marriage.

Edward and Flora are worried: For some time, about two months, an old man with a tray has been standing at the back entrance to their garden, trying to sell matches to passersby. But hardly anybody ever passes there. So what is that old man trying to do? Edward seems to be afraid of the old man; to find out what he is after, he proposes to invite him in and to put some questions to him. He asks Flora to go and get him. As he does not speak throughout the play, the old matchseller is in the radio version no more than silence, nothingness. It is one of the great advantages of radio that it is, among all the performing arts, the only one able to put the absolute void on the stage of the audience's imagination. (Ingmar Bergman's famous film *The Seventh Seal* started as a radio play; there, too, the figure of Death appeared as pure silence—far more effectively than in the film, where he had to be turned into a lay figure clad in a black cloak.) In the stage version and on television the matchseller's menace is considerably reduced when he can be seen as a very ordinary old man; and his silence, which is terrifying in the radio version, becomes a somewhat embarrassing sign of idiocy.

Edward's attempts to draw the matchseller into conversation turn, confronted with the visitor's speechlessness, into a nervous monologue, which, getting increasingly hysterical, exposes the snobbery, false intellectual pretences, and selfishness of the speaker. Edward can no longer stand it, he asks Flora to lead him out into the garden (he seems weakened; the slight ache from which he suffered initially has grown into a general loss of vitality, the start of the descent into the decay of old age).

Now it is Flora's turn to try to get the old man to speak. He reminds her of a poacher she once met in her youth:

> I had an encounter with a poacher once. It was a ghastly rape, the brute. High up on a hillside cattle track. Early spring. I was out riding on my pony. . . . Of course, life was perilous in those days. It was my first canter unchaperoned. . . . Years later, when I was Justice of the Peace for the county, I had him in front of the bench. He was there for poaching. That's how I know he was a poacher.

In other words, the encounter with the old matchseller provokes Flora into the sexual fantasies of her youth about possible first, unchaperoned "canters" and being set upon by wild men. And in spite of the old man's "vile smell" she gradually works herself up into sexual excitement about him:

> Hmmnn, you're a solid old boy, I must say. Not at all like a jelly. All you need is a bath. . . . I'm going to keep you. I'm going to keep you, you dreadful chap, and call you Barnabas.

But when Edward returns, Flora tries to keep him out of the room by pretending that the old man is dying.

Edward retorts with a furious verbal attack on his wife:
"You lying slut. Get back to your trough!" Flora goes out,
Edward is again left alone with the matchseller. Now
he talks about his youth, his athletic prowess, cricket; his
surveying the sea from a hill through a telescope, following the path of three-masted schooners. Is the old man
laughing at him? Or is he crying in grief for Edward's
plight? A fever has Edward in its grip. He falls on the
floor complaining about the germ he caught in his eyes.
Has he gone blind? It seems so, for now he believes the
matchseller looks "extraordinarily youthful." He asks the
matchseller to lead him out into the garden: "Take my
hand."

Flora has come in. The matchseller goes over to her.
She hands Edward the matchseller's tray and leaves the
room with the old man.

Who or what is the matchseller? That he is not meant
as a realistic character is clear enough. Hence his awkward effect in stage performance. One senses the incom-
patibility of his concreteness on the one hand, his obvious symbolic quality on the other.

For Edward the matchseller is the focal point of his
anxiety; he may indeed be that which starts as a slight
ache and ends with Edward's loss of his personality—
perhaps even his sight—and his expulsion from Flora's
bed. The matchseller had to stand outside the garden
gate. Now it is Edward who is handed his tray, presumably to stand outside. Edward's fate is closely analogous to Rose's in *The Room*. She, too, is visited by a symbolic figure who had been waiting for her outside. She,
too, is stricken with blindness and presumably loses her
warm home to be expelled into the cold of the basement:
death. Edward's expulsion—like Stanley's in *The Birthday
Party*—could therefore also be a metaphor for his dying.

Hence the matchseller, whom Flora experiences as the return of sexual desire, a liberation from a hated, impotent husband (the matchseller to her appears "not at all like a jelly"), is simply Edward's death. Hence the mysterious figure, whom Edward fears, represents to Flora a return to sex and to life.

In *A Slight Ache* Pinter very convincingly demonstrated that his mastery of dialogue transcended the limits of the low-life vernacular; his ear for the absurdity of the clichés of middle-class speech proved to be as mercilessly accurate as his ability to expose the idiocy of proletarian solecisms. But essentially the imagery remains the same: the intruder waiting outside, whose coming ends in the expulsion and destruction of one of the main characters, and who may be an angel of death; the tension between two closely related but antagonistic partners, which expresses itself in disputes about the finer points of language; the motherly but sexually active and aroused woman, the man who is incapable of love; the coexistence of extreme realism and the symbolism of the dream.

A NIGHT OUT

A Night Out was also originally written as a radio play, but soon after its first transmission it was also performed with great success on television, and has also since then occasionally been staged. It is the first of Pinter's plays that remains on an entirely realistic level throughout, eschewing all supernatural or openly symbolist effects as well as the elements of enigma and unexplained mystery that pervade plays like *The Birthday Party* and *A Slight Ache.*

Albert Stokes is a young man of about twenty-eight
who lives with his mother and is entirely dependent on
her—a relationship in some ways resembling that of Stanley and Meg in *The Birthday Party*. Albert's mother is
so possessive that for her his announcement that he has
to go out for the evening to an office party constitutes almost an act of desertion and rebellion.

But this time Albert is determined to have his way. He
must attend the party, which his boss is giving for an
aged colleague about to retire. At a coffee stall by a railway arch, Seeley and Kedge, two of Albert's office
friends, are already waiting for him. When Albert, having defied his mother, arrives, he is still uncertain whether
he should, in fact, go through with it and go to the party.
His friends tease him for being a mother's boy.

At the party, spirits are high. Gidney, the firm's accountant, who has a grudge against Albert, persuades
two of the secretaries to embarrass him by playing on
his shyness in the presence of girls. While the boss makes
a speech celebrating the long service of the guest of honour, one of the girls cries out that someone "touched" her.
It was, in fact, Mr. Ryan, the aged guest of honour: at
least in the television version, this is made clear by the
way he looks innocently up to the ceiling with a knowing
smile on his lips. But suspicion fastens on Albert, the
situation becomes distinctly uncomfortable, and he flees.
When he gets back home his mother receives him with a
flood of reproach and abuse. Albert loses his temper,
grabs an alarm clock, and begins to hit his mother with
it. He hears her scream and rushes out into the street,
convinced that he has gravely hurt, perhaps even killed,
her.

Back at the coffee stall, he is accosted by a prostitute;

he follows her home, as he is clearly afraid to go back to his own house.

The tart, who behaves in a most genteel, ladylike manner and talks of her little girl, whose photograph adorns the mantelpiece, tries to find out more about Albert. He does not say much, but hints that he works in films. An alarm clock in the prostitute's room recalls the incident with his mother to him. When the girl nags him about having dropped some cigarette ash onto her carpet, he becomes violent; she, too, has now recalled the image of the dominant female in his life. He rebels and throws his burning cigarette down, on purpose. When the tart protests, he grabs her alarm clock and threatens to kill her. The girl is terrified; he tears the little daughter's photograph from the frame and exposes her lies: the photograph is more than twenty years old and obviously has nothing to do with the tart. Albert throws her half-a-crown and leaves.

He is back home. His mother, surprisingly, is alive and well. She tells him that she forgives him: "You're good, you're not bad, you're a good boy . . . I know you are . . . you are, aren't you?"

But there is no reaction from Albert. As the play ends, we are left in the dark as to whether the power situation in the household has changed or not. Has Albert's show of domination over the prostitute given him the confidence to dominate his mother too? His silence could imply that. But, equally, it might mean that he has surrendered and resigned himself to a life of dependence.

The great success of *A Night Out*, particularly when it was shown on television, was based largely on the brilliantly realistic dialogue: the conversation about football at the coffee stall, the party chat, and the acutely observed tone of genteel refinement of the prostitute's speech.

The parallels to *The Birthday Party* are fairly clear, not only the analogy between Albert's dependence on his mother and Stanley's on Meg, but also the resulting fear of sex with other women. Albert, too, is being tormented by men who do know how one gets on with girls and who tease him about his innocence and bashfulness. Albert's aggression against first his mother and then the tart exactly corresponds to Stanley's attacks against Meg and Lulu during *his* party. There is a difference, however: Stanley attacks Lulu as the embodiment of the sexuality he fears; Albert raises his hand against the tart because she turns out to be exactly as nagging as his mother. But, on the other hand, it is equally clear that the attack against the prostitute also arises from Albert's feeling of inferiority, his rage about his inability to approach the prostitute as a sexual object. Albert hates both aspects of the feminine principle: the sexual demand of the prostitute, i.e. woman as a challenge to his sexual potency, and the mother's claim to dominance over him as head of her family, as a person entitled to his respect, gratitude, and servitude. The girls who tease him during the party can be seen as further embodiments of the first challenge, painful reminders of Albert's sexual inadequacy.

A Night Out can thus be regarded as an elegant and subtle set of variations on the theme of man's confrontation with aspects of the feminine principle. Albert flees from the mother who enslaves him; at the party he meets the sexual provocation of the girls from the typing pool, which reminds him of his fear of that other aspect of woman; and finally, in the prostitute, where, being a paying customer, he *could* assert his sexuality without fear of rejection, he discovers that here, too, he cannot escape the other side of the feminine principle: the nagging gentility of the mother figure. And when he returns home from his wild night out, the mother is still there; not even the extreme act of violence to which he resorted has been able to free him. Or has it?

That is the question with which we are left.

THE CARETAKER

With *The Caretaker,* Pinter finally achieved his breakthrough in the theatre. Donald McWhinnie, the radio producer who had helped Pinter over his difficult period after the failure of *The Birthday Party* two years earlier, directed the play at the Arts Theatre Club; and Donald Pleasence, one of the finest character actors on the English stage, played the part of the tramp Davies.

The Caretaker is a three-act, three-character play. Mick and Aston are brothers, the younger in his late twenties, the older, Aston, in his early thirties. Mick, we gather (one can never be quite sure about the truth of what is said about a character in a Pinter play), is a successful businessman of sorts; he owns a small van and seems to be dabbling in buying and selling properties. For his elder brother, Aston, he has bought an old, derelict house in a western suburb of London. Only one room in this house is habitable. Aston has, rather vaguely, been given the task of converting the whole house. In the meantime the one habitable room is cluttered up with old furniture and other junk Aston has acquired, and even this room has a leaking ceiling; a bucket hangs from the roof to catch the water that drips through.

Aston is a slow, awkward man who incessantly fiddles

with screwdrivers and handsaws, but he is good-natured and ready to help his fellow human beings. The play opens, after a brief, tantalizing and mysterious, silent inspection of the room by Mick, with Aston bringing in an old tramp whom he has saved from being beaten up in a brawl in a café. The tramp, Davies, informs him that he had been working as a cleaner in the café and that he had refused to remove a bucket of rubbish: "It's not my job to take out the bucket! They got a boy there for taking out the bucket. I wasn't engaged to take out buckets."

It was out of this incident that the fight developed. Davies, it seems, not only insists on doing only jobs appropriate to his station in life, he is also filled with race hatred:

> All them Greeks had it, Poles, Greeks, Blacks, the lot of them, all them aliens had it [i.e., a place to sit down in a work break]. And they had me working there . . . they had me working. . . . All them Blacks had it, Blacks, Greeks, Poles, the lot of them, that's what, doing me out of a seat, treating me like dirt.

So the old tramp emerges in the first minutes of the play as an epitome of some of the worst traits of the British workman: prone to get involved in quarrels about who should do what job, xenophobic, lazy, and ill-tempered. Moreover, he is bitter, weak, and constantly deceiving others as well as himself. He tells Aston that he is not really called Davies, for example. His name is Jenkins. At least he has got an insurance card under the name of Jenkins. Yet, when further questioned, he reverts to Davies. Davies is his real name: "Mac Davies. That was before I changed my name."

To get his papers in order, Davies, or Jenkins, has to

get to Sidcup—a southeastern suburb of London—but to get there he would need good shoes; and good shoes are hard to come by.

Aston is sorry for the old man; he invites him to stay with him in his room for a few days until he gets fixed up; he will even try to find some decent shoes for him. He gets a second bed ready. Davies can hardly believe his luck.

The next morning Aston mildly complains that Davies has been talking in his sleep. He hotly denies it and attributes it to "them Blacks. . . . Next door." Aston wants to go out. Davies is astonished to find that, nevertheless, he will be allowed to remain in the room; he can hardly understand that he is trusted not to steal some of the many pieces of junk piled high around him. He is even given the second key by Aston. But he is frightened by the electric fire and the old gas stove, which is not even connected to the mains. When he is left alone in the room, Pinter has again succeeded in establishing, out of Davies' lack of self-confidence and his nervousness about the menace of these objects, an atmosphere of threat, mystery, and horror. At this moment, Mick, the younger brother, slides into the room and eventually frightens Davies out of his wits by suddenly seizing him from behind and treating him as though he *was* a burglar.

Act II takes up the action immediately at the point where it left off—in a typically Pinteresque *coup de théâtre* shock effect—with Mick's brutal intrusion into Davies' solitude. Mick cross-examines Davies, rapidly alternating between brutality and a politeness that might be cruelly ironic or even genuine. He seizes Davies' trousers and has become very threatening again when Aston returns and Mick's attitude immediately changes to one of matter-of-fact enquiry about the house, with

Davies' presence seemingly forgotten. It is Aston who draws Davies back into the conversation by telling him that he has got his bag from the café where he had left it the night before. There follows another bout of teasing by Mick, who grabs the bag repeatedly so that it rapidly passes from one of the characters to the next in a seemingly endless round. Then, as mysteriously as he has come, Mick goes again.

> DAVIES: Who was that feller?
> ASTON: He's my brother.
> DAVIES: Is he? He's a bit of a joker, en' he?

With almost motherly solicitude Aston gives Davies a number of things he has bought for him. Even the bag, it turns out, is not really Davies'; somebody else had taken it at the café. So Aston bought another bag for him at some secondhand stall, together with a bundle of clothes.

It is clear that Aston is happy to have someone to look after. He goes so far as to offer the homeless tramp a permanent home:

> ASTON: You could be . . . caretaker here, if you
> liked.
> DAVIES: What?
> ASTON: You could . . . look after the place, if
> you liked . . . you know, the stairs and the
> landing, the front steps, keep an eye on it.
> Polish the bells.

Davies can hardly believe his good fortune; at the same time his sour, querulous nature asserts itself, and his acceptance is vague, halfhearted. What would happen if the people who are "after him" came to the door and rang the bell and he, as caretaker, had to go and open?

The same evening Davies returns to the room, having
gone out. He tries to switch on the light; it does not work.
A sudden loud and eerie noise puts him into a state of
extreme panic. Mick, who is using a vacuum cleaner, had
plugged it into the lamp socket, hence the darkness and
the sudden noise. When the light is on again, Davies is
discovered trying to defend himself by holding a knife
in his hand, ready to strike any attacker. But Mick, the
suave, quick-witted brother, has become polite and con-
siderate to Davies, complains about his brother's laziness,
and—to Davies' amazement—also offers him the position
of caretaker. Only he wants references. Davies, at first
uncertain as to which of the two brothers is the owner of
the house, promises that he will be able to bring these as
soon as he can get down to Sidcup. Recognising the obvious superiority of the younger brother, Davies now
regards him as the one he has to play up to, and, weak as
he is, he is not able to resist the temptation to speak ill of
his benefactor, Aston.

The next morning there is a growing tension between
Aston and Davies. Davies can't sleep by an open window
and complains about the rain coming in. Aston must have
fresh air to sleep. But then, obviously from a deep longing to be friends and to communicate, Aston begins to
tell Davies the story of his life. There was a time when
he was as nimble and as communicative as his brother.
Indeed, he "talked too much." And he had hallucinations.
He was taken to a mental hospital. A doctor informed
him that he ought to have treatment, something would
have to be done to his brain. But Aston refused:

> Well, I wasn't a fool. I knew I was a minor. I
> knew he couldn't do anything to me without
> getting permission. I knew he had to get per-

mission from my mother. So I wrote to her and
told her what they were trying to do. But she
signed their form, you see, giving them permission.

He tried to escape—in vain. He was subjected to
electric-shock treatment. That is why he has become
slow, unable to work except on his own, pottering about
the house he is supposed to redecorate. As Aston finishes
his long speech, the curtain falls on Act II.

This moment of Aston's self-revelation seals Davies'
fate. Weak and beset by terrible feelings of inferiority,
he simply cannot resist the temptation to take advantage
of Aston's confession; confronted with a man who has
been to a mental hospital, who admits his inadequacy,
Davies is unable to react with sympathy, with gratitude
for the maimed man's kindness, his offer of friendship.
He must enjoy the thrill of treating his benefactor with
the superiority of the sane over the lunatic. Transferred
to the lower levels of contemporary society, this is the
hubris of Greek tragedy which becomes the cause of
Davies' downfall.

As Act III opens—two weeks later—it still seems as
though Mick might really have meant his offer to Davies
that he should become his caretaker in the house and
take over the supervision of the redecoration. In a passage of ecstatic description he outlines his dream of seeing the derelict house as a luxurious penthouse: the
language of furniture advertisements and glossy weeklies
is here transformed into a kind of visionary poetry.
Davies is in a state of euphoria and sees himself as Mick's
friend; he complains about Aston and asks Mick to speak
to him and tell him that from now on he, Davies, will be
in command. But Mick, who clearly has merely been

tempting the old man to show his true nature, departs
with a mere "Yes . . . maybe I will."

Aston returns. He has at last got hold of a pair of shoes
for Davies. But Davies finds fault with them. He clearly
no longer wants to walk to Sidcup. In the night, when
Aston again complains about Davies' talking in his sleep
and making noises, Davies reacts with the anger and contempt of the dominant partner and even resorts to pull-
ing out his knife. When Aston suggests that the time may
have come for Davies to try to find somewhere else to
live, Davies retaliates by announcing that he has been
put in charge and it might be Aston who would have to
go. Aston merely puts Davies' things in his bag and hands
it to him. Davies goes, but he is sure that he will be back.

The same evening: Davies has returned, in Aston's absence, and is denouncing Aston to Mick. Mick appears
to be listening sympathetically, but when Davies goes so
far as to suggest Aston should "go back where he come
from," i.e. the mental hospital, Mick's attitude changes
abruptly to one of savage irony. He treats Davies as an
impostor who had pretended to know about interior
decoration:

> Ever since you come into this house there has
> been nothing but trouble. Honest. I can take
> nothing you say at face value. Every word you
> speak is open to any number of different inter-
> pretations. Most of what you say is lies. You're
> violent, you're erratic, you're just completely un-
> predictable. You're nothing else but a wild ani-
> mal, when you come down to it. You're a bar-
> barian. And to put the old tin lid on it, you stink
> from arse-hole to breakfast time.

In his anger Mick picks up and smashes the figure of the

Buddha which is one of Aston's favourite pieces in the room. Davies is speechless. Aston returns. The two brothers look at each other. "Both are smiling, faintly." Mick begins to speak but is unable to form a coherent sentence, probably because he cannot bring himself to confess to having smashed the Buddha, and leaves the room. Aston sees the broken pieces, then goes to his bed and begins to work on his electric plug.

Davies makes a last feeble attempt to regain Aston's favour; he withdraws any harsh words he may have said. But Aston is adamant. The play closes with Davies desperately pleading for the room, the home he has now lost, while Aston stands silently by the window with his back turned to him. Davies' words stick in his throat. He stands silently by the door as the curtain falls. We know that he will have to go, that he has lost his last chance in life.

The final scene, with one of the characters about to leave, certain to leave, yet not seen to be leaving, is strongly reminiscent of the concluding image in Beckett's *Endgame.* There Clov's leaving would mean the end of the room's owner, here it is the one who is driven away whose life is thereby forfeited. There are echoes here, too, of *Waiting for Godot:* the tramp, the two complementary brothers, the shoes that will not fit. In Beckett's play the two main characters are waiting for salvation to come, in Pinter's one of the characters is within sight of salvation and then is driven out of Paradise by his own original sin. Yet *The Caretaker* is, at least on the surface, far more naturalistic. Originally Pinter was thinking of a violent end—perhaps the killing of the old man by the two brothers. But he realised in time that this was quite unnecessary; that Davies' expulsion from Paradise would be far more tragic, precisely through Aston's apathy.

The Caretaker marks the decisive consolidation of Pinter's abandonment of obvious symbolism, supernatural devices, and even the chiaroscuro effects of the mysterious killers in *The Birthday Party*. The renunciation of the violent end was a further step in this direction.

It was a deliberate step, and one by no means lightly taken. That there was a distinct possibility of Pinter's taking a different line of development is shown by the manuscript of a hitherto unpublished and unperformed play, *The Hothouse*, which bears on its title page the handwritten note: "Final Draft. Discarded play." *The Hothouse* is undated, but it is clearly related to the synopsis for a radio play Pinter submitted to the B.B.C. on 12 November 1958, and in a further extended form on 23 December of the same year. The first idea of this play, which was to show doctors in a psychological-research station wrapped up in their own personal affairs and intrigues while the patients suffered in soundproof cells, thus clearly came between the completion of *A Slight Ache* and the emergence of Pinter's first truly realistic play, *A Night Out*.

The Hothouse takes place in a kind of psychological-research station or mental home in the country (officially referred to by the staff as a "rest home"), and is written in an idiom of grotesque farce which points in the direction of Ionesco. Yet there are a number of very significant parallels with *The Caretaker* which make it appear likely that this play took shape at about the same time and was discarded because the author realised that his future lay in the area of realism—images of the real world which are raised to metaphors of the human condition by the mysteriousness inherent in reality itself and the difficulties of drawing a line between the real, the

imagined, and the dream—rather than in the direct dis-
tortion of grotesque fantasy.

The "rest home" in *The Hothouse* is a government es-
tablishment. The inmates bear numbers instead of names,
while the staff, led by an ex-Army officer called Roote,
are grotesquely and monosyllabically named Lush, Hogg,
Beck, Budd, Tuck, Dodds, Tate, Peck, Gibbs, Lamb,
Cutts, Tibb, and Lobb. Miss Cutts, the only woman in the
cast, has an affair with the superintendent as well as with
his aide, Gibbs. Gibbs and Cutts use the newest member
of the staff, Lamb, as the guinea pig for experiments in
the course of which he is connected to electrodes and
wildly tormented, while his torturers flirt and laugh. This
can be seen as a grotesquely farcical variant on Aston's
experience in the mental hospital. Moreover, one of the
inmates of the "rest home" has died; when his mother
comes to inquire after him, she is fobbed off with a "cock
and bull" story about his having been transferred to another home. Even the name Jenkins—Davies' alias—appears briefly in *The Hothouse*, when the superintendent
discusses the possibility of giving the inmates their names
back:

> One of the purposes of this establishment is to
> instill that confidence in each and every one of
> them, that confidence which will one day enable
> them to say "I am . . . Jenkins," for example.
> Not easy, not easy, agreed, but it makes it dou-
> bly difficult if they're constantly referred to as
> 5244, doesn't it. We lose sight of their names and
> they lose sight of their names.

Lamb, the victim in *The Hothouse*, is subjected by
Miss Cutts to a cross-examination that contains elements
of Stanley's brainwashing in *The Birthday Party*, but also

relates to Aston's fear of women; in the first act of *The Caretaker* Aston tells Davies of an incident in a café when a woman suddenly touched his hand and asked him: ". . . . how would you like me to have a look at your body?" Aston's reaction is: ". . . . To come out with it just like that, in the middle of this conversation. Struck me as a bit odd."

In *The Hothouse* Miss Cutts is equally embarrassing, but in a grotesquely heightened vein:

> CUTTS: Are you virgo intacta?
> LAMB: What?
> CUTTS: Are you virgo intacta?
> LAMB: Oh, I say, that's rather embarrassing. I
>   mean in front of a lady—
> CUTTS: Are you virgo intacta?
> LAMB: Yes, I am, actually. I'll make no secret
>   of it.
> CUTTS: Have you always been virgo intacta?
> LAMB: Oh, yes, always. Always.
> CUTTS: From the word go?
> LAMB: Go? Oh, yes. From the word go.

(Pinter used that particular episode in one of his revue sketches, "Applicant.")

Strange things go on in *The Hothouse*. Not only has one patient died, but another, a woman, has given birth to an illegitimate baby. In the end Gibbs reports to a bureaucrat in Whitehall that the entire staff has been killed—by the inmates? or, indeed, by Gibbs himself?—in an orgy of bloodshed. The play ends with the poor forgotten victim, Lamb, in the soundproof room, still "sitting in the chair, earphones and electrodes attached, quite still."

It is as though Aston's experience in the hospital had been wildly heightened and exaggerated to form the subject matter of an entire play.

The grotesque figures in *The Hothouse* are caricatures, gargoyles rather than human beings, while in *The Caretaker* some of the same subject matter has been expressed through fully rounded—although still mysterious and un-motivated—*characters*. Lamb's experience in *The Hothouse* is in the form of the wild nightmare of a patient in a mental hospital; Aston's tale in *The Caretaker* is the same experience recollected in sober tranquillity. The numbered patients in *The Hothouse* have, in *The Caretaker,* been transmuted into Davies'—or Jenkins'?—anxiety about his insurance card, which after all also bears a number, but in sober reality, and *his* uncertainty about his real name and identity. The grotesque caricature of the revue-sketch dialogue about Lamb's virginity from the word go has, in *The Caretaker,* become the very real awe and fear that Aston, mentally and perhaps physically maimed by his treatment, feels towards women who put embarrassing propositions to him.

The artistic and poetic benefits of starting from a soberly realistic image clearly emerge from the comparison of the discarded play with the one that brought Pinter his first great success. The naturalistic picture of an old man trying to win a place of his own is the foundation on which, because it is so solidly built, so firmly established, the moral parable, the poetic metaphor, the archetypal symbol out of the collective unconscious, can securely rest.

In *The Room,* in *The Birthday Party,* and in *A Slight Ache* the main character was living in an undefinable dread of an outside intruder who might expel him from his home. In *The Caretaker* the situation is reversed: here a homeless wanderer is fighting to gain a foothold in a home. And this time his loss of his home is not merely the outcome of the workings of mysterious fate; it is the direct consequence of his own shortcomings: his inability to resist the easy satisfaction of glorying in his superiority over the ex-inmate of an asylum, his overconfidence in playing one brother off against the other. It is Mick who plays the role of the snake in this re-enactment of Adam's expulsion from Paradise: by apparently accepting Davies' inane boasts, his complaints about Aston, he has deliberately provoked him into revealing the worst side of his nature. Had Davies been able to show true kindness, genuine sympathy towards Aston after he had been made aware of his past history, he could have established a genuine relationship with him, could have benefited from the offer of friendship implied in that generous gesture of confidence. But poor Davies, whose own inferiority finds an outlet in his hatred of Negroes, Indians, and Greeks, is simply not capable of even realising the meaning of such a gesture. This makes Davies a highly significant and symptomatic character in an age in which an inability by large numbers of human beings to transcend such primitive emotions of racial hatred (which is merely the reverse side of their own deep feeling of inadequacy, their lack of insight and empathy into the plight of other human beings) has become one of the most dangerous threats to peace. Here again we can see that Pinter's apparent lack of political commitment by no means prevents him from dealing with the basic problems of our time.

The character of Aston throws an interesting light on that of Stanley in *The Birthday Party*. If Lamb's plight at the hands of Miss Cutts and Gibbs in *The Hothouse* exaggerates Stanley's experience into an even wilder

sphere of sadistic torture fantasies, Aston's story reduces it to the terms of sober, clinical realism. Aston tried
to escape from the shock treatment; had he succeeded
he might well have hidden, like Stanley, in some seaside
boarding house; he might well, like Stanley, have feared
the men who would be looking for him to take him back.
The reason Aston was taken to hospital was that he talked
too much and too volubly, to the point of having hallucinations; in other words he was living a life of heightened
sensibility and imagination; he was, in some senses, an
artistic personality who had to be forcibly reduced to
sober respectability. This, again in a somewhat less extravagant vein, is closely analogous to Stanley's situation, his attempts to become a concert artist. Moreover in
The Birthday Party Meg—the mother figure—is unable to
see what the sinister men who want to brainwash Stanley
are after. In *The Caretaker* the mother, from whom Aston
expected sympathy and protection, signs the document
giving the doctors permission to subject her son to
electric-shock treatment. Like Aston, Stanley is frightened of women. Aston was outraged by the woman who
propositioned him in a café; Stanley refuses Lulu's suggestion that he should "take her out."

The third character in *The Caretaker,* Mick, is the
play's most original creation. He has much in common
with Len, the equally sleek pimp of *The Homecoming;* in
some of his habits of speech, his tendency to indulge in
long and circumstantial stories which he obviously in-
vents on the spur of the moment as he tells them, he
resembles Goldberg in *The Birthday Party;* he seems, in
the end, to be taking his brother's part in dealing with
Davies; hence, at least from Aston's point of view, he is
not, as Goldberg is from Stanley's, a hostile character.

Yet we can never be sure of his motives, or, indeed, what part he played at the time of Aston's rape at the hand of the psychiatrists. The way in which the characters of the two brothers complement each other also suggests, however, that ultimately Mick and Aston—like Didi and Gogo in *Waiting for Godot*—could be seen as different sides of the same personality. Mick could then stand for the worldly, Aston for the deeper emotional aspects of the same man. Or in terms of their creator—after all, every character an author brings to life can be regarded as an emanation of one aspect of *his* personality—Mick might stand for the actor, Aston for the poet.

The solid reality of the circumstances and characters in *The Caretaker*, and the fact that this reality has all the indeterminacy, open-endedness, and mystery of real life, becomes the basis for its effectiveness on a higher plane —the plane of the poetic image, the metaphor for a greater and more general truth, the powerful, universal archetype. This, ultimately, is due to the extreme clarity and truth with which the play represents the real world (which includes the extreme lucidity of the description of its very opaqueness and mystery). The spectator's sense of reality is sharpened to the point where he suddenly perceives ordinary and everyday events he had not heretofore noticed with such intensity of insight that they transcend themselves and become symbolic of a whole category of experience. It is the experience of the Buddha's encounters with the sick man, the old man, and the corpse; or of Newton's observation of the apple falling from the tree. Here, as in the experience of a spectator confronted with a slice of real life which he is made to see in blinding clarity, the real old man, the real, ordinary apple, became archetypes of cosmic significance and illumined areas of knowledge and experience that had up to that moment remained dark and void of significance.

That sick man, that old man, that corpse who changed the Buddha's life were at that moment in history as ordinary and everyday as millions like them; by being perceived in that particular way by that particular great personality they became universal symbols, the centre of a great myth of human existence: archetypes of the human condition.

I do not want to strain the analogy too far, nor to suggest that the characters in the play we are discussing can aspire to the lofty universality of one of the great myths of mankind. I merely want to show how the realistic representation of the particular *can* transcend itself— through the poetic truth and power of the manner of the representation—and assume the significance of the symbol, the mythical, the archetypal. The individual and particular, observed with the perception and represented with the creative power of a real poet, can thus become a metaphor of its own deeper, general, all-embracing significance.

Considerations like these are, I believe, fundamental to an understanding of a play like *The Caretaker* and indeed most of Pinter's work. Mick and Aston on the one hand, Davies on the other, are meticulously observed individuals; but they are also archetypes. Archetypes, for example, of the conflict between two young men and an old one, of the battle between the sons and the father. The idea may, at first sight, seem farfetched. But there is an unmistakable indication in the text that it nevertheless has some validity. When Mick first meets Davies, his reaction is:

You remind me of my uncle's brother. . . . To be honest. I've never made out how he came to be my uncle's brother. I've often thought that maybe it was the other way round. 1 mean that my uncle was his brother and he was my uncle. But I never called him uncle. As a matter of fact I called him Sid. My mother called him Sid too. It was a funny business. Your spitting image he was. . . .

Who is one's uncle's brother? Another uncle—or one's father. As Mick's mother never called Sid his uncle, it follows that the man of whom Davies reminds Mick was Mick's father.

If Davies is a father figure, his rejection and expulsion would explain the power and poignancy of the play's final image—an old man realising that he has to go, a young man impassively accepting this fact, unwilling and unable to do anything about it. And this is the way in which Davies reaps the reward of his unthinking assumption of superiority towards Aston. There is surely here an element of the tragic guilt of all parents in their children's eyes: that they persist far too long in maintaining the stance of superiority over them that was appropriate when they were helpless infants but becomes intolerable to them when they reach adolescence and maturity. In bringing Davies home, Aston expressed a yearning for a human relationship with a father figure. He tried his best; it did not, it could not work. Mick's attitude was hostile and cynical from the outset, yet his seeming acceptance of Davies, his flattery and false politeness, also embody something of the sons' tactics towards the generation of the fathers: flattery and subservience in the sure foreknowledge that the days of their power and superiority are numbered.

The image of the sons chasing the father out of the house might also—on a different level again—be seen as a projection forward of the sons' *wish* to express their aggressiveness against the father figure. Aston's account of his experience at the hands of the doctors, his helplessness when brutally manhandled and manipulated as a passive object, contains a good deal of the child's feeling of helplessness towards the parents who decide his destiny; the doctors tormenting Aston thus become another aspect of the father figure. And it is surely significant that Aston, who appealed to his mother for help, was let down by her. As a wish-fulfillment image, Davies would be a weakened and degraded version of the father, someone who has all the presumption and arrogance of the real father but is so weak and contemptible in other ways that the sons' aggression can find a free and full outlet against him.

The Caretaker is a play without a woman, but the repressed hate/love for the mother pervades the struggle of the sons with the father figure, just as in *A Night Out* the shadow of Albert's late father falls powerfully across his love/hate relationship with his mother. The doctors in the mental hospital where Aston was treated castrated him—to punish him for his Oedipal desires—with the consent and connivance of his mother. By taking an attitude of superiority, treating him as a mental defective, as the doctors did, Davies assumes the same role. And this is what makes the two brothers finally unite against the old man.

These suggestions are not brought forward as dogmatic statements of the "true meaning" or hidden content of the play, but merely as indications of the possible sources of its power, its richness as a poetic metaphor of man's predicament. Such an indication of a possible direction in which its hidden layers of meaning might be explored does not exclude a multitude of other approaches. Aston's attempts at making his room habitable have been seen as an image of man's struggle for order in a chaotic world; it has been said that Pinter is preoccupied with the age-old human instinct to fight for territory, and that therefore his preoccupation with rooms and homes to be defended or to be conquered reflects man's deep instinctual nature. There is an element of truth in all these interpretations, provided we keep in mind that they are all *equally* relevant and that they are not intentional on the part of the author. The starting point is *not* the possible interpretation but the concrete image—two young men, an old one, a room. The more concretely, individually, and realistically this situation is enacted and thereby explored in depth, the greater its complexity and richness of human associations will become, the wider the general implications that radiate outward from this central image.

The Caretaker is the first of Pinter's plays to have achieved this complete synthesis between utter realism in the external action and the poetic metaphor, the dream image of eternal archetypes, on the deeper—or higher—levels of impact. Much of the play's initial success was undoubtedly due to the wit and accuracy of the dialogue and the number of laughs it gave rise to. Davies is a brilliantly comic creation, and audiences tend to laugh about his weaknesses and his own unawareness of them. But at the same time Davies is also a figure of menace, the intruder who might well—if Mick is not shamming—succeed in driving Aston from his room and deprive him of his place in the world.

It is Mick's mystery and indeterminacy that are thus

the pivot of the action. The economy and elegance with which this trio of interrelated characters is handled are truly remarkable. And, in contrast to some of Pinter's earlier plays, there is nothing arbitrary or forced about either the plot or the characters. Even the episode when Mick breaks the Buddha at the climax of his diatribe against Davies, which has been criticised for importing an element of spurious symbolism, is, in my opinion, quite devoid of any such aspect. Aston collects bric-à-brac of all sorts. The Buddha was one of the things he picked up as a possible ornament for the house; his bringing Davies home was another example of the same naïve tendency. Thus Mick's destruction of the Buddha at the moment when he has decided to get rid of Davies *is* a symbolic action, but one completely motivated by the real situation in which he finds himself at that moment. He vents his rage against Davies on an object that reminds him of his brother's failing that led to the appearance of Davies in the house.

The episode with the statue of the Buddha is a good example of the way in which Pinter has fused the real and the symbolic in *The Caretaker:* the presence of the Buddha in the room is a symbol, but also the direct realistic consequence of Aston's habit of picking up useless things ("Picked it up in a . . . in a shop. Looked quite nice to me. Don't know why. . . . Yes, I was pleased when I got hold of this one. It's very well made"), and its destruction by Mick has the same double character and function. In other words, what we do in life concretises itself in the objects with which we surround ourselves and these become symbolical of our character. Because Aston tends to pick up useless things without much thought, he also picks up Davies. And because Mick has no use for things that merely clutter up the place and have no function, he destroys the Buddha and brings about the expulsion of Davies.

The solidity and organic motivation of this particular symbolic element in *The Caretaker* shows what a long way Pinter had travelled since his use of the over-obvious and arbitrary symbol of the blind Negro in *The Room*, the mysterious orders for food in *The Dumb Waiter*, or even the speechless matchseller in *A Slight Ache*.

The same is true of Pinter's use of silence: Rose talks to Bert in the opening scene of *The Room* without getting an answer or a reaction. This is theatrically effective, but fairly arbitrary; we never get an explanation for Bert's silence. The same is true of the matchseller in *A Slight Ache*. He simply does not speak. In the radio version this may be due to the fact that he does not exist. In the stage version it becomes wholly arbitrary. In the final scene of *The Caretaker* we again have a character who speaks and another who does not respond: Aston who "remains still, his back to [Davies] at the window." But this time we know why Aston does not answer:

> Listen . . . if I . . . got down . . . if I was to . . . get my papers . . . would you . . . would you let . . . would you . . . if I got down . . . and got my . . . (*Long silence.*)

The long silence that closes *The Caretaker,* which is both wholly real and at the same time a powerful poetic metaphor, is anything but arbitrary. The whole course of the play has organically, logically, and inevitably led up to it.

With *The Caretaker* Pinter had acquired mastery of one of the strongest instruments in his armoury as a craftsman, and the one that is probably most characteristic of his artistic personality—the use of silence.

NIGHT SCHOOL

Night School was written for television and telecast,
by no means unsuccessfully, by Associated Rediffusion
TV in July 1960. Yet Pinter felt dissatisfied with the play,
did not include it in any of the volumes of his collected
plays, and refused to sanction further performances. He
once said that he repudiated the play because it struck
him as too obviously and mechanically "Pinteresque," as
though it were a copy of a play by Pinter rather than a
genuine work. But in the summer of 1966 he returned to
the play and rewrote it for radio in a version he regards
with far greater sympathy, and which has now appeared
in the sixth volume of his plays, published in 1967.

The theme of *Night School* is indeed a very typically
Pinteresque one. Again it is a matter of a room and a
struggle for its possession. Walter, a small-time crook who
tries to make a living by forging post-office savings books,
has just been released from prison and is being welcomed
home by his two old aunts, Annie and Milly (who mother
him in the same oversweet, sentimental manner with
which Meg looked after Stanley in *The Birthday Party*).
Walter is looking forward to getting back to his old room
in the aunts' house, but they inform him that in his absence they have been compelled to let the room. Walter
is shattered and indignant. The aunts are full of praise
for the lodger who now shares their house: Sally Gibbs,
a schoolteacher, who is pretty, intelligent, tidy, and so
keen on her further education that she attends night
school three times a week to learn languages.

Walter is determined to win back his room and above
all his bed. But when he meets Sally he also is impressed

by her; perhaps he might get back into his own room and bed by becoming Sally's lover?

Determined to impress the girl by suggesting that he is, in fact, a far more romantic type of criminal than he really is, a fierce and successful gunman, he asks her permission to look for something—a gun?—in his (now her) room by himself. Rummaging around in the cupboard he finds a photograph that shows Sally with some gentlemen in a dress and situation that suggest she is in fact working as a dance hostess in a night club. He pockets the photograph. When Sally is asked if she had been a dancer, she hotly denies that she ever goes out to dance.

Walter is determined to find out the truth about Sally, so he turns for help to an acquaintance who, he knows, is familiar with the world of night clubs: Solto, a man of Levantine origin (he speaks of his youth in Athens, but it seems more likely that he is in fact a Cypriot), is the owner of the house where Walter's aunts live and is from time to time invited to tea there. Walter, who also wants to borrow money from Solto to get started in some more legitimate business but is fobbed off by him, asks him to try to find out the identity of the girl in the photograph (without revealing that she is the lodger in the house). Solto, who is struck by the girl's looks, promises to do his best.

One evening Walter succeeds in getting himself invited to Sally's room for drinks. While the two aunts take turns listening to the conversation through the keyhole, he tries to impress Sally by wild stories about his life as a gunman and convict. When Sally seems ripe for an erotic approach after having consumed a lot of drinks, Walter takes the initiative. He begins to assert his authority by ordering Sally about:

Cross your legs. (*Pause.*) Uncross them.
(*Pause.*) Stand up. (*Pause.*) Turn round.
(*Pause.*) Stop. (*Pause.*) Sit down. (*Pause.*)
Cross your legs. (*Pause.*) Uncross your legs.
(*Silence.*)

The printed version is the radio version, so it remains
uncertain whether Sally actually does the actions she is
ordered to perform. Even in the television version the
matter might have remained uncertain by showing
Walter in closeup and leaving Sally's actions to the imagination of the audience. What is even more uncertain
is whether Walter's exercise of his authority is the prel-
ude to lovemaking or merely the expression of his
impotent infantile sadism. Using the analogy of the scene
between Albert and the prostitute in *A Night Out*, to
which it bears considerable resemblance, I should be
inclined towards the latter hypothesis. Yet the decision is
left with each member of the audience.

The scene shifts to a night club where Solto has identified the girl in the photograph, Sally. He asks the manager of the place, an old pal, to introduce him to her. As
he likes her very much, he makes up to her and invites
her to spend the weekend with him in his bungalow by
the sea; quite casually he reveals that someone called
Walter, an acquaintance of his and a small-time crook,
had asked him to try to find her. Sally is deeply upset
that Walter will now learn that she is working as a night-
club hostess (whether she is in fact a schoolteacher in
the daytime as well and is merely trying to supplement
her earnings by nightwork, or whether she is a full-time
entertainer, is left open).

The same night Solto comes to see Walter and informs
him that he has been unable to locate the girl in the

photograph. In fact he doubts whether such a girl ever existed.

The next morning Sally has gone. She evidently could not face Walter again, knowing that he knows her night-time occupation. So Walter has his room back; but he has also lost what might have been the only chance in his life to find a human being who could have become a real partner for him.

Night School combines the theme of the struggle for a room with the equally typical Pinteresque theme of the net of lies by which people mutually obscure their real selves from each other and impede genuine contact. Walter has told Sally that he is a romantic gunman. Solto has revealed to her that this was a lie. Sally has told Walter that she is a schoolteacher who goes to night school. The photograph has revealed to him that this was a lie. Neither of them can face the other in the knowledge that they know the truth. Had they had the courage to be frank about themselves, they might have found each other: after all, they are ideally suited to each other: a small-time crook who wants to go straight would be just the right partner for a girl who wants to get out of being a near-prostitute. In fact their real identities match each other far better than their fantasy personalities of the big gangster and the demure little schoolmarm.

The two tragicomic protagonists are set against three brilliantly drawn grotesques: the two aunts who eavesdrop on the young people's confrontation but are too senile and too deaf to understand what is going on (very much like Meg in *The Birthday Party*) and who spin voluptuous fantasies around food; and Solto, who also lives in his own world of fantasy: grandiose tales of his exploits in Australia and the world of opulence with which he tries to seduce Sally to spend the weekend with him.

Night School may be minor Pinter, yet it is a highly polished example of his technique and contains some of his funniest dialogue; it is also very characteristic of some of his main preoccupations. The character of Sally, who oscillates between schoolteacher and whore, foreshadows the double nature of Sarah in *The Lover* and above all Ruth in *The Homecoming,* who also fuse the respectable woman and the prostitute. Solto is a direct continuation of the Goldberg character in *The Birthday Party,* and the two aunts are expansions of the simple-minded motherliness of Rose in *The Room* and Meg in *The Birthday Party.* Walter, the small-time crook, is clearly related to the two gunmen in *The Dumb Waiter* but also contains elements of Albert Stokes, the impotent clerk of *A Night Out.* The plot with its tissue of deceptions foreshadows the much more mature treatment of the same theme in *The Collection.*

THE DWARFS

Originally written as a radio play and later transferred to the stage, *The Dwarfs* is one of Pinter's less successful works. Nevertheless it is of considerable importance for an understanding of the sources of its author's basic preoccupations. For this short play is based on, and is a distillation from, Pinter's earliest major effort as a writer, the novel *The Dwarfs,* on which he worked from about 1950 to 1956, and which thus antedates his playwriting. The novel derives directly from the milieu of his boyhood and adolescence in East London. The play therefore represents one of the earliest strata of Pinter's development and allows us to gain an insight into the motivations of his writing, particularly if we compare it with the novel.

The play *The Dwarfs* consists of a sequence of dialogues and monologues involving three characters, young men in their late twenties: Len, Pete, and Mark, who have been close friends from boyhood, when the play starts, and have drifted apart when it ends. Only once in the course of the play are all three characters together; mostly we witness encounters and conversations between two at a time, who then often discuss the third. Only one of the three, Len, appears alone in a series of monologues; Len is the one who is obsessed with the "dwarfs" of the title: he imagines these tiny, dirty creatures rummaging in his yard, offering him scraps of food. From these hallucinations it is quite clear that Len, like Aston in *The Caretaker,* is undergoing a crisis, a mental breakdown. He has been leading an irregular and eccentric life for some time, and when the play opens he is working as a porter on the nightshift at Euston Station (in the radio version; in a later stage version it is Paddington):

> The trains come in, I give a bloke half a dollar, he does my job, I curl up in the corner and read the timetables.

Mark, who, like Pinter, is of Portuguese origin ("Or at least, his grandmother on his father's side. That's where the family comes from"), is well off and frequently absent from his house, to which his two friends have access. In the original radio version his occupation was obscure; in the novel and in the later (1965) stage adaptation we learn that, like Pinter when he wrote the novel, he is an actor who occasionally goes to take up engagements outside London.

There is little action in the play, but a great deal of discussion and meditation. Len falls ill and gets better; he tells Mark that Pete thinks Mark is a fool and thereby destroys Mark's friendship for Pete. The play ends with Len's sense of loss after emerging from his mental illness: the dwarfs have left. He is alone in a prosaic, antiseptic, ordered world and regrets the glorious warmth of chaos. (Cf. Brecht's treatment of a very similar theme in *The Jungle of the Cities*, which ends with the line: "The chaos is used up. It was the best time.") In Len's words:

> . . . . they say nothing. Either they've gone dumb or I've gone deaf. Or they've gone deaf and I've gone dumb. . . . They've cut me off without a penny. . . . It's unsupportable. I'm left in the lurch. Not even a stale frankfurter, a slice of bacon rind, a leaf of cabbage, not even a mouldy piece of salami, like they used to sling me in the days when we told old tales by suntime. . . .
>
> And this change. All about me the change. The yard as I know it is littered with scraps of cat's meat, pig's bollocks, tin cans, bird brains, spare parts of all the little animals, a squelching, squealing carpet, all the dwarfs' leavings spittled in the muck, worms stuck in the poisoned shit heaps, the alleys a whirlpool of piss, slime, blood and fruit juice.
>
> Now all is bare. All is clean. All is scrubbed. There is a lawn. There is a shrub. There is a flower.

It is the desolation of the young man emerging from the wild whirlpool of steaming adolescence into the bare, ordered world of respectability.

The subject matter of *The Dwarfs* therefore is, essentially, the identity crisis that marks the transition from adolescence to maturity. While the play eliminates much of the concrete detail of this experience and reduces it to its essential, major issues, the novel is far more specific: here the bond that holds the three young men together is clearly described as that of the close community of adolescents, the tribal unit of a gang of young men:

> In fact [Pete is reported as saying in the novel] he was not sure whether they might not be said to constitute a church of a kind. They were hardly one in dogma or direction, but there was common ground and there was a framework. At their best they formed a unit, and a unit which, in his terms, was entitled to be called a church; an alliance of the three of them for the common good, and a faith in that alliance.

In the play, the relationship between the three friends from which the action starts is never so explicitly spelled out, and the audience's relative ignorance about the nature of their ties seems to me to be one of the play's weaknesses. Len occupies the centre of attention to a much greater extent, and so his problem is far more in focus. And Len's problem is clearly also that of an identity crisis:

> For me, you see, I don't grow old. I change. I don't die. I change again. I am not happy. I change. Nor unhappy. But when a big storm takes place I do not change. I become someone else, which means I change out of all recognition, I am transformed from the world in which

I suffer the changes I suffer, I retreat utterly
from the standpoint where I am subject to
change, then with my iron mask on I wait for
the storm to pass. But at the same time it is, I
admit, impossible in these moments to sit quite
still without wanting to go back. It's also impossible not to feel the itch to go forward. I must
learn restraint.

Later in the play, in a conversation with Mark, Len
broaches the central problem of human identity:

The point is, who are you? Not why or how,
not even what. I can see what, perhaps, clearly
enough. But who are you? . . . What you are,
or appear to be to me, or appear to be to you,
changes so quickly, so horrifyingly, I certainly
can't keep up with it and I'm damn sure you
can't either. But who you are I can't even begin
to recognise, and sometimes I recognise it so
wholly, so forcibly, I can't look, and how can I
be certain of what I see? You have no number.
Where am I to look, where am I to look, what is
there to locate, so as to have some surety, to
have some rest from this whole bloody racket?
You are the sum of so many reflections. How
many reflections? Whose reflections? Is that
what you consist of? What scum does the tide
leave? What happens to the scum? When does
it happen? I've seen what happens. But I can't
speak when I see it. I can only point a finger. I
can't even do that. The scum is broken and
sucked back. I don't see where it goes, I don't
see when, what do I see, what have I seen?
What have I seen, the scum or the essence?

Here—and this I consider a key to a great deal of Pinter's work—the uncertainty about the speaker's own identity merges into his uncertainty about the identity of others and into the general problem of *verification:* in a system of shifting reflections of further reflections, where there can be no certainty whether what we see is the scum or the essence, how can any firm basis be found from which to survey the world? This, we can now understand in the light of our recognition of the problem, is also the hidden mainspring of the quest for a firm point in the world which is concretised in the image of the room that Pinter's characters so often try to defend against the assaults of the outside world, or try to conquer for themselves. Len's first monologue makes this clear. His room, which is, or ought to be, the fixed centre point of his universe, is beginning to shift, and that is the onset of his mental crisis:

> This is my room. This is a room. There is wall-paper on the walls. There are six walls. Eight walls. An octagon. This room is an octagon. . . . This is a journey and an ambush. This is the centre of the cold, a halt to the journey and no ambush. This is the deep grass I keep to. This is the thicket in the centre of the night and the morning. There is my hundred-watt bulb like a dagger. It is neither night nor morning. . . . Here is my arrangement and my kingdom. . . .

But when the stability is disturbed:

> The rooms we live in . . . open and shut. . . . Can't you see? They change shape at their own will. I wouldn't grumble if only they would keep to some consistency. But they don't. . . . I am

all for the natural behaviour of rooms, doors, staircases, the lot. But I can't rely on them.

Pete also has his nightmares: he tells Len of a dream in which he saw himself in a tube station with a girl. There was some sort of panic, and suddenly the faces of all the people in that crowd were peeling off.

> When I looked at the girl I saw that her face was coming off in slabs too, like plaster. Black scabs and stains. The skin was dropping off like lumps of cat's meat. . . . Then I thought, Christ, what's my face like? Is that why she is staring? Is that rotting too?

In this scene clearly the familiar postwar nightmare of atomic-bomb attack has merged into the questioning of one's own identity.

In comparison with Len, who holds the centre in the play with his long monologues (which also devote considerable attention to the personalities of his two friends), Pete and Mark are fairly shadowy figures; they are seen from Len's point of view.

In the novel this is not so. A comparison between the novel and the play illumines a good deal of Pinter's method as a dramatist. For in the novel all the gaps which give the play its intriguing and elliptic construction are filled in. Above all we are quite clearly in the East London of Pinter's boyhood and adolescence: Hackney and Bethnal Green, the buses one takes to get to the West End both in the daytime and at night, the river Lea and the marshes, even the evil-smelling soap factory, which Pinter mentions in his own recollections of his childhood—they are all there, meticulously detailed and concrete. The three young men themselves are also far more concrete. We learn, for example, that two of them are Jewish—Len Weinstein and Mark Gilbert—while one of them, Pete Cox, is non-Jewish. We learn that Len is mad about higher mathematics and Bach and that he avidly reads the Bible, that Pete works as an accountant in a City firm but is also a skilled tailor who makes clothes for his friends. There can be little doubt that there is a wealth of firsthand observation of the real places and people of Pinter's early years in the novel, that it in fact represents a veritable storehouse of the raw material from which much of Pinter's later work is drawn. If, for example, Len was a real character whom Pinter knew as well as Pete and Mark know him in the novel (and there can be little doubt about that), we are clearly in the presence of the prototype of Aston or Stanley, while the sleek and elegant Mark bears some of the features of Mick in *The Birthday Party* or Lenny in *The Homecoming*. (On page 8 of the manuscript of the novel we even find the sentence: "It was a good homecoming.")

Pete and Mark are also manifestly the prototypes of the two men fighting for a girl in *The Basement* or jealously confronting each other in *The Collection*. For in the novel there is a fourth major character who has been omitted in the play of *The Dwarfs*, a girl, Virginia, who is a schoolteacher, like Sally in *Night School*, and who turns into a frequenter of Soho night clubs, as she does. While it is from Len that in the play Mark learns that Pete thinks him a fool, in the novel he hears it from Virginia, while making love to her, after she has deserted Pete, her boy friend of long standing. Virginia must be the prototype of numerous later split female characters in Pinter's plays, who vacillate between respectability and whoredom: the genteel prostitute in *A Night Out*, the wife/whore in *The Lover*, the faithless wife who may not have been faithless at all in *The Collection*, and, above all, Ruth in *The Homecoming*.

In the novel Virginia is rejected by Pete because she presumes to talk about Shakespeare when he maintains that she knows nothing about the subject. They are briefly reconciled, but eventually she cannot take Pete's domineering attitude, deserts him for an American to whom she has been introduced by a girl friend of hers who has become a call girl in Soho, and presumably also takes up that trade, at least part-time. It is only after she has thus changed her character and turned into a "whore" that she briefly becomes Mark's mistress. The end of the friendship between Pete and Mark comes when Mark, to revenge himself for Pete's alleged intellectual contempt for him, tells him that he slept with Sally the previous night.

The world of the four young people in the novel of *The Dwarfs* is an intensely emotional one, full of passionate intellectual discussions, midnight visits to each other's houses, an extrovert life more reminiscent of the continent of Europe than of other parts of England. But then the East End, and particularly the Jewish East End, of London must have been more like nineteenth-century Russia, Hungary, Austria, or France than the conventional pattern of English life. What is astonishing in the novel is the brilliance of the numerous dialogues, which not only foreshadows Pinter's later mastery of stage dialogue but also illustrates the high level of his awareness of language, his intense preoccupation with the nuances of spoken English, which also, to some extent, may be the outcome of his milieu: a young man, aware of alien origins and backgrounds, determined to master his environment and its language. There is a scene in the novel, when Pete Cox is shown in his office in the City encountering an old schoolmate who also works there now and is being interviewed by a senior partner in his firm, where

Pinter clearly indicates how alien and indeed ridiculously stiff the conventional English middle-class world outside the East End appeared to him at that time.

The novel of *The Dwarfs* is a very original and astonishingly finished book—and by no means imitative, although there are passages that are unmistakably influenced by Joycean internal monologue. These are especially Pete's thought sequences; Len's monologues are already very much in Pinter's own idiom. It shows his fine ear and good judgement that in the play Len's monologues have been preserved almost intact, while Pete's have been largely omitted.

The transition from the novel to the play also reveals Pinter's recognition that in the more objective genre of drama much that can be shown and discussed in a novel must go; and that, indeed, the economy and reticence of drama suited his own artistic personality far better than the more explicit narrative form. In discussing the poetry of certain writers, Len, in the novel, makes a point of immense relevance to Pinter's approach:

> Do you know what these people do? Len said. They climb from word to word, like stepping stones.
>
> He walked about the room, demonstrating. —Like stepping stones. But tell me this. What do they do when they come to a line with no words in it at all? Can you answer that? What do they do when they come to a line with no words in it at all? Can you tell me that?

To write those lines of poetry that have no words at all in them, Pinter had to turn to drama. Those lines with no words at all in them are the pauses that climax the dialogue. The poetry of the stage is indeed the only poetry that can produce great lines with no words in them at all.

Why did Pinter omit Virginia in the play of *The Dwarfs?* My guess is that he wanted to avoid the conventional subject matter of the erotic triangle; that also, perhaps, he might at that early stage in his career as a dramatist not have felt able to deal with so complex a female character; but, above all, that he felt that the girl was a mere catalyst of the breakup of the friendship, the alliance, the church of the three friends was little more than a chance motivation rather than a truly organic one; that that friendship was bound to disintegrate in any case, so that the actual reason for its disintegration was inessential and would have distracted the audience's attention from the inevitable features of the process. Such considerations certainly have a great deal of force. The question here, however, is whether, having retained so much of the framework of the novel, Pinter actually succeeded in creating a dramatic structure that could stand in its own right and fully convey what he intended without obscurity, without setting before the spectators—or the radio audience—a riddle they were unable, because ill equipped, to solve.

The play of *The Dwarfs* may be a partial failure. It nevertheless contains some of Pinter's most interesting, significant, and beautiful writing.

THE COLLECTION

Having acquired a reputation for his handling of low vernacular English with a series of plays that, with the solitary exception of *A Slight Ache*, involved working-class or lower-middle-class people, Pinter moved into the

West End of London, and into a more elegant and sophisticated milieu, with *The Collection*. The four characters in this play—originally written for television but
since then frequently performed on the stage—all come
from the world of the "rag trade." Harry Kane is a successful middle-aged man in the wholesale clothing business who lives in what is clearly a homosexual *ménage*
with a young designer, Bill Lloyd, whom he has discovered. The peace of their household is disturbed by the
intrusion of James Horne, who runs a boutique with his
wife Stella; James has been told by Stella that she had
been unfaithful to him with Bill during a visit to Leeds,
where the season's collections were being shown. According to Stella's story, Bill, who was staying at the
same hotel, had followed her to her room and, taking
advantage of her loneliness, more or less raped her.

Is Stella's story true? Can it be true? And can anyone
not directly involved ever know, ever verify, whether it
is true or not? The basic situation is reminiscent of Pirandello's *Right You Are (If You Think You Are)*, where
two, and eventually three, incompatible stories confront
each other without hope of verification. The difference is
that in Pirandello's play either one, two, or all three of
the characters involved may be mad and therefore unable to realise the true situation. In *The Collection* it is
not a matter of madness but of subtle conscious or subconscious motivations.

At first sight Bill, who has been shown as a member of
a homosexual *ménage,* seems most unlikely to have committed so brazen a heterosexual act of aggression. And,
indeed, when first confronted with James, he denies the
whole story. After a bout of rough treatment by the

wronged husband, however, he tells him another version
of the incident:

> The truth . . . is that it never happened. . . .
> All that happened was . . . you were right, actu-
> ally, about going up in the lift . . . we . . . got
> out of the lift, and then suddenly she was in my
> arms. Really wasn't my fault, nothing was fur-
> ther from my mind, biggest surprise of my life,
> must have found me terribly attractive quite
> suddenly, I don't know . . . but I . . . I didn't
> refuse. Anyway, we just kissed a bit, only a few
> minutes, by the lift, no one about, and that was
> that—she went to her room. The rest of it just
> didn't happen. I mean, I wouldn't do that sort of
> thing. I mean that sort of thing . . . it's just
> meaningless.

And yet immediately afterwards, when James tries to
substantiate his story by bringing in the further detail
that while he, James, phoned Stella, Bill was sitting on
her bed, Bill corrects him: "Not sitting. Lying." So he is
teasing James? And by outdoing James's more lurid details, throwing doubts on his own earlier, partial admis-
sions?

Harry, Bill's middle-aged flatmate, who clearly has extremely possessive feelings about the young man, has
become suspicious of the mysterious telephone calls and
the traces of secret visitors in his flat. James, the wronged
husband, on the other hand is becoming fascinated with
Bill: he tells Stella that he wants to go and see him again;
that he had dinner with him the previous evening (which
we, the audience, know is not true, or at least not entirely: this gives us a means of gauging the readiness of

the characters involved to make up stories by enlarging
and elaborating minor details). He begins to praise Bill:

> . . . . I've come across a man I can respect. It
> isn't often that you can do that, that that hap-
> pens, and really I suppose I've got you to thank.
> . . . Thanks.

While this may well be the irony of the injured party
and a way to rub salt in his wife's wounds, there is also
an element of genuine feeling behind it:

> I mean, you couldn't say he wasn't a man of
> taste. He's brimming over with it. Well, I sup-
> pose, he must have struck you the same way.
> No, really, I think I should thank you, rather
> than anything else. After two years of marriage
> it looks as though, by accident, you've opened
> up a whole new world for me.

While James goes back to visit Bill once again, Harry
comes to see Stella. When confronted with James' per-
secution of Bill, Stella denies the whole story:

> I mean, Mr. Lloyd was in Leeds, but I hardly
> saw him, even though we were staying at the
> same hotel. I never met him or spoke to him
> . . . and then my husband suddenly accused
> me of . . . it's really been very distressing.

In the meantime James and Bill are engaged in a highly
ambivalent confrontation which oscillates between extreme friendliness and sudden outbursts of hatred; it culminates in a sort of duel with knives. When Bill tries to
catch a knife thrown against his face by James, he cuts
his hand. At this moment Harry, who has been watching
them from the background, enters the conversation. He

tells James that he has it from his wife's own mouth that
the whole story of marital infidelity was pure invention.
And when James points out that Bill, after all, confirmed
Stella's story, Harry launches into a savage attack on Bill:

> Bill's a slum boy, you see, he's got a slum
> sense of humour. That's why I never take him
> along with me to parties. Because he's got a
> slum mind.

James is ready to leave and to accept his wife's latest
version of the story. But at that moment Bill offers to tell
the truth:

> I never touched her . . . we sat . . . in the
> lounge, on a sofa . . . for two hours . . . talked
> . . . we talked about it . . . we didn't . . . move
> from the lounge . . . never went to her room
> . . . just talked . . . about what we would do
> . . . if we did get to her room . . . two hours
> . . . we never touched . . . we just talked about
> it. . . .

James leaves. The last scene of the play is between
him and Stella. He repeats Bill's latest story:

> He wasn't in your room. You just talked about
> it in the lounge.
>   (*Pause.*)
> That's the truth, isn't it?
>   (*Pause.*)
> You just sat and talked about what you would
> do if you went to your room. That's what you
> did.
>   (*Pause.*)
> Didn't you?

(Pause.)

That's the truth . . . isn't it?

(Stella looks at him, neither confirming nor denying. Her face is friendly, sympathetic.)

Any of the different versions of the incident around which *The Collection* revolves may be true—or none. The point is that we have an abundance of possible motivations for each possible version. For example: Bill is a homosexual, and he is therefore unlikely to have raped Stella. Yet from Harry's wild outburst about how he found Bill in the slums, it is also possible to infer that Bill may have been made into a homosexual by an older man who offered him social advancement, a good job, life in a middle-class milieu; his homosexuality might have been imposed upon him, he might have adopted that way of life against his will or natural inclination. In that case a sudden heterosexual impulse would be understandable as a desperate attempt to escape from Harry's bondage. Or, indeed, not having the courage for a real assault on a lady, Bill might have confined his attempts to break away from the homosexual *ménage* to the world of fantasy; he might just have talked with a woman about the possibility of such an escapade without ever thinking of actually indulging in it. Conversely, Stella is clearly a somewhat frustrated wife (perhaps because James is a latent homosexual—he certainly gives some indications in this direction); she may have invented her story to make James jealous and activate his interest in her; or, again, being sex-starved she may have provoked and seduced Bill. Moreover, each of the two chief "culprits" has very good reasons why he should tell any particular version of the story at any particular moment. Bill, for example, when first confronted by James, may well be *revenging* himself for the intrusion by increasing James' suffering through tantalising details; Stella would obviously deny the whole thing to Harry, a stranger whom she does not regard as qualified to partake of her family secrets. And even the final, most plausible version, which Bill tells James at the end, may be a subtle way of revenging himself on Harry, who has just castigated him in the most cruel manner about his slum origins; by saying that he talked with Stella about lovemaking, Bill is in fact telling Harry that he is dreaming of breaking away from him, of returning to a heterosexual life.

The two objects of jealousy in the play are matched against the two sufferers from jealousy: James is jealous of Bill, but Harry is not only jealous of Stella, he is also, and perhaps more, jealous of the obvious love/hate relationship that seems to be developing between Bill and James. His outburst against Bill, for example, is clearly directed to James, whom he is warning of the ingratitude and baseness of mind of the slum urchin whom he has raised to his own level.

But *The Collection* is more than merely a highly ingenious construction, an equation with three or more unknowns, which allows of a multitude of equally valid solutions. It also contains a social comment on the situation in those strata of English middle-class society (and they are, after all, by no means insignificant) where homosexual attitudes among the men play a decisive role in determining the social climate. This aspect of the play became much clearer on the stage than it was in the original television version. On television the scene shifted between Harry's and James' apartments; on the stage they remained juxtaposed all the time—a narrow street set, with the telephone kiosk in the centre. As a result,

Stella remained in view during the scenes when the three men squabble among themselves; she sat on her sofa, playing with her kitten, terribly alone and neglected. And although Stella has a relatively brief part, measured by the lines she has to speak, she gradually emerged as the true tragic heroine of the piece: she may have been the original bone of contention between the men, yet she is soon lost from sight by them; their very involvement in fighting transforms their relationship into one of intimacy and strong personal concern with each other, a male world of rough and tumble from which the woman is forever excluded and condemned to sit at home, neglected, abandoned, playing with her kitten.

THE LOVER

Also originally a television play, *The Lover* was transferred to the stage as successfully as *The Collection,* with which it is frequently linked as a double bill. *The Lover* develops the notion of the erotic wish-fulfillment fantasy —which may well have been the source of Stella's confession of adultery in *The Collection*—and shows its function in a *happy* marriage.

Richard and Sarah live in a detached house near Windsor; Richard is the typical commuter to the city who leaves his wife behind each morning and returns to her each evening. But the very first line spoken in the play shatters the illusion of safe respectability; as he prepares to leave in the morning, Richard, having kissed his wife on the cheek, asks: "Is your lover coming today?" Equally casually, Sarah confirms that, indeed, her lover will be coming around three o'clock. Richard leaves. We see him return in the evening. And again, quite casually, after having given an account of the traffic as he was driving home:

> RICHARD: What about this afternoon? Pleasant
> afternoon?
> SARAH: Oh yes. Quite marvellous.
> RICHARD: Your lover came, did he?
> SARAH: Mmnn. Oh yes.
> RICHARD: Did you show him the hollyhocks?

Later, while the two are having an evening drink after supper, Richard questions Sarah about her feelings while she is with her lover and whether she ever thinks of *him* slaving away at his office. Sarah retorts that the picture of Richard in the office is not very convincing:

> Because I knew you weren't there. I knew you
> were with your mistress.

Richard hotly denies this:

> But I haven't got a mistress. I'm very well ac-
> quainted with a whore, but I haven't got a mis-
> tress. There is a world of difference. . . . She is
> a common or garden slut. Not worth talking
> about.

It seems as though Sarah has found Richard out. She didn't expect him to admit the existence of that whore so readily. Richard points to the importance of utter frank-ness in marriage. Sarah wonders how he, who attaches so much importance to wit and elegance in women, could be interested in a whore. His answer is:

> Why? I wasn't looking for your double, was I?
> I wasn't looking for a woman I could respect, as
> you, whom I could admire and love, as I do you.
> Was I? All I wanted was . . . how shall I put

it . . . someone who could express and engender lust with all lust's cunning. Nothing more.

The conversation returns to Sarah and her lover. What
does the lover think of her husband, Richard? "He respects you." Why does she like him so much?

SARAH: His whole body emanates love.
RICHARD: How nauseating.

We meet Richard and Sarah again next morning.
Richard is leaving. Again Richard asks whether her lover
is coming. Yes, he is. Richard promises he won't come
home too early. He'll go to the National Gallery to waste
some time.

The same afternoon: Sarah has changed into a tight,
seductive dress. She lowers the blinds. The doorbell
rings. It is the milkman. Is *he* her lover? No. He is merely
delivering some cream. Again the doorbell rings. This
time it is the lover: Richard, dressed in "a suede jacket,
casual shirt with no tie and light slacks." Sarah greets
him: "Hullo, Max."

So it is the husband himself who returns in the guise of
the lover. There now follows a sequence of erotic rituals:
first Max/Richard is playing the part of a man who mo-
lests Sarah in the park; then Richard/Max becomes a
kind gentleman who rescues her from the potential rap-
ist and, when it starts to rain, offers to sit the rain out with
her in the park-keeper's hut:

SARAH: Do you think we should? I mean, what
about the park-keeper?
MAX: I am the park-keeper.

But soon it is Sarah who becomes aggressive, and
Richard/Max who insists that he is married: he calls
Sarah by a number of different names—Dolores, Mary.

Eventually the two of them disappear under the table and the scene fades with Sarah's voice exclaiming Max's name.

When the light returns, Sarah and her lover/husband are having tea. Max is in a thoughtful, postcoital mood. He has qualms about Sarah's husband, he cannot understand how he puts up with the situation. In fact, he has come to the conclusion that the affair must stop. Because of her husband, Sarah asks? "No, nothing to do with your husband. It's because of my wife. . . . I can't deceive her any longer." Sarah cannot understand what has come over Max. But he goes on and on about his guilt feelings. Not only about his wife, but also about her children who will soon be out of boarding school. And anyway, she is too bony for his taste. Sarah still thinks it is all a joke. But Max/Richard insists: "It's no joke." He leaves.

As the clock chimes six, Richard returns home in his business clothes, complaining of the dreary conference that occupied his whole day. After a while he inquires about the lover's visit. Sarah is less than enthusiastic this time. She retaliates by asking about Richard's whore:

> RICHARD: Splendid.
> SARAH: Fatter or thinner?
> RICHARD: I beg your pardon?
> SARAH: Is she fatter or thinner?
> RICHARD: She gets thinner every day.
> SARAH: That must displease you?
> RICHARD: Not at all. I'm fond of thin ladies.

Was the complaint about the boniness of the whore merely a joke? No. Richard returns to the subject. The arrangement with the lover, which seems to have been a feature of the whole ten years that their marriage has lasted, must stop. Sarah is stunned. Richard insists she should receive her lover where she wants, but not in his house. And what about his whore? She has been paid off. Why? Because she was too bony.

Then Richard takes the bongo drum, which has been a feature of the erotic ritual with the lover, from the cupboard. He asks what is is, and as he handles it he slips into the afternoon ritual of picking up a girl in the park. Sarah at first is horrified by this breach of the rules of the game, but gradually she also gets into her part. She starts to slip beneath the table. Remarking that it is a very late tea they are having, she suggests that she should change her clothes. The play closes with Richard agreeing: "Change your clothes . . . you lovely whore."

The fantasy world of their afternoons has irrupted into, perhaps permanently taken over, the "respectable" portion of their day, of their lives. Or have they merely learned to treat their fantasies as fantasies and thus become able to switch them on and off at will, having converted a compulsion into a lighthearted game?

There is no indication in the text how we are to take the final twist in the pattern. Again we have been confronted with the shifting nature of reality: is Sarah, deep down, a whore forced by society into a guise of respectability; is she a respectable woman seeking an occasional outlet for her desires in erotic fantasy? Is Richard unable to find sexual satisfaction with a respectable woman and mother, and therefore compelled to the fantasy that he is buying satisfaction from someone experienced in "all lust's cunning"? Or is he really at heart a pimp whom society has forced into the mould of the bowler-hatted commuter?

The ambivalence of our social selves, the coexistence in all of us of the primeval, amoral instinct-dominated sensual being on the one hand and the tamed, regulated social conformist on the other, is one of the dominant themes of Pinter's writing—above all the oscillation of the image of woman between that of mother/madonna/ housewife and that of the whore/maenad. We need only recall the respectable schoolteacher Virginia in the novel of *The Dwarfs,* who turns, almost overnight and without any discernible motive, into a Soho call girl; the whore in *A Night Out,* who is revealed merely as another aspect of Albert Stokes' super-respectable mother; the dual image of woman in *The Birthday Party,* where the female principle is represented for Stanley by Meg. and Lulu; Flora, the middle-aged middle-class matron in *A Slight Ache,* who unexpectedly reveals herself as a sex-obsessed maenad thirsting after her husband's death; Stella, in *The Collection,* who, in reality or in fantasy, throws herself into the arms of a man she casually met in a lift in a hotel; and, of course, Ruth, in *The Homecoming.*

The image itself—the female as mother and as whore, split asunder into two contrasting characters or coexisting in the same person—is, indeed, one of the basic archetypes of all literature. In *The Lover,* as in some of Pinter's other works, it is, however, most originally merged with another archetypal problem, the question of the dividing line between reality and dream. Max and his whore are dream images in the minds of Richard and Sarah; their ritual is a game played by Richard and Sarah. Are Richard and Sarah therefore their true selves, Max and his whore mere figments of their imagination? Or are they not, rather, the respectable stereotypes, the clichés they enact in their daily lives, the figments, the masks, while the reckless lover and the promiscuous female represent their real selves at a far deeper level of significance and reality? The conclusion of *The Lover* suggests that it is in an integration, an interpenetration of the external mask and the subterranean instinct that a solution might emerge in the recognition that we must accept both our social self and our instinctive one, and by that acceptance learn to control them. Yet here again we might read the ending differently: that the luxuriant growth of erotic fantasy might take over altogether and destroy completely Richard's and Sarah's lives as respectable suburbanites. Or, indeed, that the whole play does not represent reality, but a dream in the mind of one or the other of the two.

The Bacchae and Genet's *The Balcony* treat the same vast subject of the conflict between tamed, socialised humanity and wild, instinct-dominated humanity on a vast and epic scale. *The Lover* deals with the theme in miniature, with elegance and dry humour, on the level of subtle, intimate comedy.

THE HOMECOMING

Pinter's third full-length play, which was received with some bewilderment in London, became a sensational success in America and established him on Broadway.

The external action of *The Homecoming* is both simple and startling: Max, a retired butcher, about seventy years old, shares his large old house somewhere in the industrial area of North London with two of his three sons— Lenny and Joey. Joey, the youngest, is an amateur boxer who hopes to become a professional but in the meantime has a job with a demolition firm. He is slow of speech and clumsy. Lenny, on the other hand, is sleek and intelligent and—at the start of the play—of uncertain occupation. Max's brother Sam, a hire-car driver, is the fourth inhabitant of Max's house.

Max talks a great deal about his boys' mother, his late wife Jessie, and of his lifelong friend and companion MacGregor, also now dead. The sons, especially Lenny, treat their father extremely badly; the old man acts as housewife and cook and has to listen to a great deal of sarcasm about his cooking. He, in turn, is extremely rude to his brother, Sam, the hire-car driver. A great mystery seems to surround the personality of the now dead mother of the family, Jessie, and Sam somehow seems connected with this mystery. Apropos of nothing, for example, Sam feels compelled to assert certain facts about Jessie's past:

> I want to make something clear about Jessie, Max. I want to. I do. When I took her out in the cab, round the town, I was taking care of her, for you. I was looking after her for you, when you were busy, wasn't I? I was showing her the West End.

As to Max's great friend MacGregor, Sam has his own opinion, too:

> Old Mac died a few years ago, didn't he? Isn't he dead?
> (*Pause.*)
> He was a lousy stinking rotten loudmouth. A bastard uncouth sodding runt. Mind you, he was a good friend of yours.

Max's reaction to this outburst is equally brutal:

> Eh Sam. . . . Why do I keep you here? You are just an old grub. . . . As soon as you stop paying your way here, I mean when you are too old to pay your way, you know what I am going

to do? I am going to give you the boot. . . . I mean, bring in the money and I'll put up with you. But when the firm gets rid of you—you can flake off.

When Sam draws Max's attention to the fact that the house is partly his as well, because it was their father's house, Max launches into reminiscences of his childhood:

> Our father? I remember him. . . . He used to come over to me and look down at me. My old man did. He'd bend right over me, then he'd pick me up. I was only that big. Then he'd dandle me. Give me the bottle. Wipe me clean. Give me a smile. Pat me on the bum. Pass me around, pass me from hand to hand. Toss me up in the air. Catch me coming down. I remember my father.

A few hours later: it is night. The inhabitants of the house have gone to bed. But two intruders stand on the threshold of the room: Teddy, Max's third and eldest son, and his wife Ruth. Teddy teaches philosophy at an American college. He and Ruth have been on a trip to Italy. On the way back they have decided to visit the house where Teddy was born and to introduce Ruth, whom Max has not yet met, to Teddy's father. Teddy still has a key to the front door; that is how he was able to get in without ringing the doorbell. Teddy does not want to wake anyone. He goes upstairs. His old room is still there. It is empty. There is some altercation between the couple. Teddy wants Ruth to come up to bed with him, she wants to stay up, perhaps go for a walk. Finally Teddy agrees. He goes upstairs. He gives Ruth the front-door key and she goes out.

Lenny, wearing his pyjamas, confronts Teddy. He could not sleep. The meeting of the two brothers after six years is very casual: Teddy merely says that he has come for a few days, he asks how his father is and where he could find sheets for his bed. Then he goes upstairs. Lenny, too, goes, the stage stays empty for a while, then Lenny returns, lights a cigarette, and sits down. Ruth comes back. The meeting between Lenny and his sister-in-law—whose identity he does not yet know, her presence has not been mentioned in his conversation with Teddy—is also strangely casual. Only after polite nothings about the weather, and whether he can offer her a drink, have been exchanged does Lenny inquire who the mysterious woman, who has just come into his house in the middle of the night, might be: "You must be connected with my brother in some way. The one who's been abroad."

When Ruth replies that she is his brother's wife, Lenny does not react at all. He merely asks her advice about his insomnia. And later in the conversation he makes it clear that he does not really believe, or has not really taken in, the fact that Ruth is Teddy's wife.

> RUTH: We are on a visit to Europe.
> LENNY: What, both of you?
> RUTH: Yes.
> LENNY: What, you sort of live with him over there, do you?
> RUTH: We're married.

Again Lenny does not react to this remark. He merely recapitulates the previous information: "On a visit to Europe, eh? Seen much of it?" And then almost immediately, after talking about Venice and his idea that, had

he not been too young to serve in the war, he might have
gone there during his war service, he asks:

> LENNY: Do you mind if I hold your hand?
> RUTH: Why?
> LENNY: Just a touch.

When Ruth asks again why he wants to hold her hand,
Lenny tries to explain by telling her a long and lurid
story about a lady who was making certain propositions
to him, whom he could have killed but merely beat up
brutally when he encountered her in a lonely spot by
the docks. And that, simply because she was "diseased."

> RUTH: How did you know she was diseased?
> LENNY: How did I know?
> (*Pause.*)
> I decided she was.
> (*Silence.*)

The absence of a reaction from Ruth to this extraordinary
long narrative of violence, which, though it is never
clearly stated, implies Lenny's connection with a world
of prostitutes and gangsters, deepens the atmosphere of
mystery.

Lenny changes the subject and inquires about his
brother. A mention of Teddy's intelligence and sensitivity
prompts Lenny to another long and equally strange narrative to explain his own brand of sensitivity. He describes how, last Christmas, he decided to do some snow-
clearing for the Borough Council one morning, not
because he wanted the money but because he likes the
work in the early morning in the newly fallen snow. During a tea break he was, he reports, approached by an old
lady who asked him to help her move a heavy iron mangle, which had been left in the wrong room when it was

delivered. He had consented to help, but when he found that the mangle was extremely heavy, and the old lady herself showed no sign of giving a hand with the job, he got extremely angry:

> So after a few minutes I said to her, now look here, why don't you stuff this iron mangle up your arse? Anyway, I said, they're out of date, you want to get a spin-drier. I had a good mind to give her a workover there and then, but as I was feeling jubilant with the snow-clearing I just gave her a short-arm jab to the belly and jumped on a bus outside.

Both of Lenny's long—and brilliantly phrased—narrations describe acts of brutality against women. He is showing off to Ruth and telling her something about himself. And as we—or, indeed, Ruth—cannot be sure whether these stories are true or merely invented on the spur of the moment, it is by no means clear what it is that Lenny wants to communicate.

Ruth has, however, understood something. When Lenny suggests that he should relieve her, first of an ashtray by her side, then of the glass from which she is drinking, a battle of wills develops between them:

RUTH: I haven't quite finished.
LENNY: You've consumed quite enough, in my opinion.
RUTH: No, I haven't.
LENNY: Quite sufficient, in my own opinion.
RUTH: Not in mine, Leonard.
    (*Pause.*)
LENNY: Don't call me that, please.
RUTH: Why not?
LENNY: That's the name my mother gave me.

(Pause.)
Just give me the glass.
RUTH: No.
LENNY: I take it then.
RUTH: If you take the glass . . . I'll take you.

Lenny is thrown by Ruth's aggressiveness. He retreats; he just wants the glass. She offers him a sip from the glass:

RUTH: Put your head back and open your mouth.
LENNY: Take that glass away from me.
RUTH: Lie on the floor. Go on. I'll pour it down your throat.
LENNY: What are you doing, making me some kind of proposal?

Ruth has won the contest of wills. She laughs, drains the glass, and merely says: "Oh, I was thirsty." Then she goes upstairs. Lenny angrily shouts after her, asking whether she had been making him some sort of proposal.

The noise has wakened Max. He comes down scolding and nagging Lenny and asking what is going on. Lenny does not—mysteriously enough—disclose the presence of either his brother or his wife and maintains that he, Lenny, had been sleepwalking. Finally he turns on his father—half in irony, half in deadly earnest—by putting a question to him:

It's a question I've been meaning to ask you for some time. That night . . . you know . . . the night you got me . . . that night with Mum, what was it like?

He enlarges on the question, describes how this torments lots of people of his age. Max is speechless with

rage. All he can say is: "You'll drown in your own blood."
Max spits at Lenny and goes back upstairs.

The next morning Max and Joey are discussing what
they will be doing during the day (evidently a Saturday
at the end of August, as it's the first day of the football
season). Max resents Sam's presence in the kitchen,
where he would like to have breakfast, but cannot stand
seeing Sam doing the washing-up there. When Sam appears, the endless bickering between the two brothers
continues. Max complains about Sam's lack of virility,
which led to their father having to take MacGregor into
the shop.

Teddy and Ruth come downstairs. Max is upset that he
has not been told of his son's arrival. When he notices
Ruth, he gets very angry: "Who asked you to bring tarts
in here?" He does not want to hear Teddy's explanation
that Ruth is his wife:

> I've never had a whore under this roof before.
> Ever since your mother died. My word of hon-
> our. . . . Take that disease away from me. Get
> her away from me.

Again overhearing Teddy's insistence that Ruth is his
wife, Max orders Joey to chuck them out. When Joey
apologises to Teddy by saying that Max is an old man,
Max hits him viciously. He himself is about to collapse
from the exertion, but when Sam tries to come to his aid,
Max hits him over the head with his stick. With Joey and
Max on the floor, Sam holding his head, Lenny, who has
appeared on the scene, and Teddy face each other in
silence. Joey is at Ruth's feet; she looks down on him.

When they are back on their feet, Max's mood is
changed. He asks Ruth if she is a mother, and when she
answers that she has three children, he is pacified. He

even offers Teddy a nice cuddle. And when Teddy con-
sents to a cuddle and kiss he exclaims in triumph: "He
still loves his father!"

So ends Act I. Act II opens the same afternoon. The
whole family have had a lunch prepared by Max, who is
flattered by Ruth's approval of his cooking. Max reminisces about Jessie, his late wife, who taught his boys
every single bit of the moral code they live by, his gen-
erosity towards her, his exertions in building up his business, and inevitably also the exploits of the late Mac-
Gregor. But almost in the same breath he calls Jessie a
"slutbitch." Teddy tells about his life on the college campus and about his and Ruth's three boys.

> MAX: All boys? Isn't that funny, eh? You've got
> three, I've got three.

But the mood of genial goodwill begins to change.
Lenny starts to needle Teddy about his philosophy. He
wants Teddy to comment on the nature of reality. What
is a table, philosophically speaking, he asks? Teddy refuses to be drawn. But Ruth suddenly intervenes:

> Look at me. I . . . move my leg. That's all it is.
> But I wear . . . underwear . . . which moves
> with me . . . it . . . captures your attention.
> Perhaps you misinterpret. The action is simple.
> It's a leg . . . moving. My lips move. Why don't
> you restrict . . . your observation to that?

The association of ideas in Ruth's mind seems to be: if
a table, philosophically speaking, is more than just a table, if there is another plane of reality behind its appearance, this is analogous to the contrast between the
outward appearance of a woman and what is beneath
that appearance: the underwear, the flesh, the sex.

Teddy has got up; he is clearly alarmed. Ruth is in a mood to make revelations about her real background, her real feelings:

> I was born quite near here.
> (*Pause.*)
> Then . . . six years ago, I went to America.
> (*Pause.*)
> It's all rock. And sand. It stretches . . . so far . . . everywhere you look. And there's a lot of insects there.
> (*Pause.*)
> And there's a lot of insects there.

The family are embarrassed. Sam has already left to go to work. Now Max, Joey, and Lenny also leave. Teddy and Ruth remain behind, alone. Teddy suggests that they should leave and go back to America immediately. But Ruth does not seem enthusiastic, although she neither accepts nor rejects the suggestion. Teddy goes upstairs to pack.

Lenny returns. He talks with Ruth about the weather, about clothes. Ruth asks whether he likes her shoes, and when he says he does, complains that they are unobtainable in America. She confesses that before she married Teddy and went to America, she was a model. Not for demonstrating clothes or hats, but "for the body." She describes a place in the country where she and other girls were photographed in the nude by a lake.

Teddy comes downstairs with his and Ruth's luggage. He asks her to go. But Lenny suggests a dance, just one, before she leaves. He puts a record on the radiogram. They dance; he kisses her.

At this point Max and Joey return from the gym where

Joey has been training. When Joey sees what is going
on he exclaims:

> Christ, she's wide open. Dad, look at that.
> (*Pause.*)
> She's a tart.

And now the youngest of the sons takes Ruth from
Lenny's arms, sits on the sofa with her, and embraces and
kisses her. Max, who was so shocked about Ruth when
he first met her, is completely casual about her behaviour.
He assures Teddy that he need not have been ashamed
when he married Ruth (he went away to America without even informing his father that he had met and married her), and praises her beauty and quality. All this
while Joey and Ruth have rolled off the sofa onto the
floor. Lenny touches her with his foot to make her get
up. She asks for something to eat and for a drink. She
has become demanding and bossy. And now she begins
to needle Teddy about his philosophy: "Have your family read your critical works?"

Teddy fights back with a defensive outburst against
his family:

> You wouldn't understand my works. You
> wouldn't have the faintest idea of what
> they were about. . . . It's nothing to do with
> the question of intelligence. It's a way of being
> able to look at the world. It's a question of how
> far you can operate on things and not in things.
> . . . You're just objects. You just . . . move
> about. I can observe it. I can see what you do.
> It's the same as I do. But you're lost in it.

The lights fade. When they come up again, it is evening. Sam and Teddy are alone in the room. Sam tells

Teddy that he always liked him best among the three boys.

When Lenny re-appears, the conflict between him and Teddy comes into the open in a quarrel about a cheese roll Lenny made for himself, put into a drawer so that he could eat it when he got back, but which has now been eaten by Teddy. Not just thoughtlessly, but intentionally. In a long speech Lenny scolds Teddy for having grown sulky in the States. Teddy hardly reacts.

Now Joey comes down from upstairs where he has clearly been spending the afternoon with Ruth. Lenny asks, coolly and clinically, how he got on with her. When Joey informs him that he didn't get all the way, Lenny is indignant. He reproaches Teddy with her being a tease. Teddy, quite unmoved and casual, merely comments: "Perhaps he hasn't got the right touch."

Lenny retorts with a long account of an exploit of Joey's and his during which they drove away two men from their girl friends and raped them on a bomb site near Wormwood Scrubs (the West London prison). When Max and Sam come in, they are also informed that Ruth is a tease. Max is equally upset: "My Joey? She did that to my boy?"

He asks Teddy if she treats him the same way. Again Teddy, quite detached, merely replies: "No."

And now, out of the blue, Max suggests that Ruth should stay in the house. Teddy, quite casually, doubts whether they should ask her to stay: "She's not well, and we've got to get home to the children."

But Max insists. How could they bear the additional cost? Perhaps by each of them contributing a little from their wages. Lenny has a better idea: she could work for a living, as a prostitute. It now turns out that Lenny, in fact, is a professional pimp who runs a string of women in Soho. She could work part-time there, not more than four hours a night. Lenny even asks Teddy to recommend her to American professors planning to come to Europe. They could give her a nice professional name, print discreet cards with her name and address. Teddy does not object or protest. He merely says: "She'd get old . . . very quickly." But this objection is dismissed by Max: there is the Health Service, after all!

Ruth comes down. And now it is her husband, Teddy, who puts the proposition to her:

> Ruth . . . the family have invited you to stay, for a little while longer. As a . . . as a kind of guest. If you like the idea I don't mind. We can manage very easily at home . . . until you come back.

And when Ruth seems pleased with the idea, it is again Teddy who draws her attention to the fact that she will have to "pull her weight. . . . Financially." When Lenny mentions the flat in which she would have to spend a certain number of hours every night, Ruth, who instantly seizes the meaning of the suggestion, drives a hard bargain: she wants at least three rooms and a bathroom, a personal maid, and is not prepared to pay back the original outlay on clothes and furnishings: "You would have to regard your original outlay simply as a capital investment."

Lenny, driven into a corner, agrees to all these conditions. Ruth wants it all drawn up as a legal contract. At this moment Sam, who has been following the scene with growing consternation, comes forward and bursts out: "MacGregor had Jessie in the back of my cab as I drove them along."

He collapses. At first they think he is dead, but he is

still breathing. They leave him lying there, while Ruth calmly concludes the bargain and Teddy merely regrets Sam's inability to drive him to London Airport. Max gives him elaborate instructions how to go by underground or taxi and a photograph of himself to show to his grandsons. Lenny and Joey also take their casual leave of Teddy. Ruth calls him, as he leaves, by a name she has not used before in the play: "Eddie." Will she change her mind? Come with him? Teddy turns. There is a pause. Ruth merely says: "Don't become a stranger."

Teddy goes. Ruth sits, relaxed, in her chair. Sam lies motionless on the floor. Joey goes up to Ruth's chair; he kneels by it. She touches his head; he puts his head in her lap. Max goes to and fro, very agitated:

> I am too old, I suppose. She thinks I'm an old
> man.
> (*Pause.*)
> I'm not such an old man.

Ruth remains impassive. Lenny stands watching the scene. Max becomes more and more pleading, more and more insistent. He begins to stammer. He falls to his knees and crawls up to Ruth, pleading all the way that he is not an old man and begging for a kiss. But Ruth remains impassive, stroking Joey's head, while Lenny stands by watching. The curtain falls.

The Homecoming shocks its audiences not only by the casual and matter-of-fact way in which sex and prostitution are discussed in it, but also, and even more, by the apparently inexplicable motivations of its main characters: why should a woman, the mother of three children and the wife of an American college professor, calmly accept an offer to have herself set up as a prostitute? How could a husband not only consent to such an arrangement but actually put the proposition to his wife? Is the author merely out to shock for the sake of shock? Is the whole story not totally incredible? Alternatively, those who admired the play's obvious theatrical effectiveness, with its sudden surprises and unexpected turns, defended it as being a cluster of symbolic images and poetic metaphors which should not be subjected to excessive scrutiny on counts of verisimilitude and realistic credibility.

It is my conviction that *The Homecoming*, while being a poetic image of a basic human situation, can also stand up to the most meticulous examination as a piece of realistic theatre, and that, indeed, its achievement is the perfect fusion of extreme realism with the quality of an archetypal dream image of wish-fulfillment.

Let us first examine the validity of the play as a realistic and perfectly explicable series of events as they could, in fact, happen to a family living in the circumstances outlined and clearly indicated by the author.

The sequence of events portrayed in *The Homecoming* is inexplicable only in terms of a convention of drama in which the past history of the characters and their motivations must be clearly outlined in the exposition. Since Pinter regards this convention not only as contrary to strict realism (people don't explain each other's past lives and motivations, already well known to them, to each other) but also somewhat presumptuous (since it postulates an omniscient author), he does not supply a neatly worked-out set of backgrounds and motivations; yet all the information is given—in the most natural manner—in the course of the play.

For example, there can be little doubt that Max was a butcher by trade, or that his friend MacGregor also started out as a butcher in the shop of Max's father. But that does not mean that Max and MacGregor could not also, and in addition, have been engaged in less savoury occupations, that they might not have been members of the London half-world of pimps and gangsters. In the very first scene, Max reminisces about MacGregor and himself:

> Huhh! We were two of the worst hated men in the West End of London. I tell you, I still got the scars. We'd walk into a place, the whole room'd stand up, they'd make way to let us pass. You never heard such silence.

At that point in the play the audience will tend to take this as empty boasting from an old man, but in the light of subsequent events it may well seem to contain at least part of the truth. And what would have been more natural than that Lenny should have followed a family tradition by taking up the profession of a Soho pimp. His story about the beating up of a diseased prostitute establishes his profession fairly early in the play. Moreover, there is a hint in this story that chauffeurs like Sam are an integral part of an organisation like Lenny's: "Don't worry about the chauffeur. The chauffeur would never have spoken. He was an old friend of the family."

Hence it becomes likely that Sam, who now works for a respectable hire-car firm, might in his youth have been a driver for prostitutes run by Max and MacGregor. His insistence to Max that he was always looking after Max's wife, Jessie, when driving her about the West End may well indicate that Jessie herself might have been one of the prostitutes involved. And this, in turn, would explain Lenny's bitter outburst when he asks his father about the circumstances of his conception. It would also explain Max's ambivalence about the mother of his children,

whom he praises to the sky at one point and then calls
a slutbitch. Even Max's statement that Jessie taught the
boys all the morality they know would then become
ironically double-edged: certainly Lenny and Joey have
the morality of pimps and rapists, which they may well
have been taught by a prostitute. Even Max's indignant
outburst when he first meets Ruth and immediately assumes that she is a tart has a double meaning:

> I've never had a whore under this roof before.
> *Ever since your mother died.* My word of hon-
> our. [My italics.]

Which might well mean that Teddy's mother *had* been
a whore.

In a family that had been living from prostitution for
decades, Max's and Lenny's final proposition to Ruth
would therefore be the most natural thing in the world;
no wonder that it is made quite casually, and received
quite casually by Teddy, the son who became an intellectual and ran away from home precisely because he did
not like the family's way of life, but nevertheless is wholly
conversant with it.

So much for the husband's complaisance. But what of
the wife's equally casual acceptance of the offer? It is
made quite clear by Ruth that when Teddy met and married her she was a nude photographic model—and this
is widely known as a euphemism for a prostitute. The
country house she so lovingly recalls as the scene of her
nude posing by the lake, where there were drinks and a
cold buffet, sounds more like the scene of orgies than a
place for photography. If Ruth therefore had been a
prostitute or near-prostitute when she first met Teddy
(and she protests when Max praises her charm: "I was
. . . different . . . when I met Teddy . . . first"), and if

both Lenny on first meeting her—he does not pay any attention to her assertion that she is married to Teddy—
and Max immediately recognise her as a tart, then surely
it is quite possible that she does not like the life of a
college professor's wife—she describes America as an arid
desert infested by insects, an unmistakable image of her
boredom in uncongenial surroundings—and that, indeed,
her marriage to Teddy is on the point of breakdown.
This would be a very believable motivation for the sudden and unannounced trip to Venice, just the kind of
last-minute attempt at a second honeymoon one would
expect to save the marriage. The likelihood is that this
trip did not produce the desired result. Ruth's refusal to
go up to the bedroom with Teddy on her first arrival in
the house could be seen in the light of her reluctance to
be exposed to what might have become a tedious or unsatisfactory sexual relationship. No doubt in the narrow
world of a university campus somewhere in Texas, Teddy's marital crisis might have given rise to embarrassing
gossip, perhaps there might even have been rumours
about Ruth's previous life. What would therefore be
more natural than that Teddy, having come to the conclusion that his marriage has broken down and that Ruth
cannot be turned into a respectable college professor's
lady, should regard the prospect of her not returning
home with a certain amount of equanimity, even relief?
Hence his eagerness to reassure Ruth that he and the
boys might well be able to manage without her.

So much then for the credibility of the events of *The
Homecoming* on a realistic level. Once we realise that
the family depicted is one that has always lived on the
fringes of the respectable, normal world; that Ruth, although a college professor's wife, might well also have

been a prostitute in the past, the actions and reactions of all the characters fall into place.

But, like most of Pinter's plays, *The Homecoming* also exists on another level: its real, its realistic action is a metaphor of human desires and aspirations, a myth, a dream image, a projection of archetypal fears and wishes. Just as the events in the *Oedipus* of Sophocles or in *King Lear* are both valid on a level of real, particular human beings, but can also be seen as dreams, nightmares of guilt and human suffering, *The Homecoming* also transcends the realistic level to become just such an archetypal image. And indeed it deals with the themes of both *Oedipus* and *Lear:* the desolation of old age and the sons' desire for the sexual conquest of the mother. That there is the strongest possible antagonism between the two younger sons, who live with Max, and their father is made clear from the very start of the play. In the first few minutes Lenny abuses his father in the rudest possible language: "Why don't you shut up, you daft prat?" And when Joey demands his evening meal from his father, Max complains:

> They walk in here every time of the day and
> night like bloody animals. *Go and find yourself
> a mother.* [My italics.]

The absence of a mother and the personality of the dead mother, Jessie, pervade the play. Max's inadequacy —or supposed inadequacy—as a cook is the most telling symbol of this state of affairs. But it is also made clear that at least one of the two younger sons, Lenny, also sees the mother as a sexual object. When he interrogates his father about the moment of his own conception, the act of sexual intercourse that gave him life, he is above all thinking of his mother in that erotic context. And his violent hatred of his father is clearly also motivated by the suffering it causes him to imagine his mother in his father's embraces; in other words, in that particular scene Lenny is a Hamlet figure.

Lenny and Joey closely resemble those other brothers, Mick and Aston, in *The Caretaker* (who are also engaged in a conflict with a father figure); like Mick and Aston, Lenny and Joey are complementary: Lenny slick and fast, Joey slow and strong, and they act as one. Lenny arouses Ruth and then hands her, without a murmur, to Joey. In fact, these two could be seen as different aspects of one personality: Lenny embodying the younger son's cunning and cleverness, Joey his strength and sexual potency. Similarly Max, the father, and Teddy, the eldest brother, could be seen as two aspects of the father figure: Max embodies the father's senility and ill temper, Teddy his superior wisdom (hence Lenny's needling of his philosophy). At the end of the play Max and Teddy have been defeated, Lenny and Joey are victorious. And what was the bone of contention between the two sides in the conflict? Ruth.

It is surely no coincidence that Ruth, Teddy's wife, like Jessie, Max's wife, has three sons. The point is underlined by Max. As the elder brother's—a father substitute's—wife, Ruth is a mother figure; she is a reincarnation of Jessie. Max's violent reaction on first meeting Ruth could then be seen as the outcome of his sudden confrontation with the image of his dead wife. ("I've never had a whore under this roof before. Ever since your mother died.")

At the end of the play Ruth again rules the household. This is the "homecoming" of the title. It is not Teddy who has come back home—after all, he left after one day —but the mother who has returned.

The mother whom the son desires in his infancy at the

moment of the first awakening of his sexuality is not an old woman but a young one. It is *her* image that dominates his dreams when he is grown up. Ruth, the mother of three boys whose ages must range from five to three, therefore represents the dreams of Lenny and Joey in that period of their lives. The final image of *The Homecoming* therefore is the culmination of their Oedipal dreams: their mother, young and beautiful, has become available to them as a sexual partner, as a "whore," while the defeated father grovels on the floor pleading for some scraps of her sexual favours. This wish-fulfillment dream is the exact reversal of the real situation that faces a young son: the father in proud possession and the son rejected, oppressed, dominated.

From the sons' point of view, therefore, *The Homecoming* is a dream image of the fulfillment of all Oedipal wishes, the sexual conquest of the mother, the utter humiliation of the father. From the father's point of view, the play is the terrifying nightmare of the sons' revenge.

The very ease with which Ruth is persuaded to take up a life of prostitution and to become a readily available sexual partner for Joey and Lenny seems, if the play is seen as a dreamlike myth, the most natural thing of all; it is merely the characteristic way in which wishes miraculously come true in dreams. Even the way in which Lenny encounters Ruth in the middle of the night, having turned up from nowhere, bears all the characteristic features of the manner in which dreams develop from a consciousness of lying in bed and imagining what one would most desire to happen. Lenny's two long stories, which he tells Ruth at this first encounter and which deal with his brutal treatment of women, fall into place as a child's attempts to convince himself that he is strong enough and big enough to impress and conquer a grown woman like his mother. Ruth, however, in the episode with the glass of water, has no difficulty in asserting her immediate and effortless superiority.

Like Sarah in *The Lover,* like Sally in *Night School,* like Stella in *The Collection,* Ruth is both mother and whore. A whore is the most passive of women, the one who can be treated as a sexual object without any consideration of her feelings or desires. The more helpess a male, the more he will tend to dream of women as obedient slaves—prostitutes. Hence the stern, unapproachable mother image must, in the sexual dreams of a child, tend to turn into the image of the whore. And that is why both Jessie and Ruth are both mother and whore.

If the view that *The Homecoming* is a wish-fulfillment dream seen primarily from the viewpoint of the young son is correct, then the character of Ruth *must* be a passive one: she is the object of male desires and, being an image in a dream, yields to these desires without putting up any resistance. Yet the play must also function on the realistic level; and here Pinter's success in making Ruth a credible character, even when seen as a real person and not just the passive object of archetypal desires, is a virtuoso achievement.

For Ruth sees herself—has resigned herself to being seen—as a passive object of desire. That is the significance of her speech about herself as a moving object in response to the discussion about the real nature of a table. Having failed in her marriage, Ruth is in a state of existential despair, a deep *accidie,* which is both fully understandable and completely motivates her behaviour. She has tried to fight her own nature and she has been defeated by it. Now she yields and surrenders to it beyond caring.

The character of Sam, on the other hand, embodies

the family's self-awareness of the true nature of the mother, Jessie, and the man who was her pimp, Mac-Gregor—who indeed, on a deeper level, merely represents Max's own activity as an underworld character, Max, in fact, when he was like Lenny. Thus Sam is the family's conscience, its superego; hence it is only natural that he collapses at the moment when the situation about which he has felt ashamed and guilty all his life is restored.

The subject matter of *The Homecoming* appears in various guises in a number of Pinter's previous plays: in *The Birthday Party* a son figure is brutally torn from a near-incestuous relationship with a loving mother figure —and the chief agent of this traumatic experience, Goldberg, has much in common with the father figure of Max; in *The Caretaker* two sons expel a father figure (and, again, the old tramp Davies has much in common with Max's garrulousness and irascibility, while Mick and Aston are very close to Lenny and Joey); in *Night School* a son (Walter) is fighting with a father figure (Solto) for the possession of a girl who is half schoolteacher (mother) and half night-club hostess (whore); in *The Lover* the hero dreams of his wife (who is a mother) as a whore. But it is in *The Homecoming* that the Oedipal theme emerges most fully and most explicitly. It is as though it had gradually risen to the surface as Pinter gained the self-confidence and formal skill that enabled him to meet it head on rather than merely obliquely.

The universality of the archetypal situation in *The Homecoming*, on the other hand, and its immense, if perhaps subconscious, relevance to theatre audiences everywhere, seems to me another explanation for the powerful impact of the play in spite of an initial reaction of incomprehension and puzzlement over its apparent surface "implausibility." However much audiences may reject

The Homecoming on the rational level, they ultimately respond to it in the depth of their subconscious. Hence the abundance of discussion and probing about *The Homecoming.*

TEA PARTY

Based on a short story which Pinter himself recorded for the B.B.C. Third Programme in April 1964 (it was broadcast on 29 April 1964) and which appeared in the January 1965 number of *Playboy,* the television play *Tea Party* was commissioned by the European Broadcasting Union to form part of a project of simultaneous, or nearly simultaneous, transmissions of television plays by major European dramatists throughout the European television networks. Pinter's contribution was preceded by plays specially written for this "largest theatre in the world" by Terence Rattigan and Fritz Hochwälder, and followed by one from François Billetdoux.

Tea Party deals with the downfall of an industrial tycoon, Robert Disson, who has risen from modest beginnings to the position of one of the most successful manufacturers of sanitary installations in Britain. This allows Pinter to start the play with a tracking shot of an elegant office suit lined with showcases displaying a selection of washbasins, lavatory bowls, and bidets. Disson's breakdown is the result of the tension between his desire for social status and respectability, represented by his second wife, Diana, a cool upper-class lady, and his sensuality, which manifests itself in his lusting after "the swelling body"—as it is repeatedly referred to in the story —of his secretary, Wendy; in other words, Disson's conflict is that of Richard in *The Lover,* except that in this case the chaste upper-class lady and the whore are different people rather than just one woman playing both parts.

The play opens with Disson's first interview with Wendy and his taking her on, on the eve of his marriage to Diana. (So he acquires the pure wife and the sexual object at the same moment.) Diana's brother Willy, who is out of a job (it seems the upper-class family is very much in need of marrying into money) is asked at the wedding reception to deliver not only the eulogy of the bride, his sister, but also, owing to the unforeseen absence of Disson's best friend, the eulogy of the bridegroom—which, as Willy does not know much good to say about his new brother-in-law, turns into a second eulogy of the bride. This starts Disson's feeling of embarrassment and inferiority towards his new wife's family. The fact that Disson's two teen-age sons, twins, from his first marriage are going to a public school and are therefore also growing into his social superiors aggravates his loss of self-confidence. Wendy, the lusty, willing social inferior, becomes a kind of haven of rest and reassurance for Disson.

When Diana, bored with being at home by herself, asks to be given a job in the family firm and becomes her brother's private secretary in the adjoining office, Disson's guilt and embarrassment grow. He suspects Wendy of flirting with his brother-in-law. When Wendy is called into Willy's office, Disson tries to watch through the keyhole what they might be up to. In the short story the scene is described as follows (Disson is the "I" in the story):

> With my eye at the keyhole I hear goosing,
> the squeak of them. The slit is black, only the

> sliding gussle on my drum, the hiss and flap of
> their bliss. The room sits on my head, my skull
> creased on the brass and loathsome handle I
> dare not twist, for fear of seeing black screech
> and scrape of my secretary writhing golden and
> blind in my partner's paunch and jungle.

In the play we see the door suddenly open: a pair of
woman's legs stands by Disson's squatting body. He looks
up. It is Diana, Disson's wife, who has been in the room
with Wendy and Willy.

Disson's discomfiture manifests itself—like Rose's in
The Room, like Edward's in *A Slight Ache*—in a failure
of his vision: he sees double or blurred images and suffers
from fits of temporary blindness. His friend Disley, who
is an eye specialist, can find nothing organically wrong.
Yet, while playing table tennis or doing carpentry with
his sons, Disson is repeatedly handicapped by his failing
eyesight.

Even in the office Disson's eyes give trouble. On these
occasions Wendy bandages his eyes with her chiffon ker-
chief, giving Disson an opportunity to touch her as she
ministers to him.

The catastrophe comes during a tea party at Disson's
office on the first anniversary of his marriage to Diana—
and of his acquisition of Wendy as his secretary. Disson's
old working-class parents have travelled down to London
from the North, Disley the ophthalmologist and his wife
are there, so are the twins, Willy, Diana, and Wendy.
Disson's eyes have again given trouble. Disley has bandaged them, just for half an hour, until the guests arrive.

The guests assemble. Disson listens to the clatter of
teacups, the snatches of party conversation. We see the
scene now and then objectively, now and then as Disson

imagines it, not being able to see what is going on. And
these imaginings become wilder and wilder. Finally he
sees Willy making love to both Diana and Wendy, who
are stretched out on Wendy's desk. Or as the story puts
it:

> Meanwhile my partner had the two women
> half stripped on a convenient rostrum. Whose
> body swelled most? I had forgotten. I picked up
> a pingpong ball. It was hard. I wondered how
> far he had stripped the women. The top halves
> or the bottom halves? Or perhaps he was now
> raising his spectacles to view my wife's swelling
> buttocks, the swelling breasts of my secretary.
> How could I verify this? By movement, by
> touch. But that was out of the question. And
> could such a sight possibly take place under the
> eyes of my own children? Would they continue
> to chat and chuckle, as they still did, with my
> physician? Hardly. However, it was good to
> have the bandage on straight and the knots
> tight.

So ends the story. In the play Disson's downfall is far
more concrete. He "falls to the floor in his chair with a
crack. His teacup drops and spills. The guests try to lift
him from the chair, but they don't succeed. Disley cuts
the bandage away. Finally they raise the chair. Disson
sits in it, motionless, with open eyes, in a catatonic trance.
Diana asks him whether he can hear or see her. She can
elicit no answer. The last shot is of Disson's face in
closeup, his eyes wide open."

Tea Party is unusual in Pinter's *œuvre* in that the age-
old English theme of the upstart who feels uneasy in his
new upper-class surroundings comes so much to the fore.

Yet it is characteristic of Pinter that even here the social theme coalesces with a sexual one. Disson feels himself not only socially but also sexually inadequate when he is with his wife; her social superiority deprives him of his manhood, for virility to him equals dominance. Hence he feels more manly, more at home with Wendy, his social inferior. And the breakdown comes when he suspects Wendy of having been taken up by his wife and brother-in-law. Indeed, his final collapse in the play is preceded by his overhearing a snatch of conversation between them:

WENDY: What me? Come to Spain?
DIANA: Yes, why not?
WILLY: Yes, of course you must come. Of course you must come.
WENDY: How wonderful.

Albert Stokes in *A Night Out* goes berserk when he discovers that the prostitute who has taken him home has the same social pretensions as his mother; Disson's collapse comes when he suspects that the vulgar and willing Wendy will rise to the social status of his upper-class wife and brother-in-law. While he sits with bandaged eyes at the tea party, Disson can hear the vulgar working-class accents of his parents on one side, the polished public-school small talk of his sons on the other. It is the tension between these two worlds that reduces him to paralysis and blindness.

In some ways Disson's emergence from the squalour of his working-class youth into the antiseptic respectability of upper-class life (beautifully symbolised by the spotless water closets and bidets) parallels Len's loss of the warm squalour of his life with the dwarfs, Aston's loss of the wild exuberance of the period before he underwent electric-shock treatment, Stanley's squalid existence in Meg's boarding house in *The Birthday Party*. Stanley, too, is propelled into respectability—and speechlessness —by an assault on his eyesight: his glasses are broken, he is reduced to near-blindness. Blindness is the punishment Oedipus inflicted upon himself for having lusted after his mother. Is it Disson's punishment for having aspired to the bed of the chaste, madonna-like Diana?

Although at first sight *Tea Party* looks like a far more conventional treatment of a more conventional subject matter, the staple of innumerable English plays, than most of Pinter's work, it does, in fact, combine many of the thematic strands of his more ambitious works.

THE BASEMENT

The Basement was first broadcast on B.B.C. Television in February 1967. Yet the script dates back to about 1963. It appears, under the title *The Compartment*, in the manuscript for a composite film planned by Grove Press, the title page of which is inscribed "Project I: Three Original Motion Picture Scripts by Samuel Beckett, Eugene Ionesco, Harold Pinter." Of the three projected films, only one, Beckett's *Film*, was made in 1964 by Alan Schneider, with Buster Keaton in the lead. The filming of Ionesco's *The Hard-Boiled Egg* and Pinter's *The Compartment* was postponed indefinitely. Yet the basic idea of the play (or film) goes back even further than that: the short story "The Examination," first published in 1959 but certainly completed by January 1958, deals with a conflict between two men, one of whom is called Kullus, at the end of which the narrator, who had been the examiner, has become the examinee, while Kullus has taken over the narrator's room. Here the conflict is, at least on the surface, not concerned with a girl. But the prose poem "Kullus," included in the collection of Pinter's early poetry published in 1968, not only introduces the girl but also contains much of the plot of *The Basement*, except that in the end it seems that the room belongs to the girl. "Kullus" is dated 1949. Thus the basic idea of *The Basement* goes back to a period when Pinter was only nineteen; it represents preoccupations that are as basic to his thinking as the subject matter of the novel *The Dwarfs*.

The Basement shows a struggle for a room and a struggle for a girl. At the beginning we see Stott, a young man in a raincoat, standing in the falling rain on a winter night outside a basement flat. Behind him, leaning against a wall, is a very young girl, Jane. Inside the large, comfortable basement room, Law, another young man, is reading a Persian love manual with illustrations. Stott rings the bell and is received as an old and long-lost friend by Law, who invites him to stay the night. After he has dried himself, exchanged some reminiscences of their previous life together with his host, and been offered a drink, Stott asks whether a friend of his, who is still waiting outside, can come in. Law readily agrees, Stott brings Jane in, they undress and immediately get into Law's bed. Law, deprived of his bed, sits by the fire and tries to read, while long sighs and gasps by Jane can be heard from the bed.

There follows a sequence of scenes in which Jane is shown exchanging confidences with Law about Stott, whom she does not appear to have known long, on a beach in summer (in the first sequence we were in winter), in a cave by the beach, and in the room, when

Jane, in bed with Stott, smiles at Law, who is sleeping on the floor.

We are back in winter. Stott and Law talk about Jane, who, Stott maintains, "comes from a rather splendid family, actually."

And now we are in summer again. On the beach, Jane caresses Law, who is afraid they might be seen by Stott.

As Law and Jane return from the beach, their towels over their shoulders, they find the room completely transformed: it is now hypermodern in a Scandinavian style.

Back in winter, but the room is still in its Scandinavian guise. Stott and Jane are in bed, Law is sitting in a chair. Stott demands some music to be played on the hi-fi.

The two men and the girl are drinking in a bar, one of the haunts of the two friends' youth.

In a field in winter, Jane is ready to act as umpire in a race between Stott and Law. She gives the sign to start. Law runs, Stott remains standing still; Law turns to look back and stumbles.

A winter night in the room with its Scandinavian look: Stott asks for some music, opens the window, and sees Law and Jane sitting outside in the moonlight, clenching their bodies with cold.

Walking in the backyard on a winter's day, Law suggests to Stott that the basement flat might be too small for three people; the town council and the Church might well object. Stott merely says: "Not at all. Not at all."

Summer again; the three are at lunch. Jane in Stott's lap. Stott demands music. Law, in looking for the Debussy record, angrily flings all the other records at the wall. Jane breaks away from Stott and runs out.

But now it is winter again, and the room looks as at the beginning. Stott and Jane, naked, are climbing into bed.

Law puts the record down, sits in his chair, and pokes the dying fire.

And now it's the backyard again, in summer. Jane is sitting by the table. Stott comes out and tries to touch her breast; she moves away. Law calls from the open window: he has found the record.

In the cave by the beach, Jane asks Law to ask Stott to go. It seems now as though Jane and Law had once lived together by themselves. Jane says:

> We had such a lovely home. We had such a cosy home. It was so warm. Tell him to go. It's your place. Then we could be happy again. Like we used to. Like we used to. In our first blush of love.

Winter again. The backyard. Law whispers to Stott that Jane is betraying him:

> . . . She has no loyalty. After all you've done for her. . . . She sullies this room. She dirties this room. All this beautiful furniture. This beautiful Scandinavian furniture. She dirties it. She sullies the room.

And now Stott lies in bed. Jane and Law discuss him as though he was about to die.

And then we see Law and Jane in a corner "snuffling each other like animals." Stott is standing by the window.

He closes the curtains. The room has again been completely transformed; it is now in the style of the Italian Renaissance, with a marble-tiled floor, tapestries, a Florentine mirror, an Italian Old Master on the wall. Jane offers Stott fruit from a bowl; Law, in a corner, plays the flute. Stott suddenly tosses the bowl of fruit across the room. He picks up a tray containing large marbles. As he throws them across the room at Law, Law uses his flute as a cricket bat. A savage and dangerous game of cricket develops; Law counters one marble by hitting it into a fish tank, the tank breaks, the fish swim across the marble tiles. Jane applauds. But then one of the marbles hits Law on the forehead; he collapses.

And now the room has become completely bare. Law and Stott advance on each other holding broken milk bottles. As the horrible weapons smash together, we see a record turning; it plays Debussy's "Girl with the Flaxen Hair."

Law and Jane are standing outside in the area in front of the basement flat; Law wears Stott's raincoat.

Inside, Stott is sitting by the fire, reading. The doorbell goes. Stott goes to open it and lets in Law, greeting him as a long-lost friend.

That this sequence of images does not tell a realistic story is only too clear; the sudden switches from summer to winter, the changes in the furniture of the room, leave no doubt on that score. Thus *The Basement* must be either a kind of dream or daydream: the first image of Stott standing outside in the rain may be a wish in Law's mind to see his old friend again—the rest would then express his hopes and fears arising out of the associations the thought of a sudden visit by Stott would conjure up in his mind. He envied his friend's superior intelligence, taste, and sexual prowess; so the thought of Stott would conjure up the image of the girl he would bring along, fears of the humiliation he would have to suffer seeing Stott make love to the girl in his bed, but also hopes of seducing her away from him. Knowing Stott's artistic leanings and wealth, he might imagine Stott furnishing the room in various sumptuous ways; and the thought of stealing the girl away from him would inevitably lead to fears of his revenge—hence the more and more savage dreams about fights with Stott (which follow the dream about Stott's sudden dying, a wish to kill him, causing instant guilt feelings). And finally, having imagined himself ousted by Stott, he begins to dream of how he would reconquer his room by the same means that Stott had used. He yearns to be as tough and ruthless as Stott, who would bring a girl with him and oust the owner of a room. The enigmatic scene in which it seems that Jane had in fact once been living with Law also fits into this pattern of a daydream. Here, too, Law merely tries out what it would feel like to be in Stott's shoes.

Alternatively, one might regard *The Basement* as no more than a sequence of images on the theme of two men fighting for a girl and for a room, an abstract, non-narrative pattern of moods and pictures which are all variations on the theme and composed, after the manner of a symphony, in a series of movements in which the different strands are contrasted, juxtaposed, varied, fused, and separated again.

Both interpretations may well be equally valid: the dream might have been the starting point, but the abstract, symphonic pattern of images the ultimate and artistically highly satisfying and sophisticated result.

Certainly the prose poem "Kullus" and the short story "The Examination" radiate a dreamlike atmosphere. Like Stott in the play, Kullus, in both the poem and the story, is associated with windows, the opening and closing of curtains:

> *Kullus took a room. The window was closed, if it was warm, and open, if it was cold. The curtains were open, if it was night, and closed if it was day.*

Why closed? Why open?
    —I have my night,
said Kullus.
        I have my day.

                                        ("Kullus")

Kullus's predilection for windows was not as-
sumed. At every interval, he retired to the window, and began from its vantage, as from a
source. . . . Neither was Kullus's predilection
for windows a deviation from former times. I
had myself suffered under his preoccupation
upon previous occasions, when the order of his
room had been maintained by particular arrangement of window and curtain, according to
day and night, and seldom to my taste or my
comfort.

                            ("The Examination")

The room again, in the poem, the story, and the play,
is symbolised by the fire in the grate. In the poem, when
Kullus and the girl invade his room, the narrator, after
they had climbed into his bed—

    . . . *placed a coat over the lamp and watched
    the ceiling hustle to the floor. Then the room
    moved to the flame in the grate. I shifted my
    stool and sat by the flame in the grate.*

At the end of the poem, when the room has become the
girl's, we have, as in the play, returned to the initial
situation:

    The ceiling hustled to the floor.
        —You have not shifted the coat from the lamp,
    I said.

Which implies that all that had happened in between might have been dreamt. In the play, Law "unbuttons his cardigan. He places it over the one lit lamp, so shading the light. He sits by the fire." The imagery of the poem has not been changed.

The dreamer sitting by the fire in the grate is thus strongly present in both the poem and the play, to a lesser extent in the story.

The Basement contains much of the youthful daydreams and preoccupations that form the matrix for Pinter's later development. Indeed, Stott and Law—or the narrator and Kullus—have much in common with the two rivals for the favours of the schoolteacher/call-girl Virginia in the novel of *The Dwarfs;* the motif of the change of role from the dominant to the dominated recurs in *A Slight Ache,* when Edward's place is taken by the formerly despised matchseller; the fight for the room, which in Pinter's other plays so often has a rather abstract character, is here still very clearly linked with the fight for the bed and the girl who will share it; only in *Night School* is this equally explicitly stated, in Walter's fight to get his bed back by becoming the lover of the girl to whom his aunts have let his room.

It is also noteworthy to observe how the more directly visual medium of television brings out the relationship between realism and the dream image in Pinter. In *Tea Party,* Disson's erotic nightmares while he is blind are made visible, and they are seen to arise directly from the naturalistic situation that has been painstakingly established. In *The Basement,* it might be argued, we are being given *only* the nightmarish vision, while the realistic basis—which may be no more than the shot of Law sitting by the fire, trying to read his book—has been whittled down to almost nothing.

LANDSCAPE

A short play, written for the stage, but withdrawn by Pinter when the Lord Chamberlain (in the last year of his tenure as stage censor) insisted on the omission of a few strong words, *Landscape* received its first performance on radio (not subject to the stage censor's power) in the spring of 1968. It reached the stage, in a double bill with its companion piece, *Silence,* in the summer of the following year.

In its style and approach, *Landscape* constitutes a new departure for Pinter: there is nothing here of the "comedy of menace." The difficulty of communication is, as in so many of Pinter's other plays, one of the main themes, but this difficulty emerges not from dialogue between people who talk to each other at length without getting through to each other, but from what are in effect two *monologues,* simultaneously delivered and intercut, but each conducted on a different level of expression.

The scene is the kitchen of a country house. By a long kitchen table sits Beth, a woman in her late forties, in an armchair. At the opposite corner of the long table sits Duff, a man in his early fifties. It is evening. A note by the author stresses the difference in levels of awareness and expression between the characters:

> Duff refers normally to Beth, but does not appear to hear her voice.
> Beth never looks at Duff, and does not appear to hear his voice.
> Both characters are relaxed, in no sense rigid.

It seems therefore that Duff, who "refers normally to

Beth," is talking to her, or at least trying to talk to her, although she does not react. Beth, on the other hand, who "never looks at Duff" and is not heard by him, seems to be talking merely to herself; her monologue is the stream of her thoughts, an *internal monologue*.

Beth's thoughts, moreover, are entirely about the past; she never refers to the present, or her present condition, while Duff is mainly concerned with telling Beth what he has been doing in the last day or two, with only an occasional reference to events further back.

Beth is dreaming of a day on the beach with a man, "my man," from whom she wanted a baby. This is the main image of her "landscape": the wide deserted beach with only a few people passing by, someone glimpsed in the distance, and Beth and her man, lying in the sand. Occasionally Beth's thoughts wander away from the beach to a scene where she arranged flowers and "he" (the same man or another? probably the same one):

> . . . . followed me and watched, standing at a distance from me. When the arrangement was done I stayed still. I heard him moving. He didn't touch me. I listened. I looked at the flowers, blue and white, in the bowl.
>
> (*Pause.*)
> Then he touched me.
> (*Pause.*)
> He touched the back of my neck. His fingers, lightly, touching, lightly, touching, the back, of my neck.

Other scenes Beth recalls—all related to the central landscape of herself and her lover at the beach—concern their visit to a hotel bar after their stay at the beach, and what preceded it: Beth meeting her man, having caught a bus to the crossroads and being picked up by him in his car to drive to the sea. And how she had got up early that day to do her housework; and how she wore her blue dress on that beautiful autumn morning. Bess speaks about her skill in drawing and that on that day at the beach she might have drawn a portrait of her man. The final image of the play is Beth's memory of that day on the beach:

> He lay over me and looked down at me. He supported my shoulder.
>   (*Pause.*)
> So tender his touch on my neck. So softly his kiss on my cheek.
>   (*Pause.*)
> My hand on his rib.
>   (*Pause.*)
> So sweetly the sand over me. Tiny the sand on my skin.
>   (*Pause.*)
> So silent the sky in my eyes. Gently the sound of the tide.
>   (*Pause.*)
> Oh my true love I said.

Beth does not even try to communicate. She has shut herself off from the present, the world that now surrounds her. Duff, on the other hand, *wants* to tell *her* what he has been doing, he also clearly wants to elicit an answer from her. "Do you remember the weather yesterday? That downfall?" He informs Beth that the dog has disappeared, that he sheltered under a tree in the rain, that he went to a pub and had a beer and got into an argument with another guest who complained about the quality of the beer.

Duff's conversation also gives a lot more detail about his and Beth's background and how they come to be sitting in that large kitchen on that evening. It emerges that he and Beth were taken on by the owner of the large country house as a team of domestic servants, housekeeper/cook and handyman/chauffeur. And that the owner of the house was called Mr. Sykes. And that now they are living in Mr. Sykes' house by themselves:

> That's where we are lucky in my opinion. To live in Mr. Sykes' house in peace, no-one to bother us.

That they are not just keeping the house warm for Mr. Sykes, but, in fact, seem to have become its owners, emerges from Duff's next sentence:

> I've thought of inviting one or two people I know from the village in here for a bit of a drink once or twice but I decided against it. It's not necessary.

Duff dwells on the fact that Beth was "a first-rate housekeeper. . . ."

> He could rely on you. He did. He trusted you, to run his house, to keep the house up to the mark, no panic.

Was it because of Beth's skill and reliability as a housekeeper that the couple were left the house by Mr. Sykes? He must have had a very compelling reason, for he was by no means all alone in the world:

> Mr. Sykes gave a little dinner party that Friday. He complimented you on your cooking and the service.

(Pause.)

Two women. That was all. Never seen them
before. Probably his mother and sister.

Or did Mr. Sykes have other reasons? Although Duff
considers that he was "a gloomy bugger" who led a
"lonely life," he was very attentive towards Beth:

> That nice blue dress he chose for you, for the
> house, that was very nice of him. Of course it
> was in his own interests for you to look good
> about the house, for guests.

Was this the blue dress that Beth wore that day when
she went to the beach with her man? It seems so; she
does not seem to have had another one: "I wore my blue
dress."

How have Beth and Duff come to their present condition of non-communication? Duff recalls what must
have been the decisive, traumatic incident:

> You used to wear a chain round your waist.
> On the chain you carried your keys, your thim-
> ble, your notebook, your pencil, your scissors.
> *(Pause.)*
> You stood in the hall and banged the gong.

This was after Mr. Sykes had gone, had in all probability
died.

> Standing in an empty hall banging a bloody
> gong. There's no one to listen. No one'll hear.
> There's not a soul in the house. Except me.
> There's nothing for lunch. There's nothing
> cooked. No stew. No pie. No joint. Fuck all.

(The last phrase was the principal cause for the Lord
Chamberlain's ban.) It was seeing Bess banging the

gong, as no doubt she had always done when Mr. Sykes was there, that made Duff wild. He tore down Beth's insignia of her office of housekeeper:

> I took the chain off and the thimble, the keys, the scissors slid off it and clattered down. I booted the gong down the hall. . . . I thought you would come to me, I thought you would come into my arms and kiss me, even . . . offer yourself to me. I would have had you in front of the dog, like a man, in the hall, on the stone, banging the gong. . . .

Is this merely fantasy, or did Duff, after tearing off Beth's chain with her keys and sewing things, really try to rape her there and then?

> I'll bang the gong on the floor, if the sound is too flat, lacks resonance, I'll hang it back on its hook, bang you against it swinging, gonging, waking the place up, calling them all for dinner, lunch is up, bring out the bacon, bang your lovely head, mind the dog doesn't swallow the thimble, slam—

These are Duff's last words in the play; from them the image is cross-cut to Beth's final fantasy of her man lying tenderly above her at the beach.

Thus the play's main image is one of contrast: the contrast between the tenderness and delicacy of the woman's memory of her past love, and the man's brutal coarseness, whether he is talking about the duck-shit that lay on the paths after the rain, whether he uses the strongest of taboo words, or dreams of sex in terms of banging a gong, bringing home the bacon, and slamming, beating, bashing.

There is, as always in Pinter's *œuvre*, a delicately balanced ambiguity in *Landscape*. Who is the man Beth remembers so tenderly? Is it Duff, who is clearly her husband, or another man, perhaps Mr. Sykes, her employer?

That there might have been a period when Duff himself was as tender as Beth is suggested in the text. The man who watched her so tenderly when she was arranging the flowers had remarked, says Beth, on her gravity:

> My gravity, he said. I was so grave attending
> to the flowers.

While Duff remembers:

> I was thinking . . . when you were young . . .
> you didn't laugh much. You were . . . grave.

So it might well have been Duff who watched her arrange the flowers and who spoke to her about her gravity. Duff recalls another episode that shows not only that he had a certain delicacy in former times but that there had been genuine love and understanding between them. He speaks of an occasion when he returned from a trip to the north with his employer:

> I told you that I'd let you down. I'd been un-
> faithful to you.
> (*Pause.*)
> You didn't cry. We had a few hours off. We
> walked up to the pond, with the dog. We stood
> under the trees for a bit. . . . When we got
> back into this room you put your hands on my
> face and you kissed me.

If Duff is the man whom Beth remembers so tenderly, the man who loyally confessed his transgression to her and begged forgiveness and was forgiven, then what we are seeing is the tragic operation of time, which turns men coarse and brutal by throwing them together with coarse drinking companions in pubs where they argue about the quality of the ale and boast about their expertise on the handling of beer (there is a long passage in Duff's text in which he parades his knowledge of the professional jargon of cellarmen), while the women retain the warmth and delicacy of feeling that blossomed in the beautiful erotic experiences of their youth.

But the man whom Beth remembers may well *not* be Duff; indeed, there is much in the text to indicate the likelihood that it was Mr. Sykes who was Beth's lover, Mr. Sykes who gave her the blue dress and took her to the beach and to tea at a hotel, and who, when he died, left her his large, empty house. In that case it may well be the grief at her lover's passing that has turned Beth into a silent recluse; in that case there is irony in the fact that Duff, when he was unfaithful, confessed, but that the tender and delicate Beth calmly went on deceiving her husband. If it was Duff who took Beth to the beach, for example, why should she have secretly gone off by herself by bus to the crossroads, to be picked up by him in the car later? If Mr. Sykes allowed Duff to use his car, they could have left together from the house; after all, they were man and wife. But if, Duff having been given some other job, Mr. Sykes had been driving the car himself, then he could not have set off with Beth, then the subterfuge would have been necessary. And in that case *Landscape* would present us with another variant of the eternal triangle: the coarse, bluff fellow Duff, who loves his wife deeply but in a rough-and-ready, earthy way; the gentleman lover with his gentle ways; and the woman who, having tasted the delicacy and gentleness of a social superior, rejects the coarse wooing of her pro-

letarian spouse and cuts herself off from him in grief and
loathing.

The point is, of course, that we will never be quite
certain what the truth might be: perhaps Beth merely
imagines all that beautiful episode by the sea, perhaps
she only dreamt of having such an outing with her employer, or, indeed, her husband; or perhaps she did experience that beautiful day, but with an entirely different
man. The landscape of memory, the landscape of the
soul, is dark, inaccessible, and shrouded in the mists of
eternal uncertainty.*

What is remarkable about *Landscape* as a virtuoso
piece of writing is not only the subtle control of its
rhythms, but also the immense feat of compression Pinter
has accomplished. Like Beckett's *Play*—with which *Landscape* and its companion piece *Silence* have many affinities—the matter of what might otherwise have occupied

---

* In a letter to the director of the first German production
of *Landscape* (Hamburg, January 1970) which was—by a
misunderstanding and against Pinter's wishes—published in
the programme brochure, Pinter told the director, Hans
Schweikart: ". . . the man on the beach is Duff. I think there
are elements of Mr Sykes in her memory of this Duff, which
she might be attributing to Duff, but the man remains Duff.
I think that Duff detests and is jealous of Mr Sykes, although
I do not believe that Mr Sykes and Beth were ever lovers. I
formed these conclusions after I had written the plays [the
same letter also refers to *Silence*] and after learning about
them through rehearsals." That Pinter himself came to this
conclusion *after* having written *Landscape* and having seen
it in rehearsal, does of course, by no means invalidate the
fact that for the *audience* the identity of the man on the
beach must remain indeterminate; for it is precisely that indeterminacy, the question whether the man she still dreams
of *could* have been Duff or Mr Sykes, which is the essential
content of the statement which *Landscape* makes.

a three-act play or a full-length novel is here compressed
into a bare half hour. The sparseness of the style, the
extreme skill with which minute clues are subtly interwoven, creates a picture of depth and density with a bare
minimum of words. It is out of the silences and pauses
that the landscape of these three lives emerges—a landscape that opens out onto a vast horizon.

SILENCE

Of all of Pinter's writings, *Silence* is the most lyrical,
but also the most mysterious and difficult. Like *Landscape*, *Silence* consists of cross-cut monologues, only here
there are not two but three characters; also, occasionally,
two of the characters are shown in dialogues that are
flashbacks to the past. Also, whereas in *Landscape* the
two characters, though never making contact with their
minds, are physically together in the same room, a realistically conceived kitchen in a definite house, in *Silence*
they are also—except in the flashback dialogues—physically separated. The stage direction is extremely laconic:

> Three areas.
> A chair in each area.

So, in fact, the three characters seem to live apart, each
in his own room.

These three characters are—according to the list provided by the author—Ellen, a girl in her twenties; Rumsey, a man of forty; and Bates, a man in his middle
thirties.

It is clear that Ellen has, or has had, relations with
both these men. The play opens with Rumsey talking
about going for a walk in the country with his girl:

> I walk with my girl who wears a grey blouse
> when she walks and grey shoes and walks with
> me readily wearing her clothes considered for
> me. Her grey clothes.

Ellen's opening passage starts with the essential information that:

> There are two. One who is with me sometimes,
> and another. He listens to me. I tell him what I
> know. . . . I lead him to a tree, clasp closely to
> him and whisper to him, wind going, dogs stop,
> and he hears me.
> But the other hears me.

The other, it appears, is Bates, the younger of the two men. He seems less tender, a rougher type than the lyrical Rumsey, for he describes how he took a girl (who is clearly Ellen, as later appears from an enactment of the scene in flashback) to the town by bus, walked with her through the backstreets and:

> Brought her into this place, my cousin runs it.
> Undressed her, placed my hand.

Both Rumsey and Bates are country men; but it seems that Rumsey is socially superior to Bates. He has his own house, where, as Ellen tells in her next passage, she visited him once, while Bates, who had to take her to a place —a pub, or hotel?—run by his cousin, seems to be a farm labourer without his own house.

As Ellen says, clearly referring to Rumsey:

> One time visited his house. He put a light
> on, it reflected the window, it reflected in the
> window.

Whereupon Rumsey, taking up his cue, describes what seems to be the same visit from his point of view, how she walks from the door to the window:

> . . . . to confirm that the house which grew nearer is the same one she stands in, that the path and the bushes are the same, that the gate is the same.

Bates, on the other hand, recalls how he used to stand waiting for the girl in the open:

> How many times standing clenched in the pissing dark waiting? The mud, the cows, the river.
>
> You cross the field out of darkness. You arrive.

And Ellen sums up:

> There are two. I turn to them and speak. I look them in their eyes. I kiss them there and say, I look away to smile, and touch them as they turn.

There follows the stage direction: *Silence*. That this is not just the usual *pause* that punctuates Pinter's dialogue is clear from the fact that the stage direction *Pause* also occurs in the text. Here the "*Silence*"—which gives the play its title—has a doubtlessly far greater significance. It marks the end of a chapter. But it also has a dramatic meaning of its own.

At the end of this first caesura of silence we are no longer in the situation where Ellen was in contact with the two men. Now Rumsey speaks of his being alone with his animals. He has, he says, lost nothing. He finds it pleasant to be alone. Bates, on the other hand, describes his anger and dismay at living next door to young people who make noisy music and noisy love. These young people have called him Grandad. And he sighs: "Were I young . . ." The Bates who is now talking is no longer "a man in his middle thirties" but an old man. So presumably is Rumsey in the preceding speech, and Ellen in the one that follows Bates' complaint about the noisy young neighbours, for she speaks of a drinking companion, an elderly woman who constantly asks her about her early life and sexual adventures. That she is no longer in her twenties becomes clear when she muses about her appearance: "But I'm still quite pretty really, quite nice eyes, nice skin."

At this point Bates moves to Ellen's area. They enact the scene he described in the first section of the play, leading up to his invitation that they should take a bus to town to a place his cousin runs. But Ellen's response in this flashback scene is "No." Followed by another *Silence*. Did she eventually accept the invitation? Or had Bates merely been dreaming about what might have been when he spoke of the visit to the place run by his cousin, where he undressed her?

After the second silence we hear only Rumsey and Bates. Rumsey talks about the heat, about a visit to his horse. Bates speaks of his imagined walks, his inability, in the real world, to get out of the walls. And he remembers a little girl:

> I took it for walks. I held it by its hand. It looked up at me and said, I see something in a tree, a shape, a shadow. It is leaning down. It is looking at us.
>
> Maybe it's a bird, I said, a big bird, resting. . . .

Where, in the time scale of the play, are we here, in

this brief section comprising just one short speech by Rumsey, one by Bates, between two silences? As Rumsey is alone, as Bates is living in town, we must assume that we are again in a period when they are no longer with Ellen, when, though perhaps not yet very old, they are older than at the time when they were having their relationship with her. Who, then, might the little girl be whom Bates took for walks? It seems that this, too, might have been Ellen at an even earlier stage in their relationship. For in a subsequent section, in a flashback scene between Rumsey and Ellen in which they re-enact her visit to Rumsey's house, Rumsey asks her whether she can remember when she last visited his house. She says she can remember. And Rumsey adds: "You were a little girl." So we must assume that Ellen grew up with both Rumsey and Bates having known her almost all her life.

But before we come to the passage that takes us back to Ellen's visit to Rumsey, there is a brief section, between two silences, in which Ellen as well as Rumsey speaks of what seems to be an ecstasy of lovemaking:

> ELLEN: When I run . . . when I run . . . when I
> run . . . over the grass . . .
> RUMSEY: She floats . . . under me. Floating . . .
> under me.
> ELLEN: I turn. I turn. I wheel. I glide. I wheel.
> In stunning light. The horizon moves from the
> sun. I am crushed by the light.
> (*Silence.*)

Then we are back with Rumsey and Bates much later, lonely and old. Then Ellen moves to Rumsey's acting area, and we are in the scene where she visits his house. She offers to cook for Rumsey, Rumsey offers to play music for her. They notice her reflection in the window—

which was mentioned by Ellen in the first section. The reflection is due to the darkness outside:

> ELLEN: It's very dark outside.
> RUMSEY: It's high up.
> ELLEN: Does it get darker the higher you get?
> RUMSEY: No.
> (*Silence.*)

And now we are back in the old age of the three characters. Ellen talks of the night around her:

> Around me sits the night. Such a silence. I can hear myself. Cup my ear. My heart beats in my ear. Such a silence. Is it me? Am I silent or speaking? How can I know? Can I know such things? No one has ever told me. I need to be told things. I seem to be old. Am I old now? No one will tell me. I must find a person to tell me these things.

Bates speaks about his landlady asking him for a drink and inquisitive about his former life: has there been no pleasantness, no loveliness in it? Bates reacts: "I've had all that. I've got all that. I said."

Ellen remembers that visit to Rumsey's house: he sat her on his knee by the window and asked her if he could kiss first her right, then her left cheek.

> I said yes. He did.
> (*Silence.*)

There follows an enigmatic passage: both Bates and Rumsey recall a similar incident with Ellen. Rumsey talks about something that Ellen said and he could not hear, Bates about something he said that Ellen could not hear. Bates briefly recalls—presumably while old—how happy horses are in the country. Then Ellen moves to Rumsey's acting area: Rumsey is telling her to find a young man for herself. She refuses because young men are stupid and she hates them.

Again there is silence. We are back, very briefly, in Ellen's and Bates' younger life. Bates talks about the shapes in the trees, which are just birds. Ellen speaks of her two friends:

> There are two. They halt to laugh and bellow
> in the yard. They dig and punch and cackle
> where they stand. They turn to move, look
> round at me to grin. I turn my eyes from one,
> and from the other to him.
> (*Silence.*)

Briefly Bates is interpolated—old again; the young people next door are silent now:

> Sleep? Tender love? It's of no importance.
> (*Silence.*)

Ellen—old—speaks of her life in town among people through whom she walks without noticing them. Her drinking companion has asked her for the hundredth time whether she had ever been married:

> This time I told her I had. Yes, I told her I
> had. Certainly. I can remember the wedding.

And now, with ever more frequent intervals of silence, the rest of the play is taken up by brief snatches from the speeches we have heard, cross-cut in an intricate pattern of memory which, as the snatches of speech become briefer, seems to run down, to ebb away until they merge into one long silence as the lights fade.

Even more than *Landscape, Silence* recalls Beckett's

Play, where the device of repeated fragments of speech running down is used to suggest the way the last moments of awareness of a dying person might remain suspended in a limbo forever, echoing on and on through eternity, while gradually losing their intensity but unable ever to fade away completely. Are the cross-cut thoughts and memories in *Silence* also the dying thoughts of the three characters before they are engulfed in total silence, the silence of death? The possibility is by no means excluded. But the play might, on the other hand, also try to portray the way in which memory gradually fades in the process of living and aging, the way in which the most intense emotions gradually flatten out and lose their impact and intensity. As we age, our awareness of the past dims and runs down—and the rest is silence.

Be that as it may, *Silence* is an attempt to tell a story by a technique that breaks the chronological sequence more decisively than is usually done even in intricately woven patterns of flashback. The story is presented simultaneously from three different points of *view* and from two, perhaps three, different points in *time:* the time of the relationship itself, and one or even two later periods. It is remarkable that with this highly intricate technique the story that emerges is probably less ambiguous than that of many of Pinter's other, less intricately patterned plays. Ellen, it seems pretty clear, grew up in the country, and two men who knew her as a little girl fell in love with her. Rumsey, the older of the two, later broke with her and advised her to look for younger men. She may have gone away with Bates, but as she loved Rumsey more, their relationship broke up. So Rumsey lived on, fairly contented on his lonely farm, while Bates and Ellen both stayed in town, unhappy, isolated, and longing for the country. It is a simple tale, but out of it

Pinter has made an intriguing attempt at a truly lyrical
theatre of strong images and vividly recreated emotions,
interwoven like the themes of a symphonic poem.

SKETCHES

The short sketches Pinter contributed to two revues in
1959, some of which were broadcast or performed sub-
sequently, are little more than limbering-up exercises to
try out characteristic innovations in dialogue technique.
But precisely for this reason, they contain a good deal
that is of interest for a deeper understanding of Pinter's
style.

The Lyric Revue *One To Another,* which opened at
the Lyric, Hammersmith, on 15 July 1959 and transferred
to the Apollo Theatre on 19 August 1959, contained two
sketches by Pinter: *Trouble in the Works* and *The Black
and White.*

Trouble in the Works is set in a factory. Mr. Fibbs, the
manager, interviews a personnel officer, Wills, about the
unrest among the workers. The reason, Mr. Wills asserts,
is that "they seem to have taken a turn against some of
the products." To his horror Mr. Fibbs learns that they
no longer like the brass pet cock, the hemi unibal spheri-
cal rod end, that "they have gone vicious about the high
speed taper shank spiral flute reamers" and a number of
other wildly named mechanical contraptions. This is
clearly an exercise for the much subtler use of technical
language in *The Caretaker*—Aston's relish of the names of
various saws, Mick's delight in new material for furniture.

In *The Black and White,* two homeless old women
late at night in a milk bar, which stays open till the early
hours of the morning, discuss late-night buses, the

chances of being picked up by the police, and the dangers of talking to strangers. It is a study in the pathos of meaningless conversation. For example: "[An all-night bus] don't look like an all-night bus in daylight, do it?"

The revue *Pieces of Eight,* which opened at the Apollo Theatre on 3 September 1969 contained four sketches by Pinter: *Getting Acquainted,* the manuscript of which now seems lost; *Request Stop; Special Offer;* and *Last To Go.*

In *Request Stop,* a woman who has asked a little man in a bus queue how she could get a bus to Shepherds Bush showers abuse on him because he allegedly made insinuations about her in his reaction to the question. When the bus comes, she remains behind and accosts another man, asking him how to get to Marble Arch. Clearly she is merely seeking an outlet for her hatred of foreigners.

In *Special Offer* (reprinted in Arnold P. Hinchcliffe's monograph on Pinter in the Twayne "English Authors Series"), a B.B.C. secretary is outraged by what happened to her in the staid London store of Swan & Edgar: in the rest room she was handed a card offering "men for sale."

In *Last To Go,* the barman and an old newspaper seller at a coffee stall muse on what was the last evening paper to be sold: "Yes, it was the *Evening News* was the last to go tonight." "Not always the last though, is it, though?" "No. Oh no. I mean sometimes it's the *News.* Other times it's one of the others. No way of telling beforehand." This speculation is cross-cut with musings about a man called George, whom neither seems to know and whom neither has seen for a long time. A study in the futility of human conversation.

A group of nine revue sketches broadcast by the

B.B.C. Third Programme in 1964 contained some of the above-mentioned sketches together with some hitherto unperformed ones.

That's Your Trouble presents two men in a park discussing whether the sandwich board they see around a sandwich-man's neck will give him a headache or a back and leg ache. They cannot agree:

> B.: You just don't know how to listen to what other people tell you, that's your trouble.
> A.: I know what my trouble is.
> B.: You don't know what your trouble is, my friend. That's your trouble.

In *That's All,* two old women laboriously discuss the reasons why a friend who used to visit Mrs. A. for a cup of tea on Wednesdays now comes sometimes on Thursdays. "She comes in. She doesn't come in so much, but she comes in." (*Pause.*)

> Mrs. B.: I thought she didn't come in.
> (*Pause.*)
> Mrs. A.: She comes in. (*Pause.*) She doesn't come in so much. That's all.

In *Applicant,* a very efficient lady subjects an applicant for a job to various rigorous tests. This is a fragment from the discarded play *The Hothouse.*

In *Interview,* a pornographic bookseller, Mr. Jakes, is subjected to the usual pre-Christmas radio or television interview about seasonal trade. He puts holly around the shop, but it doesn't seem to make much difference. Gradually Mr. Jakes reveals that he is dreaming of imprisoning all his customers, because every single one of them is a Communist.

Dialogue for Three (also published in the quarterly

review *Stand*) is a dialogue between two men and a woman. The first man tells wildly extravagant stories of exotic adventure to the second man (who only gets in one line) while the woman pesters him with questions about whether he thinks her too feminine, too masculine, or not masculine enough, and reminds him of their first meeting. Some of the lines also come from the discarded play *The Hothouse,* notably the memorable statement: "The snow has turned to slush."

For *Mixed Doubles,* a programme of miniature plays about marriage, in which his wife took part, Pinter wrote the sketch *Night* (1969): A man and a woman remember their first meeting years ago, which led to their getting married and founding a family. But *her* memories contradict his. Did they meet at a party or on a bridge? Did he "take her" on a rubbish dump or pressed against some railings? Perhaps he remembers an incident with another girl, she with another man. . . . .

SCREENPLAYS

Apart from faithful transpositions of his own plays (*The Caretaker,* 1962; *The Birthday Party,* 1968; *The Homecoming,* 1969, not yet in production at the time of writing) and the short film *The Compartment* for Grove Press's *Project I,* which later became the television play *The Basement,* Pinter's work for the cinema has been confined to adaptations of novels by other writers. These are: *The Servant,* from the short novel by Robin Maugham, 1963; *The Pumpkin Eater,* from the novel by Penelope Mortimer, 1963; *The Quiller Memorandum,* from the spy story *The Berlin Memorandum,* by Adam Hall, 1966; *Accident,* from the novel by Nicholas Mosley,

1966; *The Go-Between,* from the novel by L. P. Hartley, 1969.

Clearly the adaptation of other writers' work for the screen is an exercise of craftsmanship rather than the wholly creative process of shaping themes and images that have sprung entirely from the artist's own imagination. Yet it is probably no more than the conditions under which the film industry works, which do not favour the commissioning of entirely original work from dramatists, that provides the reason why Pinter has not as yet produced a film wholly his own. That the cinema as a medium attracts him is shown by his skill in writing television plays and in the success of his screen adaptations. After all, the cinema is perhaps even more effective in mirroring the impenetrably mysterious surface of events, the silences between the words, than the stage. As Pinter himself has said in connection with *Accident:*

> In this film everything happens, nothing is explained. It has been pared down and down, all unnecessary words and actions are eliminated. If it is interesting to see a man cross a room, then we see him do it; if not, then we leave out the insignificant stages of the action. I think you'll be surprised at the directness, the simplicity with which Losey is directing this film: no elaborations, no odd angles, no darting about. Just a level, intense look at people, at things. As though if you look at them hard enough they will give up their secrets. Not that they will, for however much you see and guess at, there is always something more. . . . (Pinter, interviewed by John Russell Taylor, in *Sight and Sound,* Autumn 1966.)

Hence all Pinter's screen adaptations not only contain passages of dialogue highly characteristic of Pinter but also mirror some of his basic preoccupations and imagery. *The Servant,* for example, the story of a rich young man who is gradually being reduced to complete dependence and servitude by his manservant, is closely akin to Pinter's theme of "changing places," as in *A Slight Ache* and *The Basement.* A comparison between the novel and the screenplay shows how Pinter made that motif, which undoubtedly is already present in the story, considerably more explicit in the concrete imagery of the action. In the novel the story is told by a narrator who was a friend of the hero, Tony. Pinter's screenplay eliminates the subjective source of the narration, as the cinema can show the objective surface of events. Tony's fiancée (Sally Grant in the novel, Susan Stewart in the film), who is the sinister manservant's chief antagonist, steps into the narrator's shoes in incidents in which he was involved in the novel: for example, Barrett, the manservant, has brought his girl Vera into the house as his niece in the novel, his sister in the film, in order to seduce Tony away from his fiancée and get a hold over him. In the novel, the *narrator,* passing Tony's house while he is out of London, sees a light burning in Tony's room, goes up, and finds the servant in bed with his alleged niece. He then tells Tony, and Tony sacks his manservant. In the film Tony, who wants to resume his relationship with his fiancée, returns from a visit to the country with her and has asked her to spend the night with him for the first time; when they go to Tony's bedroom they find Barrett in bed with the girl whom he has introduced as his sister. Pinter's version of the incident has clearly greatly sharpened the situation and focussed what is a series of loosely related coincidences in the story into a highly compressed image.

In the novel the final image is of the narrator visiting Tony for the last time and finding him completely under Barrett's spell; as he leaves, a girl arrives who has obviously been procured by Barrett for Tony's and his own amusement. In the film it is Susan who is coming to the house to try to redeem Tony from final subjection; she finds an orgy involving several girls in progress and, as though to arouse Tony into realising his position, kisses Barrett, thus emphasising the very Pinteresque point that the servant and the master have changed places.

There are many highly characteristic touches in the dialogue involving Susan's aristocratic relatives, and, above all, there is the scene in the French restaurant in Soho where Susan makes an attempt to get Tony to rid himself of Barrett. To counterpoint the action, Pinter introduces three other dining couples in the background: a bishop (played by Patrick Magee) taking out a curate (played by Alun Owen—there is a private joke here in introducing two of Pinter's colleagues from the Anew McMaster company); an older woman giving lunch to a younger one, with hints of a lesbian relationship; and a society man (played by Pinter himself) lunching a débutante. There are delicious touches of absurd-sounding snatches of dialogue between these three pairs which are intercut with the tense scene between the hero and his fiancée, who is struggling to save him.

The Pumpkin Eater—the story of a woman who wants more and more children and her husband who escapes from too much domesticity into relations with other women—is more remote from Pinter's own preoccupations. He has, however, brilliantly dramatised the climactic situations of the plot, and occasionally introduces passages of dialogue that bear his unmistakable hallmark, notably in the scene where Jake, the heroine's faithless husband, meets the jealous husband of his latest conquest:

JAKE: . . . . How is your wife, by the way?

CONWAY: Tip top. She's at a reception tonight for the Duchess of Dubrovnik.

JAKE: I thought she *was* the Duchess of Dubrovnik.

CONWAY: My wife? No, not at all. Not at all. Not at all.

JAKE: Well, you're not the bloody Duke anyway.

(*Jake's glass slips from his hand, falls on Conway's lap and then to the floor. Whisky stains Conway's trousers.*)

CONWAY: You've made me wet.

There is more than a hint here of the confrontations between the jealous men in *The Collection* or *The Basement*.

In *The Quiller Memorandum,* Pinter's touch gave the modish spy story about a Western agent who penetrates a Nazi underground organisation a gloss of tautness, dryness, and economy, particularly in the scenes between Quiller and the German girl, where we sense that he knows she is not what she pretends to be, and that she knows he knows, and that he knows that too, while yet carrying on as though neither of them suspected anything beneath the surface of what looks like an ordinary love affair. The dialogues between two high British civil servants back in Whitehall, which counterpoint the melodramatic action in Berlin with cosy upper-class aloofness, also—and more obviously—display Pinter's style, the style of his revue sketches.

Accident, the second film Pinter wrote for Joseph Losey, whose direction of *The Servant* had revealed his affinity with Pinter's approach, is on an entirely different and higher level than *The Quiller Memorandum.* Nicholas Mosley's novel, set among dons and students at Oxford, was faithfully adapted and yet wholly transformed by Pinter. The screenplay follows the novel closely, but, by transforming the story from a first-person narrative by the hero, Stephen, to a sequence of images that, though most of them are seen from his point of view, are objectified merely by being stripped of any commentary or description of feelings, Pinter and Losey succeeded in turning it into a wholly original work of art. The script is laconic and enigmatic, and provides a minimum of explanation—but the theme emerges strong and clear: the tension between the university teacher's responsibility towards his pupils and his desire for the girl student; the tension between his love for his wife and children and the urge to indulge in a last adventure; the way in which the actions of the other people around Stephen mirror and act out all his desires (his friend and fellow don, Charley, seduces the beautiful student); and his final fall from grace, when after the girl's student fiancé has been killed in an accident outside Stephen's house, and he has her in his power because he could testify that he found her in the driver's seat, drunk and without a licence, he takes advantage of her helplessness and dependence. (This last, telling touch is Pinter's; there is no hint of this consummation of Stephen's desire in the book.)

Among the many original uses of the medium in the screenplay is the fusion of silent images with dialogue

belonging to the same incident but not synchronous, in
the episode when Stephen recalls a brief escapade with
a former girl friend whom he looks up in London to escape his preoccupation with the beautiful aristocratic
student. The wild game involving the beautiful girl's
equally aristocratic fiancé—a version of the Eton Wall
Game played in that particular family on social occasions—is reminiscent of the confrontations between rivals
in *The Collection, The Basement,* and *Tea Party.* Pinter
himself appeared briefly as a television producer in an
episode when Stephen tries to become a television don,
like his more successful rival Charley.

The screenplay for *The Go-Between* (also written for
Joseph Losey) tackles what undoubtedly is the most considerable literary work Pinter has yet adapted—a minor
classic and a masterpiece. The screenplay, even more
laconic and elliptic than *Accident,* does it full justice. In
the book, the narrator finds his old diary, which contains
the account of the climactic episode of his childhood.
He then tells the story it recalls: his stay with a rich
school friend in Norfolk in the summer of 1900, his carrying of messages between a couple of illicit lovers, and his
final discovery of them while making love, which leads
to the suicide of the man, and finally, in the epilogue, his
visit half a century later to the place of these dramatic
events and his meeting with the girl involved, now an
old woman. Pinter has telescoped the action into that
last visit and brilliantly parallels the narrator's arrival,
inspection of the place as it now is and meeting with the
old lady, with the flashbacks of the ancient events, so
that the whole culminates in the complete fusion of past
and present in the mind of the spectator, who has been
gradually drawn into a complex pattern of past and
present images and relationships.

Pinter's ability to enter into the spirit of other writers' work, and, while respecting their personality and intention, infuse them with the unmistakable hallmark of his personality, is proof of the high degree of professionalism that is also the basis of his achievement as an artist in those works which are wholly the product of his own imagination, a professionalism that, incidentally, marks him out among many of the other talented playwrights of his generation.

IV

LANGUAGE AND SILENCE

That Pinter has added a new band of colours to the spectrum of English stage dialogue is attested by the frequent use of terms like "Pinteresque language" or "Pinterese" in current dramatic criticism. Some of the more obvious features of his use of language, such as recurrent tautological repetition, on the pattern "He's old. Not young. No, I wouldn't call him young. Not youthful, certainly. Elderly, I'd say. I'd call him old" have been copied to the point of self-parody by a large number of aspiring authors. And the bad imitations have inevitably cast a shadow over the original user and, indeed, discoverer of these linguistic absurdities, which had hitherto largely escaped the observant ears of playwrights. Yet these most easily recognisable features of Pinter's dialogue are, on the whole, the most superficial aspects of his artistry; even their function in the over-all picture has been largely misunderstood. While Pinter undoubtedly has an uncannily accurate ear for the linguistic solecisms of the English vernacular spoken by ordinary people, it is neither his special intention nor foremost dramatic purpose merely to amuse his audience by confronting them with accurately observed examples of linguistic nonsense and thus giving them the pleasure of *recognising* the linguistic mistakes of others and feeling superior to them. It may be true that a good deal of Pinter's initial success was due to this kind of audience reaction, and he may even, occasionally, have succumbed to the temptation of exploiting it. Yet if his work is seen as a whole it will be recognised that he has also resisted this temptation, and with considerable success, not only by discarding plays like *The Hothouse* (which might have been regarded as an overindulgence in Pinterese) but also by moving out of the sphere of low-life dialogue in the plays that followed the success of *The Caretaker* (*The Lover, The Collection,* and later *Tea Party* and *The Basement*); by avoiding the tricks of the more obvious Pinterese in a play that might well have given a great deal of opportunity for self-copying and self-parody—*The Homecoming;* and finally by abandoning naturalistic action and dialogue altogether in the next phase of his development—the highly compressed stage poetry of recollected experience in *Landscape* and *Silence.*

A true understanding of Pinter's use of language must, I believe, be based on deeper, more fundamental considerations. It must start from an examination of the function of language in stage dialogue generally—and indeed from considerations of the use of language in ordinary human intercourse itself. For here—at least as far as the English language is concerned—Pinter has given us added insight into—has, in a certain measure, even *discovered*—the fact that traditional stage dialogue has always greatly overestimated the degree of logic that governs the use of language, the amount of information that language is actually able to impart on the stage, as in life. People on the stage, from Sophocles to Shakespeare to Rattigan, have always spoken more clearly, more directly, more to the purpose than they would ever have done in real life. This is obvious enough in verse drama, which had to obey not only the rules of prosody but also those of the ancient art of rhetoric, which concerned itself with the ways in which speech could be made as clear, well proportioned, and easily assimilated as possible. So strong was this tradition that it even persisted in naturalistic drama, although it was sometimes superficially disguised: the finest speeches in Ibsen or Shaw are as brilliantly rhetorical as those of Cicero or Demosthenes. And even in the scenes of light conversation in the exposition of these plays, the main emphasis lies on the elegance with which the essential *information* about the antecedents of the plot, the motivation of the characters, is conveyed, broken up perhaps into seemingly casually arranged fragments, but nevertheless in a discursive, explicit style.

It was only gradually that a certain defectiveness of communication between characters—who talk past each other rather than to each other—was introduced by dramatists like Strindberg or Wedekind; and that "oblique" dialogue in which the text hints at a hidden subtext was brought in by Chekhov, as in the climactic scene of *The Cherry Orchard* discussed in an earlier chapter of this book, when the real action—Lopakhin's failure to declare himself to Varya—is taking place beneath a trivial exchange about a missing article of clothing. But this scene was elaborately *prepared* by Chekhov: he had taken care in the preceding scene to make it quite explicit to the audience that they were to expect Lopakhin's offer of marriage. Pinter's technique continues Chekhov's use of such "oblique" dialogue, but carries it much further.

A comparison between two climactic closing scenes by the two playwrights might serve to illustrate this point: In the closing scene of Chekhov's *Uncle Vanya*, the chief characters have lost their hope of love and fulfillment. Vanya turns to Sonia and expresses his feelings in a highly explicit outburst:

> My child, there's such a weight on my heart!
> Oh, if only you knew how my heart aches!

And Sonia replies:

> Well, what can we do? We must go on living!
> (*A pause.*) We shall go on living, Uncle Vanya.
> We shall live through a long, long succession of
> days and tedious evenings. We shall patiently
> suffer the trials which Fate imposes on us; we
> shall work for others, now and in our old age,
> and we shall have no rest. . . .

Having described the reality of their lives to come,
Sonia turns to talk of their last remaining great hope of
eternal rest—in death:

> We shall rest! We shall hear the angels, we
> shall see all the heavens covered with stars like
> diamonds, we shall see all earthly evil, all our
> sufferings swept away by the grace which will
> fill the whole world, and our life will become
> peaceful, gentle and sweet as a caress. I believe
> it, I believe it. . . . Poor, poor Uncle Vanya,
> you're crying. . . . You've had no joy in life, but
> wait, Uncle Vanya, wait . . . we shall rest . . .
> We shall rest. . . . We shall rest!

A magnificent piece of writing, but surely very far re-
moved from the way in which a girl like Sonia would
use language in a real situation of this kind. The rhetorical heritage is still very strong in Chekhov's style.
There *is* an element of "obliqueness" present even here,
however, for while Sonia professes to *believe* in the joys
of eternal bliss in heaven, we know that what she is saying is *not* what she really believes; she is using the picture of heavenly bliss as a last despairing attempt at

bringing consolation to Uncle Vanya. It is in the contrast between what is being said and what lies behind it that the poignancy and also the innovatory modernity of Chekhov's approach to language in drama appears.

Pinter, in the final scene of *The Birthday Party,* which portrays a situation that is analogous to the close of *Uncle Vanya*—the loss of the hope of love suffered by Meg—goes infinitely further than Chekhov. Pinter's characters do not talk explicitly about the situation at all. Meg knows, deep down, that Stanley has gone, but she cannot and will not admit it to herself; and Petey is too inarticulate to offer a speech of consolation like Sonia's:

> MEG: I was the belle of the ball.
> PETEY: Were you?
> MEG: Oh yes. They all said I was.
> PETEY: I bet you were too.
> MEG: Oh, it's true. I was.
>   (*Pause.*)
>   I know I was.

Four times Meg repeats that she was the belle of the ball—the disastrous party through which her substitute son was destroyed and taken away from her. It is quite clear that she does not in fact want to say anything about the impression she actually made at that party. She is merely trying to hang on to the illusion that everything is still as it was, that the disastrous party was not a disaster but the success she had hoped for. The fourfold *repetition* of the statement does not derive from any desire to say the same thing four times; it is no more than a sign of the desperateness of her attempt, her pitiful determination not to let the realisation of the disaster dawn on her. Hence the repetition of the statement is more relevant than the statement, and the explicit, "discursive" content of the statement itself. Similarly Petey's affirmation that the statement is true merely expresses his compassion, his despair, and, above all, his inability to do anything towards making Meg acknowledge or realise the true position. The dramatic effect of this brilliantly moving, brilliantly economical and concise passage of dialogue is entirely due to the complete contradiction between the words that are spoken and the emotional and psychological *action* that underlies them. Here the language has almost totally lost its rhetorical, informative element and has fully merged into dramatic action.

It is true that in a passage of dialogue like this there is little verbal communication between the characters, in that neither Meg nor Petey informs the other of any fact she or he wants him or her to know. Yet to sum up this state of affairs by labelling such a passage a "dialogue of non-communication" completely misses the point. Pinter is far from wanting to say that language is incapable of establishing true communication between human beings; he merely draws our attention to the fact that in life human beings rarely make use of language for that purpose, at least so far as spoken language is concerned. People interact not so much logically as emotionally through language; and their tone of voice, the emotional colour of the words, is often far more significant than their exact meanings by their dictionary definition. We all know that an outburst of name-calling by one person against another is basically an act of aggression, an assault by verbal blows in which the violence of the emotion behind the words is far more important than their content. Where animals use physical action and physical contact (such as sniffing each other, catching each other's fleas), human beings, through the power of speech, can substitute verbal contact and verbal action (small talk about the weather, exchange of information about one's minor ailments, abuse or words of endearment). What matters in most oral verbal contact is therefore more what people are *doing* to each other through it than the conceptual content of what they are saying.

In drama, dialogue is ultimately a form of *action;* it is the element of action, the interaction between the characters, their reactions to each other, that constitutes the truly *dramatic* element in stage dialogue, its essential aspect in the context of drama, apart from, and over and above, all the other values embodied in the writing: its wit, lucidity, elegance of structure and logical development, depth of thought, persuasiveness, rhythm, imagery, mellifluousness, and sheer beauty as poetry—all the rhetorical and literary qualities that *could also* be appreciated *outside* the context of drama.

Being essentially action, dramatic dialogue is not necessarily the dominant element in the playwright's armoury: it may be equally important as, or even less so than the nonverbal actions of the characters and, indeed, their silences. Traditionally, however, because of the origins of dramatic writing in the art of oratory, dialogue has been the dominant element in drama. Hence the tendency for drama to involve highly articulate characters, the only ones who would naturally interact in terms of brilliantly phrased speech. This showed itself in the need to *stylise* verbal expression by the use of verse, which relieved the playwright of the need to imitate the real speech of characters who in reality would have been inarticulate, or at least far from possessing the powers of expression with which they seemed to be endowed on the stage; or, in later naturalistic drama, the tendency to place the action among people who would be highly articulate in real life: the elegant wits of Wilde, the eloquent intellectuals of Shaw. Only when it was recognised that the verbal element need not be the dominant aspect of drama, or at least that it was not the content of what was said that mattered most but the action that it embodied, and that inarticulate, incoherent, tautological, and nonsensical speech might be as dramatic as verbal brilliance when it was treated simply as an element of action, only then did it become possible to place inarticulate characters in the centre of the play and make their unspoken emotions transparent. Pinter is among the discoverers of this highly significant aspect of drama.

If we examine some of Pinter's favourite linguistic and stylistic devices in the light of these considerations, we shall find that, far from being mere verbal absurdities held up to ridicule, they do in fact illuminate the mental processes that lie behind the ill-chosen or nonsensical words; and that in each case superficially similar quirks of language may serve quite different dramatic functions.

Take the most obvious of these, the one most frequently attributed to Pinter as a mere mannerism: repetition. Each time Pinter's characters repeat themselves, or each other's phrases, the playwright employs the device of repetition to fulfill a definite function in the action; if, for example, at the beginning of *The Birthday Party* Meg, having served Petey his corn flakes, asks:

> MEG: Are they nice?
> PETEY: Very nice.
> MEG: I thought they'd be nice.

the emptiness of the dialogue clearly indicates the emptiness of the characters' relationship with each other, the boredom of their lives and yet their determination to go on making friendly conversation. So this short dialogue of no more than ten words, three of which are repetitions of "nice," which on the surface conveys no worthwhile *conceptual* information whatever, does in fact compress a very considerable amount of dramatic *information*— this being the exposition of the play—and dramatic *action,* i.e. the vain attempt at conversation, the desire to be friendly, into an astonishingly brief space.

If, on the other hand, Davies in *The Caretaker,* talking about his ex-wife's slovenliness, mentions the saucepan in which he found some of her underclothing, repeats himself, saying: "The pan for vegetables, it was. The vegetable pan . . ." the repetition serves a completely different purpose: it shows us this inarticulate man's struggle to find the correct word, the *mot juste.* Traditional stage dialogue tended to err on the side of assuming that people have the right expression always ready to suit the occasion. In Pinter's dialogue we can watch the desperate struggles of his characters to find the correct expression; we are thus enabled to observe them in the—very dramatic—act of struggling for communication, sometimes succeeding, often failing. And when they have got hold of a formulation, they hold on to it, savour it, and repeat it to enjoy their achievement, like Gus in *The Dumb Waiter,* when he recalls the time they killed a girl:

> . . . . It was a mess though, wasn't it? What a mess. Honest I can't remember a mess like that one. They don't seem to hold together like men, women. A looser texture, like. Didn't she spread, eh? She didn't half spread. Kaw!

The pleasure with which Gus dwells on the words *mess* and *spread* is evident: not because he enjoyed killing the girl, quite the contrary, but because, being an inarticulate person who has trouble finding the expressive phrase, he loves to play with and savour it once he has got hold of it, and does not want to let it go. He is delighted to have found the expressive image of the girl's body dissolving like butter: "she spread." So while, on one level, he is worried and unhappy about his job as a killer and deplores having had to liquidate that girl, on another he revels in the happy feeling of having expressed his thought well. This is another example of how dialogue that is primitive and crude when judged by the standards of rhetoric can be astonishingly subtle, ironic, and psychologically penetrating if considered as an expression of character in action—drama.

As against the use of repetition to show a character's *enjoyment* at having found the *mot juste,* there is repetition as a form of hysterical irritation: for example, so obsessed is McCann in *The Birthday Party* with the unpleasantness of what he and Goldberg will have to do to Stanley that he breaks out:

> Let's finish and go. Let's get it over and go.
> Get the thing done. Let's finish the bloody thing.
> Let's get the thing done and go!

McCann's hysteria emerges not only from the frantic rhythm with which these sentences are phrased but also from the obsessive permutation of the same elements—"finish," "go," "get done."

Conversely, Pinter uses repetition to show how a character gradually learns to accept a fact that at first he had difficulty taking in. Having been terrorised by Mick, Davies in *The Caretaker* asks Aston:

> DAVIES: Who was that feller?
> ASTON: He's my brother.
> DAVIES: Is he? He's a bit of a joker, en' he?
> ASTON: Uh.

DAVIES: Yes . . . he's a real joker.

ASTON: He's got a sense of humour.

DAVIES: Yes, I noticed.

> (*Pause.*)

> He's a real joker, that lad, you can see that.

> (*Pause.*)

ASTON: Yes, he tends . . . he tends to see the funny side of things.

DAVIES: Well, he's got a sense of humour, en' he?

ASTON: Yes.

DAVIES: Yes, you could tell that.

> (*Pause.*)

Here the manner in which Davies takes up Aston's phrase about the "sense of humour" and the way in which he punctuates his realisation of Mick's character with "I noticed," "you can see that," and "you could tell that" allows the audience to witness the slow sinking in of the facts, the gradual evaluation of the man he met, his eventual and increasingly bitter coming to terms with these facts. Two repeated phrases are interlocked in this passage ("He's a joker/got a sense of humour" and "I noticed/can see/can tell that") and again their various permutations in the mouth of first the one and then the other character give the dialogue a definite poetic shape, a musical form of theme and variations, of strophe and antistrophe: psychological realism and a poet's control over the formal element in language are here fused in a way highly characteristic of Pinter.

Repetition, which, as Pinter has discovered, is an aspect of real speech that stage dialogue had neglected under the influence of the rhetorical tradition (which rejects recurrence of the same word as stylistically inelegant), is, of course, also one of the most important elements of poetry—particularly in the form of whole phrases that recur as refrains, for example in ballad metre —on the realistic level. Pinter uses the refrain-like recurrence of whole sentences to show that people in real life do not deliver well-thought-out set speeches but tend to mix various logical strands of thought, which intermingle without any apparent connection; while the structure of rhetorical or written language tends to be logical, that of spoken language is associative. In the first act of *The Caretaker*, Aston tells Davies that there is a family of Indians living in the house next door. Davies immediately reacts:

> DAVIES: Blacks?
> ASTON: I don't see much of them.
> DAVIES: Blacks, eh?

The conversation then turns to other matters, and Davies embarks on his story about his odyssey to the monastery at Luton, where he had been told the monks handed out shoes to the poor. Having reached the climax of that story, he is about to introduce the punch line:

> . . . . You know what that bastard monk said to me?
> (*Pause.*)
> How many more Blacks you got around here then?
> ASTON: What?
> DAVIES: You got any more Blacks around here?

Without any *logical* motivation the question about the Blacks re-emerges a minute or more after it was first mooted. But the association is clear enough: the hatred and indignation Davies feels for the monk who treated him so badly has reawakened the emotion of fear and hatred against that other arch-enemy of his—the coloured community.

Similarly, in Davies' long speech of hatred against Aston, when he believes that Mick will support him in giving him control of the house and he tries to assert his superiority over Aston as a former inmate of a mental institution, we find several lines of thought mixed to give a refrain-like effect:

> . . . . I'm a sane man! So don't start mucking me about. I'll be all right as long as you keep your place. Just you keep your place, that's all. *Because I can tell you, your brother's got his eye on you.* He knows all about you. I got a friend there, don't worry about that. I got a true pal there! Treating me like dirt! Why'd you invite me in here in the first place if you was going to treat me like this? You think you're better than me you got another think coming. I know enough. They had you inside one of them places before, they can have you inside again. *Your brother's got his eye on you!* They can put the pincers on your head again, man. . . . [My italics.]

It is clear that this type of associative structure, in which several basic thoughts (I am better than you because I am sane, you have been in a mental institution—your brother is my friend, he has his eye on you) intermingle in ever-recurring variations belongs on the whole to characters of Davies' primitive mentality. But Pinter also uses it, in an appropriately modified form, in the mouth of one of his most sophisticated characters, Harry, the rich clothing manufacturer in *The Collection*:

Bill's a slum boy, you see, he's got a slum sense of humour. That's why I never take him along to parties. Because he's got a slum mind. I have nothing against slum minds *per se,* you understand, nothing at all. There's a certain kind of slum mind which is perfectly all right in a slum, but when this kind of slum mind gets out of the slum it sometimes persists, you see, it rots everything. That's what Bill is. There's something faintly putrid about him, don't you find? Like a slug. There's nothing wrong with slugs in their place, but he's a slum slug; there's nothing wrong with slum slugs in their place, but this one won't keep his place—he crawls all over the walls of nice houses, leaving slime, don't you, boy? He confirms stupid sordid little stories just to amuse himself, while everyone else has to run round in circles to get to the root of the matter and smooth the whole thing out. All he can do is sit and suck his bloody hand and decompose like the filthy putrid slum slug he is. . . .

Here the structure is apparently one of rigid logic, even of syllogism, but only apparently. The real motivation for the erection of this structure of pseudo-logic is to give an opportunity to hammer away at the humiliating terms *slum* and *slug;* the repetition indicates the degree of Harry's obsession with Bill and his hatred of him, it is also deliberately used by him as a means of aggression, of mental torture and humiliation towards Bill. And again the refrain-like recurrence of the same type of phrase ("I have nothing against," "There is nothing wrong") gives this highly realistic and closely observed reproduction of genuine speech patterns a musical-poetic structure.

In Harry's diatribe the emotional charge of jealousy, hatred, and contempt underlies the associative structure of his speech. In other instances it is the absence of emotion, the determination to avoid saying what ought to be said, that leads to associative and equally repetitious sequences of words. When Davies, in *The Caretaker,* first encounters Mick, is frightened by him and asks who he is, Mick, who wants to torment him by keeping him on tenterhooks, embarks on a long diatribe, which is quite obviously intended to convey no information whatever:

> You know, believe it or not, you've got a funny kind of resemblance to a bloke I once knew in Shoreditch. Actually he lived in Aldgate. I was staying with a cousin in Camden Town. This chap, he used to have a pitch in Finsbury Park, just by the bus depot. When I got to know him I found out he was brought up in Putney. That didn't make any difference to me. I know quite a few people who were born in Putney. Even if they weren't born in Putney, they were born in Fulham. The only trouble was, he wasn't born in Putney, he was only brought up in Putney. It turned out he was born in the Caledonian Road, just before you get to the Nag's Head.

Not only is this passage, in its total nonsensicality, highly comic, not only does it prolong Davies' and the audience's suspense, it also shows the thought process that prompts Mick: one London place name simply leads him on to the next. We can clearly follow his method in making up a long and meaningless speech, which ironically apes the exchanges of reminiscences between new acquaintances who want to break the ice between themselves by recalling mutual friends with a maximum of circumstantial detail. So transparent is the associative mechanism here that we are also fully aware that Mick is malevolently enjoying himself at Davies' expense.

It is by an analogous use of associative linguistic structure that Pinter indicates that a character is lying. Here, too, the story is being made up as it goes along, and often merely from the *sound* of the words, as in Solto's reply to the question how he got to Australia, in *Night School:*

> SOLTO: By sea. How do you think? I worked my
> passage. And what a trip. I was only a pubes-
> cent. I killed a man with my own hands, a six-
> foot-ten Lascar from Madagascar.
> ANNIE: From Madagascar?
> SOLTO: Sure. A Lascar.
> MILLY: Alaska?
> SOLTO: Madagascar.
>   (*Pause.*)
> WALTER: It's happened before.
> SOLTO: And it'll happen again.

It is quite clear that Solto thought of Madagascar only because the term Lascar suggested it. Walter's interjection, that it happened before, indicates that he is fully aware of the spuriousness of the story and the intention behind it; namely, the braggart's desire to impress. Hence by his remark he shows himself unimpressed, while Solto, by insisting that it happened and will happen again, feebly insists on his veracity, but without carrying any conviction.

The braggart is a stock figure of comedy and has been from time immemorial, and so, of course, have been the braggart's stories and lies. Here Pinter is therefore moving along very traditional lines; where his special talent shines through is in his ability to make the often very pathetic thought-processes behind the tall stories utterly transparent to the audience: these liars are carried along, almost passively, by the limited range of their imaginations, the paucity of possible associations that can lead them on from one word to the next. When Walter, again in *Night School,* brags to Sally about his success as a prison librarian, for example, he is, very much against his will and better judgement, driven into a mention of rare manuscripts:

> . . . . Well, funny enough, I've had a good bit to do with rare manuscripts in my time. I used to know a bloke who ran a business digging them up. . . . Rare manuscripts. Out of tombs. I used to give him a helping hand when I was on the loose. Very well paid it was, too. You see, they were nearly always attached to a corpse, these manuscripts, you had to lift up the pelvis bone with a pair of tweezers. Big tweezers. Can't leave fingerprints on a corpse, you see. Canon law. . . .

(The germ of this speech is already contained in Pinter's early novel *The Dwarfs,* where Pete tries to impress a girl during a party. In the passage in *Night School,* however, the idea has been considerably and brilliantly developed and expanded.) It is only superficially that a speech like this one is funny. On a deeper level, it reveals an underprivileged individual's desperate attempt to impress the girl, the mixture of ignorance and half-baked information with which his mind is stocked, the vagueness of his ideas. Rare manuscripts to him suggest archae-

ology, and archaeology, tombs. Somehow he has to in-
vent for himself a way in which these two vague ideas
can be related, hence the suggestion that rare manuscripts are found in tombs. Hence the association with
skeletons; hence, again, the urge to mention one of the
few technical terms from anatomy he knows—"pelvis"—
which leads to the association with the cliché of the soap
opera involving an operation: it is here that tweezers
are always mentioned. And this brings the ex-convict
Walter back to his own sphere: to explain the tweezers
he gets back to his own world, that of the petty thief
who does not want to leave fingerprints. To retrieve this
lapse he has to take covering action by mentioning canon
law. While it is unlikely that the audience will be wholly
conscious of the exact way in which such a chain of associations is built up, they can certainly follow the main
line of the underlying thought-process and thus partake
in the *action* that this speech portrays, Walter's desperate attempt, on the one hand, to establish his intellectual and social superiority and his equally desperate efforts, on the other, to extricate himself from the more
and more difficult traps and pitfalls he creates for himself.

Always, in Pinter's world, personal inadequacy expresses itself in an inadequacy to cope with and to use
language. The inability to communicate, and to *communicate in the correct terms,* is felt by the characters as a
mark of inferiority; that is why they tend to dwell upon
and to stress the hard or unusual "educated" words they
know. Solto, in the rodomontade quoted above, casually
introduces the unusual, and to him no doubt highly refined, term "pubescent," Walter talks about "canon law,"
"pelvis," "rare manuscripts"; Mick in *The Caretaker,* on
his first confrontation with Davies, speaks of someone
the tramp reminds him of, who had a *penchant* for nuts:

Had a penchant for nuts. That's what it was.
Nothing else but a penchant. Couldn't eat
enough of them. Peanuts, walnuts, brazil nuts,
monkey nuts, wouldn't touch a piece of fruit-
cake.

Note, again, the laying bare of the mechanism of the
lie: the false circumstantial detail contained in the associative use of the names of different kinds of nuts. The
introduction of the "refined" term *penchant*, however,
serves to emphasise Mick's claim to superior education,
intelligence, and *savoir-faire*. It is thus equivalent to an
act of aggression. Again and again veritable duels of this
type develop among Pinter's characters. The memorable
dispute about whether one says "light the kettle" or "light
the gas" in *The Dumb Waiter* belongs in this category.
Words like "penchant" and "pubescent" are proofs of
superior general education. The use of technical terms
and professional jargon, on the other hand, establishes
the speaker's superiority in his own chosen field and gives
him the advantages of belonging to a freemasonry, an
inner circle of people who are able to exclude intruders
and interlopers. The use of technical jargon thus corresponds to the enclosed rooms and protected spaces that
Pinter's characters tend to covet and to defend against
outsiders. When Mick finally turns against Davies and
initiates the move that will expel him from the home he
has been seeking, he overwhelms him with a demonstra-
tion of his ignorance of the skills he alleges Davies
claimed when applying for the post of a caretaker in his
house:

> MICK: . . . . I only told you because I under-
> stood you were an experienced first-class pro-
> fessional interior and exterior decorator.

DAVIES: Now look here—

MICK: You mean you wouldn't know how to fit teal-blue, copper and parchement linoleum squares and have those colours re-echoed in the walls?

DAVIES: Now, look here, where'd you get—?

MICK: You wouldn't be able to decorate out a table in afromosia teak veneer, an armchair in oatmeal tweed and a beech frame settee with a woven sea-grass seat?

DAVIES: I never said that!

MICK: Christ! I must have been under a false impression!

DAVIES: I never said it!

MICK: You're a bloody impostor, mate!

Davies' inability to comprehend the technical jargon of the interior decorator seals what, in effect, is his death sentence. In fact he had never directly claimed any such knowledge, but had merely tacitly nodded his approval when Mick, using the selfsame terms, had tempted him with the job of caretaker while outlining his grandiose plans for converting the derelict dwelling into a "penthouse." Incomprehension and the inability to express himself is clearly stated to be the reason for his loss of favour with Mick:

Honest. I can take nothing you say at face value. Every word you speak is open to any number of different interpretations. Most of what you say is lies. You're violent, you're erratic, you're just completely unpredictable. You're nothing else but a wild animal, when you come down to it. You're a barbarian. . . .

The ability to communicate is here equated with civilisation, even the possession of a claim to being human. The loser in a contest about words and their meaning loses his claim to live. Power, the power over life or death, derives from the ability to make one's opponent accept the meaning of words chosen by the dominant partner. When Davies, earlier in the play, ventures to remark that Aston, Mick's brother, is "a bit of a funny bloke," Mick stares at him in indignant amazement:

> MICK: Funny? Why?
> DAVIES: Well . . . he's funny . . .
> MICK: What's funny about him?
>   (*Pause.*)
> DAVIES: Not liking work.
> MICK: What's funny about that?
> DAVIES: Nothing.
>   (*Pause.*)
> MICK: I don't call it funny.
> DAVIES: Nor me.

His surrender is both abject and complete. A disagreement about the meaning of a term has become a fundamental, existential contest of wills. Words are thus of vital importance. And yet, it is not so much the words themselves as the existential situations they conceal and reveal. It is no coincidence that the climactic turning point of *The Homecoming* arises from a "philosophical" discussion, Lenny's attempt to draw his brother Teddy into an argument about being and nonbeing, words and the realities behind them:

> LENNY: Well, for instance, take a table. Philosophically speaking. What is it?
> TEDDY: A table.

LENNY: Ah. You mean it's nothing else but a table. Well, some people would envy your certainty, wouldn't they, Joey? For instance, I've got a couple of friends of mine, we often sit round the Ritz Bar having a few liqueurs, and they are always saying things like that, you know, things like: Take a table, take it. All right, I say, *take* it, *take* a table, but once you've taken it, what you going to do with it? Once you've got hold of it, where you going to take it?

MAX: You'd probably sell it.

LENNY: You wouldn't get much for it.

JOEY: Chop it up for firewood.

(*Lenny looks at him and laughs.*)

RUTH: Don't be too sure though. You've forgotten something. Look at me. I . . . move my leg. That's all it is. But I wear . . . underwear . . . which moves with me . . . it . . . captures your attention. Perhaps you misinterpret. The action is simple. It's a leg . . . moving. My lips move. Why don't you restrict . . . your observations to that? Perhaps the fact that they move is more significant . . . than the words which come through them. You must bear that . . . possibility . . . in mind.

Perhaps the fact that the lips move is more significant than the words that come through them! This key sentence not only touches the basis of Pinter's practice of the use of dramatic dialogue, it also reveals his fundamental philosophical attitude, his search, through and in spite of an obsessive preoccupation with language, its nuances, its meaning, its beauty, for the area of reality that lies

behind the use of language. It is not the word "table"
that matters, but the way you *take* the table, how you
act on it and how it *acts* on you, what it does to you. The
lips that move are more significant, ultimately, than the
words that come through them, the leg and the underwear that moves with it have more reality, because they
are an action that creates an immediate response, than
any of the polite words that a respectable professor's wife
like Ruth might utter. Or, to put it differently, it matters
little whether Mick's or Davies' interpretation of the
word "funny" is the correct one; what is essential and
existentially important is that Mick makes Davies accept
his definition of the word's meaning.

Again and again in Pinter's plays, language becomes
the medium through which a contest of wills is fought
out, sometimes overtly, as in the disputes about the correct expression to be used or about the correct meaning
of a given word or phrase, sometimes beneath the surface of the explicit subject matter of the dialogue. The
brainwashing of Stanley by Goldberg and McCann in
The Birthday Party shows the transition from the one
mode to the other with particular clarity. It opens with
specific questions referring to Stanley's real situation:

> Why do you behave so badly, Webber? Why
> do you force that old man out to play chess?

Yet gradually the questions become more and more
fantastic, more and more abstract, until in the end we
are indeed made aware that it is the lips that are moving,
and the rage with which they move, that matter, rather
than the words they utter. Nevertheless the words are of
the utmost importance; not through their surface meaning, but through the colour and texture of their sound

and their *associations* of meaning. At first Goldberg and McCann bombard Stanley with questions about specific crimes, which, however, are so contradictory that it is clear that he could not really have committed all of them. At one point he is asked: "Why did you kill your wife?" A few lines later his crime is: "Why did you never get married?"

As the cross-examination proceeds, it becomes ever more obvious that it is an expression of Stanley's *general* feelings of guilt, of his tormentors' general conviction that he deserves punishment. The long list of venial and mortal sins, major and minor transgressions, which is unleashed upon poor Stanley—"You stuff yourself with dry toast. You contaminate womankind. Why don't you pay the rent? Why do you pick your nose? What about Ireland?"—covers the whole gamut of possible sources of guilt feelings, from embarrassment over social gaffes (picking one's nose), collective national guilt feelings about crimes committed by one's country (in Ireland for the Englishman Stanley Webber), minor lapses (such as eating too much toast), to the major sins of lechery and, worst of all, cheating at the national sport: "Who watered the wicket in Melbourne?" (which so baffled the first translator of the play into German that he rendered it by a sentence which, translated back, reads: "Who urinated against the city gate of Melbourne?") until it culminates in the final, existential question of why the chicken crossed the road, and which came first, the chicken or the egg—in other words why Stanley has the effrontery to exist, to be alive at all. The proliferation of images, grotesquely juxtaposed and subtly intensified, establishes this long scene as a kind of poem, a structure of images which constitutes a set of variations on a basic theme. The chief character of the play is thrown, as it were, into a whirlpool of language, which batters him into insensitivity.

Ten years after Pinter wrote *The Birthday Party*, Peter Handke, a young protagonist of the theatrical avant-garde in Germany, achieved considerable success with a new kind of dramatic spectacle, which he called *Sprech-stücke* (word plays); these consist of long structures of pure language uttered by speakers who do not represent any specific characters. By confronting the audience with permutations of words and associations on a given theme (the future; cries for help; insults; or the sources of guilt feelings) these set up linguistic fields of force, from which each member of the audience must, willy-nilly, assemble his own personal experience of hope, helplessness, rage, or guilt. Pinter not only anticipated this "new" experimental form, but also demonstrated how it could be integrated and made to work within a more traditional framework of drama.

Brilliant as the brainwashing scene in *The Birthday Party* is, Pinter's use of language became far subtler in his later plays. When Lenny first meets Ruth in *The Homecoming*, he tells her two long, and seemingly gra-tuitous, stories. As in *The Birthday Party's* brainwashing scene, these are linguistic structures designed to evoke feelings of guilt and terror in the listener; but they are far more subtly orchestrated, far less obviously abstract *tours de force*. Having just met Ruth late at night and alone in his house, Lenny at first engages her in the usual small talk. Then suddenly, out of a speech about her visit to Venice and his feeling that he might have seen Venice had he served in the last war, he confronts her with a clearly erotic proposition:

LENNY: . . . . Do you mind if I hold your hand?
RUTH: Why?
LENNY: Just a touch.
   (*He stands and goes to her.*)
   Just a tickle.
RUTH: Why?
   (*He looks down at her.*)
LENNY: I'll tell you why.
   (*Slight pause.*)

Lenny then launches into his first long story, which seems totally unrelated to the question he promised to answer; namely, why he wants to touch Ruth. The story starts on a formal linguistic level, almost like the opening sentences of a novel:

> One night, not too long ago, one night down by the docks, I was standing alone under an arch, watching all the men jibbing the boom, out in the harbour, and playing about with the yardarm—

Note the use of technical terms of nautical language as an indication of expertise, of being an insider. Ruth and the audience will now expect to hear that Lenny (whose occupation is a mystery) might turn out to have something to do with the sea. But at this point the story—and the language—suddenly change gear: "—when a certain lady came up to me and made me a certain proposal."

Now we are in terminology of the British popular press when it deals, as politely and respectably as is possible under the circumstances, with sexual matters, and above all sex crimes:

> This lady had been searching for me for days. She'd lost track of my whereabouts. However,

the fact was she eventually caught up with me, and when she caught up with me she made me this certain proposal. Well, this proposal wasn't entirely out of order and normally I would have subscribed to it. I mean I would have subscribed to it in the normal course of events. The only trouble was—

and here the language again enters, abruptly, another sphere altogether:

—The only trouble was she was falling apart with the pox.

This is another field of technical jargon: the professional talk of pimps and prostitutes. Lenny has shown his hand; he has indicated that this is his world. What is more, he goes on to discuss, very dispassionately and coolly, his desire to kill the girl there and then:

. . . . and the fact is, that as killings go, it would have been a simple matter, nothing to it.

and concludes the story with his decision *not* to kill her:

But . . . in the end I thought . . . Aaah, why go to all the bother . . . you know, getting rid of the corpse and all that, getting yourself into a state of tension. So I just gave her another belt in the nose and a couple of turns of the boot and sort of left it at that.

Again it is the switching from the polite language of the newspaper crime report to the brutal vernacular of the criminal himself that makes the point. In answer to Ruth's question why he made her an erotic proposal, Lenny has told her that being engaged in the business of prostitution, and being in a position to reject such pro-

posals from other girls, he feels himself entitled to make
such claims, and that, indeed, such claims should be regarded as an honour by the women to whom they are
addressed. Ruth's reaction shows that she has understood
the import of the story only too well. Displaying no surprise whatever, she instinctively or deliberately falls into
the same technical jargon:

> RUTH: How did you know she was diseased?
> LENNY: How did I know?
> > (*Pause.*)
> I decided she was.
> > (*Silence.*)
> You and my brother are newly-weds, are you?

Having, by her lack of surprise and the technical language of her question, revealed that she comes from the
same world, Ruth is, in Lenny's answer, sharply re-
minded by him that his power over his girls is absolute.
If he decides that a girl is diseased, then she is diseased.
The point is made. Lenny can change the subject and
return to polite small talk. But it is merely a short break
in the contest of wills. Again, to establish his determination to be brutal to women, be they helpless and old,
Lenny tells his second long story about the lady who
asked him to move her mangle while he was employed
to clear the snow in the streets on a winter morning, but
failed to give him a helping hand with the heavy object:

> So after a few minutes I said to her, now look
> here, why don't you stuff this iron mangle up
> your arse? Anyway, I said, they're out of date,
> you want to get a spin-drier. I had a good mind
> to give her a workover there and then, but as I
> was feeling jubilant with the snow-clearing I

just gave her a short-arm jab to the belly and
jumped on a bus outside. Excuse me, shall I take
this ashtray out of your way?

The narration of a brutal assault on an old woman is
directly linked to the seemingly trivial question about
the ashtray. But in fact the ashtray and the glass that
stands beside it become the focus for the first direct confrontation between Ruth and Lenny. She does not want
to move the ashtray, and she wants to keep the glass, as
she is still thirsty. And having been told of Lenny's capacity to be brutal to women and having taken it all in,
Ruth openly challenges him: "If you take the glass . . .
I'll take you." And she goes over to the attack:

> (*She picks up the glass and lifts it towards
> him.*)
> RUTH: Have a sip. Go on. Have a sip from my
> glass.
> (*He is still.*)
> Sit on my lap. Take a long cool sip.
> (*She pats her lap. Pause.*)
> (*She stands, moves to him with the glass.*)
> Put your head back and open your mouth.
> LENNY: Take that glass away from me.
> RUTH: Lie on the floor. Go on. I'll pour it down
> your throat.
> LENNY: What are you doing, making me some
> kind of proposal?
> (*She laughs shortly, drains the glass.*)

Ruth has turned the tables completely. She has become the girl who makes a proposal to Lenny; but Lenny
fails to do to her what he had boasted he had done to
the girl who had made him that proposal.

The audience, witnessing the play for the first time, will of course not be consciously aware of *all* the information the playwright has subtly supplied in the shifts of linguistic levels, the echoing and re-echoing of key words (e.g. "proposal"). To them the strange night scene with its long and seemingly pointless narrative passages and the sudden contest of wills must seem "enigmatic," provocatively suggestive but barely penetrable. Dramatically this is an advantage, because it generates one of the most important elements in all drama—suspense. Yet, as in the best detective fiction, the clues are all provided, and with scrupulous fairness. They are present in the language itself, which lets us see through it into the depths of the unspoken thoughts and emotions of the two characters: Lenny propositions Ruth because he has sensed that she is like the girls with whom he deals in his profession. When she asks *why* he has propositioned her, he tells her, by gradually falling into the brutal trade language of the pimp, what he is and—by implication—what he thinks she may well be. And by her reaction—or rather the absence of a shocked reaction, the acceptance of a man who uses that kind of language as a matter of course—she clearly indicates that she does in fact belong to that same world. Hence Ruth's acceptance of the role of a prostitute when it is offered to her towards the end of the play, which tends to shock audiences so deeply, has already been anticipated in this scene of her first confrontation with Lenny. And so has the sovereign, disdainfully businesslike attitude with which she settles the terms of her new life by driving an exceedingly hard bargain; for in that first contest of wills she has shown herself fully Lenny's equal in ruthlessness.

In fact, if one analyses Pinter's work closely, one will find that behind the apparently random rendering of the

colloquial vernacular there lies a rigorous economy of
means; each word is essential to the total structure and
decisively contributes to the ultimate, over-all effect
aimed at. In this respect also, Pinter's use of language is
that of a poet; there are no redundant words in true
poetry, no empty patches, no mere fill-ins. Pinter's dramatic writing has the density of texture of true poetry.

That is why—as in poetry, the caesura; as in music, the
pause—silences play such a large and essential part in
Pinter's dialogue. Pinter uses two different terms for the
punctuation of his dialogue by passages without speech:
"Pause" and "Silence." In the above example, which has
been analysed in some detail, when, at the end of Lenny's
first narration, Ruth asks how he knew the girl in question was diseased (and thus reveals her lack of surprise
and her familiarity with the vocabulary), Lenny's reaction is:

> How did I know?
> (*Pause.*)
> I decided she was.
> (*Silence.*)
> You and my brother are newly-weds, are you?

The repetition of the question "How did I know?" shows
Lenny's surprise at Ruth's reaction; he can hardly, as yet,
believe that she would react in so matter-of-fact a way.
The pause bridges the time he needs to take in the whole
import of that reaction and to think out his reply. The
silence after his reply and before he changes the subject
indicates the much deeper caesura of the end of that
section of the conversation. When Pinter asks for a *pause*,
therefore, he indicates that intense thought processes
are continuing, that unspoken tensions are mounting,
whereas *silences* are notations for the end of a movement,

the beginning of another, as between the movements of a symphony.

The pauses and silences in Pinter's play are the answer to Len's question in the novel *The Dwarfs*, when he was speaking about those poets who climb from word to word like stepping stones: "What do they do when they come to a line with no words in it at all?" The answer to that question is that *drama* is a kind of poetry that *can* find room for the emotional charge of the unspoken line. What speaks on the stage is the situation itself: the characters who confront each other in silence; what has gone before and the expectation, the suspense as to what will happen next. Pinter's pauses and silences are often the climaxes of his plays, the still centres of the storm, the nuclei of tension around which the whole action is structured: there is the "long silence" at the end of *The Caretaker*, when Davies' pleading for permission to remain in Aston's room elicits no answer. This "long silence" is the death of hope for the old man, Aston's refusal to forgive him, his expulsion from the warmth of a home—death. But as the curtain falls before he is seen to leave, it may also be the long silence before that final word of forgiveness is pronounced: the "line with no words in it" thus has all the ambiguity and complexity of true poetry, and it is also a metaphor, an image of overwhelming power.

At the close of *The Collection*, after Bill's "final" confession, his last version of the incident with James' wife, Stella—namely, that nothing happened between them at all—Pinter calls for a "long silence," after which James leaves the house. And then the silence continues as Harry and Bill remain sitting, facing each other. That silence contains an image of the despair and horror of their mutual dependence, above all of Bill's final failure to free himself from Harry's domination. As the light fades on that image, James is seen returning to his own home and confronting his wife:

> JAMES: You didn't do anything, did you?
> (*Pause.*)
> He wasn't in your room. You just talked about it, in the lounge.
> (*Pause.*)
> That's the truth, isn't it?
> (*Pause.*)
> You just sat and talked about what you would do if you went to your room. That's what you did.
> (*Pause.*)
> Didn't you?
> (*Pause.*)
> That's the truth . . . isn't it?
> (*Stella looks at him, neither confirming nor denying. Her face is friendly, sympathetic.*)

Stella's silence, her refusal to confirm or deny the story, is, in the true dramatic sense, an *action*, the pause that echoes each of James' questions *is a line of dialogue;* it is also a poetic image of one human being's mystery and impenetrability for another. Neither of these, it must again be stressed, has anything to do with man's *inability* to communicate with his fellow man; what is being demonstrated is man's—or in this case woman's—*unwillingness* to communicate, and indeed her partner's inability ever to be certain that, whether she speaks or remains silent, he can get hold of the real, the inner, personal truth of the matter.

The silence that is a *refusal* to communicate is one of the dominant images of Pinter's plays, from Bert's nonresponsiveness to Rose in his first play, *The Room,* to

Beth's inability or unwillingness to hear, and to respond to, what Duff tells her in *Landscape.*

There is another speechlessness, however, in Pinter's work, the speechlessness of annihilation, of total collapse: we find it in Stanley's inarticulate "uh-gughh" and "caaahhh" at the end of *The Birthday Party,* in Edward's silent acceptance of the matchseller's tray in the closing moment of *A Slight Ache,* in Disson's catatonic collapse at the close of *Tea Party.* This also is the silence that gives its title to the play *Silence*—the silence of the gradual fading of memory, the gradual, inevitable dissolution of human personality itself.

To be filled, to be meaningful, Pinter's silences and pauses have to be meticulously *prepared:* only if the audience knows the possible alternative answers that might be given to a question can the absence of a reply acquire meaning and dramatic impact; only because we know what Disson might want to say—and the way in which he is torn between the conflicting desires and fears he is unable to keep under control—are we moved by his inability to speak. The effectiveness of the pauses and silences is, in Pinter's technique, the direct consequence of the density of texture of his writing: each syllable and each silence is part of an over-all design, all portions of which are totally integrated. Another way to put this would be to say that Pinter writes with the utmost economy, there are no redundant parts in his work. It is the economy by which a door, a simple ordinary door, can become a source of nameless fear and menace, merely because the character in the room has been shown to dread the intrusion of the outside world; the economy by which a character who has been kept silent through most of the play can cause an effect of overwhelming surprise by suddenly starting to speak; the economy of words that can invest the most threadbare cliché with hidden poetic meaning.

Teddy's departure in *The Homecoming* might be cited as a telling, final example of this supreme economy. Ruth, Teddy's wife, has consented to stay behind with the family and to become a prostitute. Teddy is returning to America alone. He has said goodbye to all the men in the room. He has not spoken to Ruth. He goes to the door. Then Ruth speaks: she calls him "Eddie."

Throughout the play Ruth has never addressed Teddy by his name. Talking to the others she has referred to him, as they have, as Teddy. The fact that she now calls him by a different name, the name that no doubt was the one she used when they were alone, thus acquires a particular force. "(*Teddy turns.*)" Quite clearly he feels that the use of a name Ruth regarded as part of their intimacy in earlier times, may indicate that she has changed her mind, that she may yet come with him. But having turned and having waited, he is greeted with silence. Pinter indicates a *pause*. Then Ruth merely says: "Don't become a stranger."

"Don't become a stranger" is a cliché, an idiom without any emotional force. It is what one says to a casual acquaintance after the holiday is over, the cruise has come to an end; if one were to explain the phrase in a dictionary of idioms one would translate it with no more than "We may meet again," or "See you some time." This, clearly, is also how Teddy understands it. For he goes and shuts the front door. Pinter indicates a *silence*. But in that silence, which concludes Teddy's visit, which sets a full stop to his appearance in the play and probably in the lives of the other characters, surely there will also echo something of the *literal* meaning of that phrase "Don't become a stranger," rather like a last despairing lament of a wife for the husband whom she has now lost, who has, in fact, at that very moment become a stranger to her.

Only five words, only eight syllables are actually spoken in that whole passage: "Eddie. . . . Don't become a stranger." But through the surprise use of a name, through a pregnant pause and an utterly final silence, and through the subtle ambiguity of a phrase that is both a weak cliché and yet carries a strong literal meaning of deep, tragic impact, Pinter has put a wealth of drama, psychological profundity, suspense, irony, and pathos into those eight syllables.

Such economy and subtlety in the use of language, such density of subtext beneath the sparseness of the text itself, are surely the hallmarks of a real master of the craft of dialogue.

V

EVALUATION

How does a writer like Pinter fit into the over-all pattern of contemporary drama? How important is he? What values does he contribute to the theatre of our time? What has he to say to us? And is what he has to say worth saying? Will his work endure?

It is only too clear that to give a definitive answer to these questions with any claim to lasting validity at a time when the playwright concerned has barely reached the age of forty is impossible. Nevertheless judgements, however provisional they may have to be, can and must in some cases be made. They are made each time a theatre decides for or against performing a play by an author and, indeed, each time an individual playgoer, television viewer, or buyer of a movie ticket decides for or against seeing one of his works. Already the literature on Pinter is growing, not only articles but also books devoted solely to him; and it is growing precisely because there *is* a demand for such an interim assessment, from professional and amateur directors about to embark on staging Pinter's plays, from members of the audience who want to gain a deeper understanding of what they have seen, and even from critics and reviewers who want to approach their author with some background knowledge.

Yet in trying to place Pinter in his context; to define the true nature of his approach, subject matter and message; in analysing his technique—or mannerisms—and his very personal style as first steps towards an evaluation of his importance and degree of originality, one must beware of easy generalisations. Pinter has been explained as an existentialist dramatist par excellence, as a "playwright of the ambiguous," as a member of the "angry young men" or "kitchen-sink school" of British playwrights, and even as an exponent of man's instinctual territorial drive. Each of these views contains some portion of the truth at a more or less profound, more or less journalistically superficial, level. Yet none of them does justice to the complexity and integrity, the richness and the simplicity of his achievement in the first forty years of his life, the first thirteen of his career as a dramatist.

The classification of Pinter as one of the generation of angry young men has no more than a certain chronological validity: he emerged at about the same time as Osborne, Wesker, Kops, Alun Owen, and John Arden, to mention only the best-known of that highly successful and talented wave of young playwrights born around 1930 who came to the fore after 1956. Like most of these, Pinter represented the first generation of beneficiaries of the new postwar educational system in Britain, by which talented young people without distinction of their class origin were given access to higher education. (Pinter went to the Royal Academy of Dramatic Art with a grant from the London County Council.) These were the playwrights who replaced the middle-class idiom, which had dominated the British stage, with regional and lower-class vernaculars of various kinds, and thereby, initially, shocked many of the older critics and playgoers. Yet apart from this superficial family likeness, each of the playwrights concerned pursued totally different objectives and embodied very different basic attitudes—quite apart from the fact that some were more talented than others. While some of the members of this "new wave" were spoiled by premature success or failed to fulfill their early promise for other reasons, Pinter has remained in the forefront of contemporary, and not merely British, dramatists and has steadily consolidated his position. This, while surely no indication of ultimate, enduring success, nevertheless must be regarded as empirical evidence not only of growing acceptance by critics and audiences but of a genuine contribution to contemporary drama, its style, idiom, subject matter, and flavour. That this aspect of Pinter's achievement is real is amply attested to by the number of his imitators.

Even more telling is the fact that Pinter *has* largely resisted the temptation to imitate himself. His output of stage plays has been relatively small and widely spaced out: more than three years elapsed between the completion of *The Homecoming* (late 1964) and *Landscape* (1967/1968). He has been able to limit his truly personal writing to work for which he feels a real creative need by his skill as a brilliant craftsman in the field of screen adaptation of other writers' novels and as an actor and director, which relieves him of having to turn out stage plays to make a living. Pinter's immense professionalism as a master of dramatic technique and dialogue has thus become a protective shield for his deeper, creative capacity, his integrity as a poet.

That his attitude of complete devotion to the demands of his work as a poet has been consistently maintained since his very beginnings as a writer is shown by a letter Pinter wrote to a friend who had deplored the lack of a "moral" (i.e. ideological) standpoint in his writing, as long ago as 1955, when he was twenty-four:

> If I write about a lamp I apply myself to the demands of that lamp. If I write about a flower, I apply myself to the demands of that flower. In

most cases, the flower has singular properties as opposed to the lamp. . . . Flower, lamp, tin-opener, tree . . . . tend to take alteration from different climate and circumstance and I must necessarily attend to that singular change with the same devotion and allowance. I do not intend to impose or distort for the sake of an ostensible "harmony" of approach.

What you want from my writing is not self expression but self confession, and you're not going to get it. You want me to open wide my doors (possibly from a "moral standpoint"). That is neither my inclination, nor, more important, my purpose.

The sources of Pinter's accuracy as an observer are his ability to hear the real speech of real people and to note it down with the objectivity of a tape recorder; this objectivity is *self-expression* insofar as it proceeds from an urge to communicate his own personal mode of experiencing the world—his own existential emotion:

. . . I am not trying to assert myself when I write, or rarely. [My subjects] present themselves to me in their separate guises. I sharpen my tools for them. I stand them in front of the window with the light behind them, I place them in a corner in the shadows. I am there, of course—I am writing the stuff. There are many corridors and many rooms, many climates, in my possession. I am not a fixed star. Of course I am there—everywhere—I crawl on all fours—I declare war—I abdicate—it is my world. But I do not sit in a cosy didactic corner in *one* room,

speaking through a loudspeaker. My preoccupation is not a cosy corner. It is the house.

I am stuck neither to a style, in the limiting,
self-conscious sense, to a room, or to a proph-
ecy. I am concerned with penetration to the
root of the immediate matter, the matter in
hand. My aim is stringency, shading, and accuracy. Where I indulge in word-warfare, it is
no longer for highjinks, but simply where I feel
it demanded. Of course I recognise forms and
employ them, or rather, go to meet them—a
continuous voyage, and my seed within them,
they expand or snap. There is no such thing as
a static mode of expression. There is no form
which does not take alteration with one artist's
approach. . . .

Sometimes, in poems, I am only dimly conscious of the grounds of my activity, and the
work proceeds to its own law and discipline,
with me as go-between, as it were. But as you
say, if not conscious, so much the better. . . .

Thus this very early—and remarkable—self-examina-
tion goes with penetrating insight to the very heart of
Pinter's method and artistic personality: on the one hand
the objective, meticulous recorder of the world around
him; on the other the poet who knows that his work
flows from deep subconscious sources, by its own law
and discipline. He records the world as dispassionately
as he can, but, of necessity, this is a world recorded by
him, seen through *his* eyes, which notice and select each
detail by the inner law of *his* personality; hence the
world thus recorded is *his*, the poet's own, personal
world. At one and the same time it bears the lineaments

of real, external objects, real people whom he has encountered; and yet, because it has been observed by that
particular personality obeying its own inner law and discipline, it is also an image, a metaphor of his *inner* world.
The external world, objectively and meticulously recorded, must, of necessity, be fragmentary, disconnected,
unmotivated, and without a clearly discernible structure; segments of reality are like that. But because these
fragments have been noted down by a highly individual
personality whose very act of perception must be an expression of his individual mode of experiencing the world
around him, simply because certain objects or images
will touch him more than others, the disconnected ingredients will coalesce into an organic structure, express-
ing its own inner consistencies—obeying its own inner
law as an individual's personal vision of his own personal world.

Hence the dual nature of Pinter's work, the simultaneous coexistence within it of the most extreme naturalism of surface description and of a dreamlike, poetic
feeling, which, as indeed often happens in dreams, is
by no means inconsistent with an uncanny clarity of outline. This explains also the duality of the impact Pinter's
plays tend to have on their audiences: the amusement
about the accuracy of observation, combined on a deeper
level with the unease, the mixture of horror and fascination evoked by a subconscious response to implications
that spring from the author's own subconscious. On the
surface we may laugh about Davies' impotent antics and
stupid lies; deep down we sense that this laughter expresses some of the contempt—and the fear—sons feel for
their fathers. We may feel amused by the game husband
and wife play with each other in *The Lover*, yet deep
down we respond to the fact that husbands do indeed

dream of their wives as prostitutes, wives of their husbands as suave lovers or brutal rapists.

If, as is sometimes suggested, the ambiguity and uncertainty of Pinter's plays really are no more than the outcome of a deliberate manipulation of his audience by a clever craftsman of theatrical trickery, his use of repetition and absurdly inconsequential conversation no more than mechanical mannerisms, his work would be highly ephemeral and have no chance of making an impact on future generations of playgoers, who would no longer be taken in or shocked by such superficially effective devices. If, on the other hand, as I believe it to be the case, the uncertainties, ambivalences, and ambiguities of plot and language in these plays are the expression of a genuine perplexity about the nature of our experience of the world, the distillation of a deeply felt, painfully sifted, and conscientiously recorded creative process, then they will surely endure not only as works of brilliant craftsmanship (which is already beyond doubt) but as considerable artistic achievements.

What speaks for the latter view is the undoubted evidence of a steady development in Pinter's style, his consistent refusal merely to reproduce the mannerisms and technical achievements of his early successes. *Landscape* and *Silence* in particular are so radically different from the formula of what is commonly regarded as Pinteresque, so uncompromisingly remote from cheap seeking after success, that the view of Pinter as a mere manipulator of mechanical formulae must surely break down. In these plays the *poet* following his own inner law and discipline is again to the fore. "My last two plays," said Pinter in an interview before the first night of *Landscape* and *Silence*, "are really rather different. They had to be from my point of view: I felt that after *The Homecom-*

ing, which was the last full-length play I wrote, I couldn't any longer stay in the room with this bunch of people who opened doors and came in and went out. . . ." (Interview with Michael Dean, B.B.C. TV, reprinted in *The Listener.* 6 March 1969.)

If Pinter felt like that, one is tempted to think, it must be due to the fact that the fears and subconscious anxieties connected with his obsession with these images of menace have been overcome. *The Homecoming* finally brought the true nature of these anxieties to the surface by showing the connection between these fears and the duality of the female figure who oscillates between mother and harlot. These anxieties were the anxieties of an adolescent, a young man coming to terms with his own personality. In *Landscape* and *Silence* we are in an entirely different sphere: the area of nostalgia for lost love and innocence, regret for past mistakes and meditation about the gradual obliteration of consciousness in silence, oblivion, and death. This is the world of a man no longer young, but one that lies beyond the watershed *"nel mezzo del cammin di nostra vita"* of middle age. The curve of the playwright's development as a human being is thus being followed by his work; yet because the world he reproduced in his plays was a poetic evocation, in precise and realistic images, of his *inner* world, Pinter's plays are free of the concentration on autobiographical subject matter that has become a problem for such contemporaries of his as Osborne and Wesker (by presenting them with the difficulties of having to mirror a more opulent but less interesting external life). Pinter's ability to transcend the merely autobiographical puts him, in my opinion, in a different class from most of the other, social-realist playwrights of his generation in Britain.

Moreover, and surprisingly, since so much of his effect

in his own country derives from his witty use of local speech patterns, Pinter's plays have been as successful in America and in Europe across the Channel as they are in England. In English-speaking countries, Pinter's language retains much of its appeal through his evident skill in the handling of rhythm, pace, and pause, and the fascination of his vocabulary. In translations—some of which, like the first German version (since revised), were full of inaccuracies and downright howlers—these purely linguistic features are bound to lose much of their impact, although some elements, like the use of repetition, can be preserved. Yet enough remains to hold an audience: the "oblique" character of the dialogue, the poetic power of "motiveless" action, the menace and suspense, the philosophical implications of the existential uncertainties that are being demonstrated—but above all the depth of insight into the subconscious mainsprings of human action; the archetypal imagery, expressed through *situations* rather than explicit statement or discursive argumentation, by which they are brought to life by Pinter on the stage.

The unquestionable impact of Pinter's work notwithstanding, it has been said that he lacks the wide sweep, variety of subject matter and character that mark a major playwright, a Brecht, Shaw, Ibsen, or Shakespeare; that Pinter is no more than a miniaturist, a minor master with a narrow range. Yet surely the importance of a writer lies in the *depth* of his insights rather than in the width of his subject matter. Those writers who are primarily interested in society, politics, history, and the external world certainly need this kind of richness; others, whose main preoccupations are the inner life of man, his basic existential problems, which, of necessity, are few, have undoubtedly been of comparable stature. Beckett, one of

Pinter's avowed literary models, is a case in point. These are, in the main, lyricists rather than epic poets, absurdists rather than realists. The extreme accuracy of Pinter's images from reality (which corresponds to the meticulous descriptive pedantry of Kafka, the earthy naturalism of Beckett's detail) must not blind us to the fact that essentially his is a *lyrical* vision which builds up a communication of an individual's otherwise inaccessible and inexpressible experience of living from a complex structure of verbal and situational imagery. The observation of surface detail is not an end in itself, but a means to an end, which is the elevation of a situation (a man afraid of the persecutors behind a closed door; an old man being expelled from his home; two people separated by the gulf that yawns between the different levels of emotion on which they live, in *Landscape*) into a poetic metaphor, an image within a pattern of images. The range of such a work may *appear* narrow, and as a mere representation of external reality it may seem extremely simple; yet if we examine its ability to express the inexpressible, to transcend the scope of language itself and to evoke a response at the deepest level of the direct communication of emotion and experience, then such a work will have to be acknowledged as in fact going *further* in range than anything that can be accomplished on a merely discursive level, and being, also, far more complex. To achieve such a communication, a multitude of elements operating on a multitude of different levels must be brought to bear at one and the same time; it is from the tensions between the laughter about the accurately observed verbal blunder and the pathos of the situation, between the poverty of vocabulary and the wealth of emotion it hides, between the triviality of the outside circumstances and their power as an archetype

of existence, that these high points of poetry in the theatre are sparked into being and fused into flashes of insight, which are communication on a higher level than
can be attained by any prose—these are the "lines with
no words in them" of which one of Pinter's early characters spoke.

Clearly not all of Pinter's work can aspire to be judged
on this high level. Some of his early plays are trial runs;
his revue sketches are no more than exercises in the technique of dialogue; some of the radio and television plays
were tailored to the needs of the media and their mass
audiences. *A Slight Ache, A Night Out,* and *Night School*
are highly efficient and amusing examples of professional
craftsmanship; *Tea Party* was written for a specific project involving a vast international audience. Yet other
television plays, notably *The Collection, The Lover,* and
The Basement, do achieve at least some degree of that
higher level of communication. Pinter's major claims
must, however, rest on his best work for the stage: *The
Dumb Waiter* among his first efforts; the three full-length
plays, *The Birthday Party, The Caretaker* and *The
Homecoming,* and the two short lyrical pieces in a new
vein, *Landscape* and *Silence.*

The three longer plays have, in my opinion, proved
themselves beyond a doubt. *The Birthday Party* and *The
Caretaker* have stood the test of repeated revival; *The
Homecoming* also seems to me, after a considerable number of encounters with the play, fresher and more dur-
able each time and able to preserve its impact and
essence even in .bad translations and abominable performances. These three plays are classics of our time,
even though only future generations will be able to judge
whether they can become classics for all time.

As to Pinter's new manner, the static, condensed poetic

idiom of *Landscape* and *Silence,* judgement is obviously even more difficult at this moment. Will audiences *learn* to penetrate into the depths of these extremely compact poetic structures so that they will not strike them, as they undoubtedly tended to do on first acquaintance, as obscure and beyond comprehension? Will the mastery of construction, the economy of the storytelling, the subtlety of language, which closer study and analysis yield, become transparent to future audiences? If one considers how obscure and impenetrable Beckett, Ionesco, and, indeed, Pinter himself appeared to audiences in the fifties and early sixties and how readily the same plays are now understood and appreciated, the answer to these questions may well be "yes." If so, will the static, lyrical mode in which these plays are couched be capable of development? That question cannot be answered; it is merely the measure of the challenge that faces a playwright of Pinter's stature at the height of achievement on the threshold of middle age.

Yet of that stature itself there can, on the strength of what he has already accomplished, be little doubt. In a wave of young playwrights which is richer in talent than any generation of British dramatists since the Restoration, Harold Pinter clearly stands in the front rank, as a craftsman, a master of dialogue, a technician of suspense, laughter, surprise, and emotion, and as an artist, a true poet of the stage, who has created his own personal world in his own personal idiom, wholly consistent, wholly individual, an expression of his own anguish, peopled from *his* wound, which yet, as great poetry always does, re-echoes in the depths of the minds of a multitude of individuals and is therefore capable of giving voice to unspoken fears, sufferings, and yearnings shared by all mankind.

BIBLIOGRAPHY

I. PINTER'S WRITINGS:

Plays

The Birthday Party, London: Encore Publishing Co.,
1959.

"*The Birthday Party*" *and Other Plays*, London:
Methuen, 1960. Also contains *The Room* and *The
Dumb Waiter*.

The Caretaker, London: Methuen, 1960.

"*A Slight Ache*" *and Other Plays*, London: Methuen,
1961. Also contains *A Night Out, The Dwarfs,* and
five revue sketches ("Trouble in the Works," "The
Black and White," "Request Stop," "Last to Go,"
"Applicant.")

"*The Collection*" *and* "*The Lover,*" London: Methuen, 1963. Also contains the story "The Examination."

The Homecoming, London: Methuen, 1965.

"*Tea Party*" *and Other Plays*, London: Methuen,
1967. Also contains *The Basement* and *Night
School.**

Landscape, London: Emanuel Wax for Pendragon
Press, 1968, edition limited to 2000 copies, num-
bered 1–1000 for Great Britain, 1001–2000 for the
United States.

The Homecoming, London: Karnac/Curwen, 1968,

* Later, revised printings of the volumes of the Methuen
edition, contain highly significant cuts and revisions when
compared to the first editions.

edition limited to 200 copies, with nine lithographs
by Harold Cohen, each signed by the author and
the artist.

"Landscape" and *"Silence,"* London: Methuen, 1969.
Also contains *Night*.

American editions of the plays

"The Birthday Party" and *"The Room,"* New York:
Grove Press, 1961.

"The Caretaker" and *"The Dumb Waiter,"* New
York: Grove Press, 1961.

*Three Plays: The Collection, A Slight Ache, The
Dwarfs,* New York: Grove Press, 1962.

The Homecoming, New York: Grove Press, 1966.

The Lover, Tea Party, The Basement, New York:
Grove Press, 1967.

A Night Out, Night School, Revue Sketches, New
York: Grove Press, 1968.

Landscape, in *Evergreen Review,* No. 68, July 1969.

"The Dwarfs" and *Eight Revue Sketches,* New York:
Dramatists Play Service. Contains the following
revue sketches: "Trouble in the Works," "The
Black and White," "Request Stop," "Last to Go,"
"Applicant," "Interview," "That's All," "That's Your
Trouble."

(Further revue sketches: "Dialogue for Three," in
Stand, Vol. VI, No. 3, 1963. "Special Offer" reprinted
in *Harold Pinter,* by A. P. Hinchcliffe, New York:
Twayne, 1967, pp. 73–74.)

Other writings by Pinter

Poems, selection by Alan Clodd, London: Enitharmon Press, 1968. This selection contains most of

Pinter's poems which have appeared in periodicals; it omits "Rural Idyll" and "European Revels" in *Poetry London,* No. 20, November 1950, and "One a Story, Two a Death," in *Poetry London,* No. 22, Summer 1951. In both these issues, Pinter's name is spelled "Harold Pinta."

"Beckett" in *Beckett at Sixty. A Festschrift,* London: Calder & Boyars, 1967.

Mac, London: Emanuel Wax for Pendragon Press, 1968; limited edition, like *Landscape* (see above). A brief autobiographical sketch, recalling Pinter's association with the Irish actor-manager Anew McMaster.

"Tea Party" (story), in *Playboy,* January 1965.

"Memories of Cricket," in the *Daily Telegraph Magazine,* 16 May 1969.

"Between the Lines," speech at the Seventh National Students Drama Festival, Bristol, in the *Sunday Times* (London), 4 March 1962.

Manuscript notes and a page of the typescript of *The Homecoming* are reproduced in *London Magazine,* New Series No. 100, July/August 1969.

II. INTERVIEWS WITH HAROLD PINTER

Interview with John Sherwood, B.B.C. European Service, in the series "The Rising Generation," dated 3 March 1960 (duplicated ms.).

Interview with Hallam Tennyson, B.B.C. General Overseas Service, 7 August 1960 (duplicated ms.).

Interview with Kenneth Tynan, B.B.C. Home Service, recorded 19 August 1960, broadcast 28 October 1960 (duplicated ms.).

Interview with Carl Wildman and Donald McWhinnie, B.B.C. Network Three, in the series "Talking of Theatre," 7 March 1961 (duplicated ms.).

Interview with Laurence Kitchin and Paul Mayersberg, in the programme "New Comment," B.B.C. Third Programme, broadcast 10 October 1963.

Interview with Marshall Pugh, "Trying to Pin Down Pinter," in the *Daily Mail* (London), 7 March 1964.

Interview with Lawrence M. Bensky in *The Paris Review*, No. 39 (1966). Reprinted in *Writers at Work: The Paris Review Interviews*, Third Series, New York: Viking Press, 1967; London: Secker & Warburg, 1968.

Interview with John Russell Taylor, in *Sight and Sound*, Autumn 1966.

Interview in *The New Yorker* ("Talk of the Town"), 25 February 1967.

Interview with Kathleen Tynan, "In Search of Harold Pinter," Part 1 in the *Evening Standard* (London), 25 April 1968; Part 2, 26 April 1968.

Interview with Michael Dean, B.B.C. TV, "Late Night Line-Up," reprinted in *The Listener*, 6 March 1969.

Interview with Joan Bakewell, B.B.C. 2 TV, 11 September 1969.

III. SOME TRANSLATIONS OF PINTER'S PLAYS

Into French:

La Collection suivi de l'Amant et de Le Gardien, trans. Eric Kahane, Paris: Gallimard, 1967.

Le Retour, trans. Eric Kahane, in *L'Avant-Scène,*
No. 378, 15 April 1967.

L'Anniversaire, trans. Eric Kahane, Paris: Gallimard,
1968.

Into German:

*Die Heimkehr, Der Liebhaber, Die Kollektion, Tee-
gesellschaft, Tiefparterre,* trans. Willy H. Thiem,
Hamburg: Rowohlt, 1967.

*Die Geburtstagsfeier, Der stumme Diener, Das Zim-
mer, Die Zwerge,* trans. Willy H. Thiem (revised), Hamburg: Rowohlt, 1969.

*Der Hausmeister, Eine Nacht ausser Haus, Abend-
kurs, Ein leichter Schmerz,* trans. Willy H. Thiem
(revised), Hamburg: Rowohlt, 1969.

Dramen (the content of the above paperbacks plus
new translations *Landscape* and *Silence* (trans.
Renate & Martin Esslin) Hamburg: Rowohlt,
1970.

Into Czech:

Správce (The Caretaker), trans. Milan Lukeš,
Prague: Orbis, 1965.

Navrat Domu (The Homecoming), trans. Milan
Lukeš in "Svetlova Literatura," No. 4, 1966.

Norozeniny (The Birthday Party) and *Navrat
Domu,* trans. Milan Lukeš in *Anglicke Absurdni
Divadlo,* Prague: Orbis, 1966.

Into Spanish:

El Amante and *La Colección,* trans. Luis Escobar,
in *Primer Acto,* No. 83, 1967.

El Conserje (*The Caretaker*), trans. Josefina Vidal & F.M. Lorda Alaiz in *Teatro Ingles*, Madrid: Aguilar, 1966.

El Cuidador (*The Caretaker*), *El Amante, El Montaplatas* (*The Dumb Waiter*), trans. Manuel Barbera, Buenos Aires: Nueva Vision 1965.

El Portero (*The Caretaker*), trans. T.R. Trives in "Primero Acto," January 1962.

Into Dutch:

De Kamer, De Dienstlift, De Huisbewaarder, De Collectie, De Minnaar (*The Room, The Dumb Waiter, The Caretaker, The Collection, The Lover*), Amsterdam: Uitgeverij De Bezige Bij, 1966.

Into Italian:

Il Gardiano e altri drammi, trans. Elio Nissim (also contains: *La Stanza* and *Il Calapranzi*) Milan: Bompiani, 1962.

Una Serata Fouri and *Un leggero malessere,* trans. Laura del Bono & Elio Nissim in *Teatro Uno,* ed. L. Codignola, Turin: Einaudi, 1962.

Into Portuguese:

O Monte Cargas (*The Dumb Waiter*), trans. Luis de Stau Moneiro, in *Tempo de Teatro,* No. 3, Lisbon, n.d.

Feliz Aniversario, trans. Artur Ramos & Jaime Salazar Sempaio, Lisbon: Preto, 1967.

Into Serbo-Croat:

Bez Pogovora (*The Dumb Waiter*), in Avangardna Drama, Belgrade, 1964.

Into Turkish:

Dodumgünü Partisi (*The Birthday Party*), trans. Memet Fuat, published by de yayinevi, 1965.

Into Danish:

Vicevaerten (*The Caretaker*), trans. H. C. Branner, Fredensborg: Arena, 1961.
En Tur i Byen (*A Night Out*), trans. Klaus Rifbjerg, in "En Tur i Byen—Moderne Engelsk Dramatik i TV og Radio," Fredensborg; Arena, 1962.

Into Hungarian:

A Gondnok (*The Caretaker*), trans. Tibor Bartos, in *Mai Angol Drámák*, Budapest: Europa, 1965.

Into Swedish:

Mathissen (*The Dumb Waiter*), trans. Lars Göran Calsson, in *I En Akt*, ed. Ingvar Holm, Stockholm, Aldus, 1966.

Into Polish:

Urodziny Stanleya (*The Birthday Party*), trans. Adam Tarn, in "Dialog," No. 10, 1960.
Powrot do Dumo (*The Homecoming*), trans. Adam Tarn, in "Dialog," No. 12, 1965.
Kochanek (*The Lover*), trans. B. Taborski, in "Dialog," No. 8, 1966.

IV. ON PINTER

Bibliography

Gordon, Lois G., "Pigeonholing Pinter: A Bibliography," *Theatre Documentation,* Fall 1968. An excellent annotated list of books and articles, as well as selected reviews of performances.

Monographs

Allgaier, Dieter, *Die Dramen Harold Pinters, Eine Untersuchung von Form und Inhalt* (dissertation), Frankfurt: 1967.

Esslin, Martin, *Harold Pinter,* No. 38 in the series "Friedrichs Dramatiker des Welttheaters," Velber bei Hannover: Friedrich Verlag, 1967.

Hayman, Ronald, *Harold Pinter,* in the series "Contemporary Playwrights," London: Heinemann Educational Books, 1968.

Hinchcliffe, Arnold P., *Harold Pinter,* in "Twayne's English Authors Series," New York: Twayne, 1967.

Kerr, Walter, *Harold Pinter,* No. 27 in the series "Columbia Essays on Modern Writers," New York & London: Columbia University Press, 1967.

Salem, Daniel, *Harold Pinter, Dramaturge de l'ambiguité,* Paris: Denoël, 1968.

Other books

Armstrong, William A. (ed.), *Experimental Drama,* London: Bell, 1963.

Esslin, Martin, *The Theatre of the Absurd,* revised

edition, London: Pelican Books, 1968; New York: Doubleday Anchor Books, 1969.

Fricker, Robert, *Das moderne englische Drama,* Göttingen, 1964.

Kitchin, Laurence, *Mid-Century Drama,* 2nd edition, London: Faber, 1962.

Kitchin, Laurence, *Drama in the Sixties: Form and Interpretation,* London: Faber, 1966.

Marowitz, Charles; Milne, Tom; and Hale, Owen (editors), *The Encore Reader: A Chronicle of the New Drama,* London: Methuen, 1965.

Taylor, John Russell, *Anger and After,* London: Methuen, 1962 (revised edition, 1969).

Tynan, Kenneth, *Right & Left,* London: Longmans, 1967.

Williams, Raymond, *Drama from Ibsen to Brecht,* London: Chatto & Windus, 1968.

Articles and essays in periodicals

Ashworth, Arthur, "New Theatre: Ionesco, Beckett, Pinter," in *Southerly,* 1962.

Bernhard, F. J. "Beyond Realism: The Plays of Harold Pinter," in *Modern Drama,* September 1964.

Boulton, James T., "Harold Pinter: *The Caretaker* and Other Plays," in *Modern Drama,* September 1963.

Brown, John Russell, "Mr. Pinter's Shakespeare," in *The Critical Quarterly,* Autumn 1963.

Brown, John Russell, "Dialogue in Pinter and Others," in *The Critical Quarterly,* Autumn 1965.

Cohn, Ruby, "The World of Harold Pinter," in *Tulane Drama Review,* Vol. VI, No. 3, March 1962.

Cohn, Ruby, "Latter Day Pinter," in *Drama Survey,* Winter 1964.

Dick, Kay, "Pinter and the Fearful Matter," in *Texas Quarterly,* IV, 1961.

Dukore, Bernard, "The Theatre of Harold Pinter," in *Tulane Drama Review,* Vol. VI, No. 3, March 1962.

Dukore, Bernard, "A Woman's Place," in *Quarterly Journal of Speech,* 1966.

Esslin, Martin, "Pinter Translated," in *Encounter,* March 1968.

Gallagher, Kent G., "Harold Pinter's Dramaturgy," in *Quarterly Journal of Speech,* October 1966.

Goodman, Florence J., "Pinter's *The Caretaker:* The Lower Depths Descended," in *Midwest Quarterly,* Winter 1964.

Habicht, Werner, "Theater der Sprache: Bemerkungen zu einigen englischen Dramen der Gegenwart," in *Die Neueren Sprachen,* July 1963.

Habicht, Werner, "Der Dialog und das Schweigen im 'Theater des Absurden,'" in *Die Neueren Sprachen,* 1967.

Hinchcliffe, Arnold P., "Mr. Pinter's Belinda," in *Modern Drama,* September 1968.

Hoefer, Jacqueline, "Pinter and Whiting: Two Attitudes Towards the Alienated Artist," in *Modern Drama,* February 1962.

Hutchings, Patrick, "The Humanism of a Dumb Waiter," in *Westerly* (University of Western Australia), April 1963.

Knight, Wilson, "The Kitchen Sink," in *Encounter,* December 1963.

Lahr, John, "Pinter the Spaceman," in *Evergreen Review,* No. 55, June 1968.

Morris, Kelly, "The Homecoming," in *Tulane Drama Review,* Winter 1966.

Schechner, Richard, "Puzzling Pinter," in *Tulane Drama Review*, Winter 1966.

Schenker, Ueli, "Versuche zur Ordnung: Harold Pinter und sein *Caretaker*," in *Neue Zürcher Zeitung*, 13 April 1969.

Schlegelmilch, Wolfgang, "Der Raum des Humanen: Zu Harold Pinters *The Caretaker*," in *Die Neueren Sprachen*, 1964.

Thornton, Peter C., "Blindness and the Confrontation with Death: Three Plays by Harold Pinter," in *Die Neueren Sprachen*, 1968.

Walker, A., "Messages from Pinter," in *Modern Drama*, May 1967.

V. BOOKS ON WHICH PINTER BASED HIS SCREEN ADAPTATIONS

Hall, Adam, *The Berlin Memorandum*, London: Collins, 1965.

Hartley, L. P., *The Go-Between*, London: Hamish Hamilton, 1953.

Maugham, Robin, *The Servant*, London, Falcon Press, 1948; republished by Heinemann, 1964.

Mortimer, Penelope, *The Pumpkin Eater*, London: Hutchinson, 1962.

Mosley, Nicholas, *Accident*, London: Hodder & Stoughton, 1965.

INDEX

Absurd, literature of the, 44
Accident (film), 21, 199, 200, 204–5
Aggression (aggressiveness) theme and treatment of, 73, 85, 131, 149, 225. *See also* Violence; specific plays
Alienation, theme and treatment of, 29, 70–71. *See also* Fear; Identity; Reality
Ambiguity, 30, 37, 38, 185 ff., 244
"Anaesthetist's Pin, The" (Pinter), 55
"Angry young men," Pinter as a member of, 244–46
Anxiety. *See* Fear (anxiety)
Applicant (Pinter), 18, 105, 198
Arden, John, 244
Ashcroft, Peggy, 22, 23
Associated Rediffusion TV (ARD), 13, 15, 16, 18

Bacchae, The, 143
Badel, Alan, 18
Balcony, The (Genet), 143
Basement, The, 21, 22, 35, 56, 127, 171–78, 199, 205, 253; analysis of, 171–78; basic situation in, 172
Bate, Anthony, 16, 23
Bates, Alan, 13, 16
B.B.C., 5, 11, 12, 13, 15, 17, 18, 19, 20, 21, 22, 166, 171
Beckett, Samuel, 9, 10, 21, 73, 82, 102, 171, 187, 194–95, 254; influence on Pinter, 27, 29, 44, 251–52
"Beckett" (Pinter), 257
Bensky, Lawrence M., interview with Pinter by, 26, 258
Bergman, Ingmar, 88
"Between the Lines" (Pinter speech), 38–39, 257
Billetdoux, François, 166
Birthday Party, The, 7–11, 12, 13, 19, 22, 54, 91, 94, 107–8, 116, 119, 120, 127, 142, 165, 253; analysis of, 28, 30, 34, 37, 74–87;

basic situation in, 74–75; critics on, 7, 8–11, 115; film, 22, 199; language in, 44, 53, 211–12, 214, 216, 229–31, 240; levels of interpretation of, 85–86
Black and White, The (Pinter), 12, 18, 196–97
Blindness, theme and imagery of, 81, 88, 90, 168–69, 171
Brearly, Joseph, 3
Brecht, Bertolt, 43, 122
Bristol University Drama Department, 6, 7, 38
Bryant, Michael, 19, 21

Campton, David, 46
Caretaker, The, 13–16, 17, 23, 95–115, 121, 162, 165, 253; analysis of, 34, 37, 43, 45, 95–115; basic situation in, 95–102; critics on, 13–16; filming of, 17–18, 199; language and silences in, 43, 54, 55, 115, 196, 215, 216–17, 218–19, 221–22, 224–27, 238; symbolism in, 107–10, 114–15
"Chandeliers and Shadows" (Pinter), 4, 52, 53
Chekhov, Anton, 41, 209–11
Cherry Orchard, The (Chekhov), 41, 209
Clodd, Alan, 256
Codron, Michael, 7
Cohen, Harold, 256
Collection, The, 16, 17, 20, 120, 127, 130–37, 142, 164, 205, 253; analysis of, 37, 130–37; basic situation in, 131–35; language and silences in, 219–21, 238–39
"Comedies of menace," 46, 179
Comedy (humor), 45–46, 248–49. *See also* specific plays
Communication (non-communication). *See* Language
Compartment, The (Pinter), 21, 171, 199
Counterpoint, 17